SCIENTIFIC ASPECTS OF GRAPHOLOGY

SCIENTIFIC ASPECTS OF GRAPHOLOGY

A Handbook

Edited by

BARUCH NEVO, Ph.D.

Director, National Institute for
Testing and Evaluation
and
Senior Lecturer
Department of Psychology
University of Haifa
Israel

CHARLES C THOMAS • PUBLISHER
Springfield • Illinois • U.S.A.

Published and Distributed Throughout the World by
CHARLES C THOMAS • PUBLISHER
2600 South First Street
Springfield, Illinois 62708-4709

© *1986 by* CHARLES C THOMAS • PUBLISHER
ISBN 0-398-05245-X
Library of Congress Catalog Card Number: 86-5698

Printed in the United States of America
Q-R-3

Library of Congress Cataloging in Publication Data
Scientific aspects of graphology.

Includes bibliographies and index.
1. Graphology. I. Nevo, Baruch. [DNLM: 1. Behavior.
2. Handwriting. BF 901 S416]
BF891.S36   1986   155.2'82   86-5698
ISBN 0-398-05245-X

CONTRIBUTORS

Mrs. Ursula Ave-Lallemant
Researcher in Psychology and Graphology
München, West Germany
Address: Postfach 340255
D-8000 - München, West Germany

Dr. Maya Bar-Hillel
School of Social Work
The Hebrew University
Jerusalem, Israel
Address: Paul Baerwald School of Social Work
The Hebrew University
Mount Scopus
Jerusalem 91905, Israel

Dr. Gershon Ben-Shakhar
Department of Psychology
The Hebrew University
Jerusalem, Israel
Address: Department of Psychology
The Hebrew University
Mount Scopus
Jersualem 91905, Israel

Dr. James Crumbaugh
Clinical Psychologist
Veterans Administration Medical Center
Gulfport, Mississippi, U.S.A.
Address: Tally Arms no.32
Church & 16th Streets
Gulfport, MS 39501, U.S.A.

Dr. Amos Drory
Department of Industrial Engineering & Management
Ben-Gurion University of the Negev
Beer-Sheva, Israel
Address: Department of Industrial Engineering & Management
Ben-Gurion University of the Negev
Beer-Sheva 84105, Israel

Mrs. Anat Flug
Research Assistant
Department of Psychology
The Hebrew University
Jerusalem, Israel
Address: Department of Psychology
The Hebrew University
Mount Scopus
Jerusalem, Israel

Prof. Lewis R. Goldberg
Department of Psychology
University of Oregon
Eugene, Oregon, U.S.A.
Address: Institute for Management of Personality
1201 Oak Street
Eugene, OR 97401, U.S.A.

Dr. Hay Halevi
Clinical Psychologist and Psychoanalyst
Jerusalem, Israel
Address: 4, Mane Street
Jerusalem, Israel

v

Dr. Giora Keinan
Ray D. Wolfe Center for Study of Psychological Stress
University of Haifa
and
Tel-Aviv University
Tel-Aviv, Israel
Address: Department of Psychology
Tel-Aviv University
Ramat-Aviv
Tel-Aviv 69978, Israel

Prof. Elchanan I. Meir
Department of Psychology
Tel-Aviv University
Tel-Aviv, Israel
Address: Department of Psychology
Tel-Aviv University
Ramat-Aviv
Tel-Aviv 69978, Israel

Prof. Lothar Michel
Department of Psychology
University of Mannheim
Mannheim, West Germany
Address: Lehrstuhl Psychologie II
University of Mannheim
6800 - Mannheim, West Germany

Dr. Med. Arie Naftali
Handwriting Analyst
Tel-Aviv, Israel
Address: 124, Hayarkon Street
Tel-Aviv 63573, Israel

Dr. Baruch Nevo
National Institute for Testing & Evaluation, Jerusalem
and
Department of Psychology
University of Haifa
Haifa, Israel
Address: National Institute for Testing & Evaluation
6a Chaim Yachil Street
Jerusalem 93593, Israel

Mr. I. Odem
Address: Ein Harod 18965
Hakibbutz Hame'uchad
Israel

Prof. Anat Rafaeli
Department of Management Sciences
California State University
Hayward, California, U.S.A.
Address: Department of Management Sciences
California State University
Hayward, CA 94542, U.S.A.

Mrs. Hava Ratzon
Psychographologist
The Kibbutz Psychological Counseling Center
Tel-Aviv, Israel
Address: P.O. Box 33035
Tel-Aviv, Israel

Mrs. Thea Stein Lewinson (Hall)
Graphologist, former chief of the U.S. Government Handwriting Assessment Section (retired)
Bethesda, Maryland, U.S.A.
Address: 9109, North Branch Drive
Bethesda, MD 20817, U.S.A.

Mrs. Emilie Stockholm
Research Director
International Graphoanalysis Society
Chicago, Illinois, U.S.A.
Address: International Graphoanalysis Society
111, North Canal Street
Chicago, IL 60606, U.S.A.

Dr. Martin Wirthensohn
University of Zurich
Zurich, Switzerland
Address: Rosenbergstrasse 32
CH-8304 Wallisellen
Switzerland

PREFACE

A SPECIFIC DOMAIN of behavior can be considered a legitimate object of research in differential psychology if:

a) People differ from one another in respect of this behavior;
b) The behavior is reasonably stable and can be recorded and measured reliably;
c) The behavior is significant on its own merits or is related to some other interesting psychological trait or behavior.

Using more familiar terminology, these three requirements are: heterogeneity, reliability and validity. There is no point in studying a behavioral variable if it is invariant across subjects, unstable or without any potential for association with other interesting variables.

In this book, we examine almost all of the scientific evidence that has been published in the area of handwriting behavior in the last fifty years. It is our opinion—in which we hope the reader will eventually share—that there is in writing behavior the potential embodiment of the necessary characteristics, mentioned above, and that it therefore deserves consideration by psychologists and other behavioral scientists.

Writing is a self-recorded behavior which lends itself comfortably to a variety of research designs: longitudinal, cross-sectional, correlational, etc. As a diagnostic source of information, handwriting certainly has a level of face validity at least equal to that of some of the more standard projective techniques. For these reasons, and others, some of the most prominent psychologists in the first quarter of the 20th century became interested in the behavioral domain of handwriting (e.g., Binet, Allport). Nevertheless, scientific handwriting psychology today is a neglected area; it was banished to a far corner of the academic arena many years ago, and has remained there. It is typical that not a single comprehensive textbook on handwriting behavior research has been published till now.

What are the historical reasons for the suspicious attitude of the psychological establishment towards graphology? There appear to be three major sources:

a) Negative findings (regarding the validity of handwriting interpretations) which were reported in a few papers at the turn of the century;

b) The lack of ethics, low professional standards and pretensions of hundreds of "graphologists" — many of whom lacked any formal education in psychology;

c) Language barriers which hindered the communication between American and European scientists and deprived them of mutual benefits.

None of these obstacles — alone or in combination — is sufficient to justify the continuing scientific neglect of graphological research. In the following chapters it will be indicated how these difficulties could be overcome.

This book was written from a constructive point of view. The editor takes the position that graphology (or handwriting psychology, which is a **broader** concept), could become a legitimate subdiscipline of psychology, if certain conditions were to be fulfilled. Researchers should study handwriting, employing their scientific methods, and practitioners should then implement the findings in diagnostics, selection, forensic problems, etc., employing their professional and ethical standards. There is no sense in fighting phony graphologists by ignoring the whole domain of handwriting behavior. Relinquishing graphology into the hands of non-professionals has already caused great damage.

In contrast to this basic attitude of the editor, not all of the authors who contributed to this book present a positive attitude towards graphology. The book was opened to expressions of criticism, doubts and warnings. There was no attempt to ignore the serious problems inherent in this field of research and every effort was made to create a balanced picture. Whether or not we have achieved this aim, the reader will decide.

Baruch Nevo

ABOUT THIS BOOK

THIS BOOK was written for psychologists, students of psychology, and other scholars who are interested in the human behavioral sciences in general and in handwriting behavior in particular. The reader will not become an expert in handwriting analysis from this book, but will obtain a comprehensive view of its scientific aspects.

Nineteen authors have contributed to this "encyclopaedic" handbook, representing a prominent group of experts from America, Europe and Israel. The contributors tried to incorporate into their chapters, material from publications in at least three languages: English, German and French. Original works and new findings are presented side-by-side with literature surveys and re-analyses.

Most of the chapters are critical, integrative and contain up-to-date summaries of the work that has been done in the area since the early nineteen-thirties. In other words, the book covers fifty years of research activity in graphology.

The book consists of four parts:

- Most of Part I deals with applied graphology. Classic, as well as new schools of graphology are presented. In this part, the reader is expected to gain some familiarity with the basic concepts and methods of practicing graphologists.

- The chapters in Part II relate to developmental and situational factors and the ways in which they affect handwriting. Various types of stresses are among the factors which are discussed in this part.

- Part III is the major part in terms of the number of chapters. It is dedicated in its entirety to the question of validity; do graphological evaluations truly reflect the characteristics of the writers? Are graphological ratings significantly related to behavioral indices? No absolute answer is provided by the chapters in Part III, but a variety of methods and findings is presented to the reader.

- Part IV consists of chapters which discuss methodological issues; some are orientated towards existing problems, while others are oriented towards the future — what can and should be done in order to facilitate the scientific study of handwriting.

A few words of apology: This book is an international project. The authors live and work in various countries and they wrote in several languages. Much translation work was required before a reasonable level of English was achieved. To the authors whose articles lost something in the translation and to the readers who will have to be content with this, please accept the editor's apologies. A further apology is due, in view of the strict limitations placed on the length of chapters, for obvious objective reasons. The editor was in many cases obliged to shorten the material he received, and the integrity of presentation of not a few chapters was undoubtedly marred in the process.

It is our hope that this book will facilitate the future development of research into handwriting behavior and applications of such research.

Baruch Nevo
Jerusalem
Editor

ACKNOWLEDGEMENTS

MANY PEOPLE and institutions assisted in this project. Lack of space precludes mentioning more than a few:

Ms. Ruth Zucker, who introduced me to the field of graphology;

Ms. Iris Atzmon, Ms. Simone Kessler, Ms. Dvora Lifshitz and Ms. Tzippi Stern, who assisted with the secretarial work, graphics and typing; Ms. Karinna Michal, Ms. Nurit Goldenberg and Mr. Ted Goralnik, who assisted with the translations;

The Alexander von Humboldt Foundation, which invited the editor to Germany and enabled him to study the subject at close hand;

The Research Foundation of Haifa University, which enabled the editor to commence an independent research project on the subject.

Many thanks to them all.

Baruch Nevo

CONTENTS

Part III: Validity Studies

Part IV: Methodological Considerations

SCIENTIFIC ASPECTS
OF GRAPHOLOGY

PART I
MAJOR SCHOOLS OF GRAPHOLOGY

1

CLASSIC SCHOOLS OF GRAPHOLOGY

THEA STEIN LEWINSON

Introduction

THE TWENTIETH CENTURY has seen a dramatic development of dynamic handwriting analysis as a scientific technique, a process which is by no means concluded. Unfortunately, most of the representative works were never translated into English as the philosophical and psychological basis of phenomenology and the humanities (Geisteswissenschaften) was foreign to the clear-cut, rational Anglo-Saxon mind. In this chapter, the methods of seven representatives who made valuable contributions to the new field of dynamic handwriting analysis will be discussed. They are: Ludwig Klages, Max Pulver, Robert Heiss, Rudolph Pophal, Rhoda Wieser and the Mueller-Enskat team. Most of them based their theories on the science of expression developed by Ludwig Klages who is generally considered to be the founder of modern graphology. They all used (with different emphasis) the following indicators: the size of the middle-zone, upper and lower lengths and their relationship to the middle zone, direction and fluctuation of line, distance between lines, width of the writing, breadth of the letters, slant and fluctuation of the slant, left and right tendency, distance between words, width of margins, strength and placement of pressure, degree of connection, form originality in its various modifications (i.e., the divergency from the school copy), contraction and expansion of the letter contour, forms of connection and the characteristics of the stroke (sharpness, pastiness, elasticity-stiffness, etc.), although they developed different standards of evaluating the handwriting, which could at times change the emphasis on a particular graphic indicator. In general, however, they all contributed to the improvement and refinement of the new method and eventually came to similar conclusions in the analysis of handwriting.

Widespread use and results of various research studies supported the value of these newly-developed psychodiagnostic techniques, even though none of them should be viewed as perfect.

References and quotations in this chapter refer to the principal work of each scholar as named at the start of each section, unless otherwise specified.

LUDWIG KLAGES

Born in Hanover, Germany, on December 10, 1872. Died in Kilchberg, Switzerland on July 23, 1956. Studied: Philosophy, Psychology, Chemistry. In 1905, gave privately the first seminar on the science of expression. Dr. Phil.

Principle work: *Handschrift und Character* (1940)

Ludwig Klages is usually considered the founder of modern handwriting psychology. Philosopher, psychologist and graphologist, Klages is not well known in non-German speaking countries partly due to the difficulty in translating his works, but also due to his unique, intuitive philosophy on which all the interpretations of his objective findings are based.

Klages's work is divided into four parts, each dependent on the other in pyramid-like fashion: philosophy, characterology, the science of expression and graphology. Accordingly, "Graphology is one aspect of the science of expression which, in its turn, is an aspect of the science of character; the science of character, however, is an indispensable element of the potential knowledge of the essence of the world."

The Science of Expression

The three main types with which we are concerned are the expressive movement, the impulse-movement and the volitional movement. What differentiates them from each other is their relationship to their aims. The expressive movement has no ulterior aim, but carries its meaning within itself; the impulse-movement has its aim in the environment; and for the volitional movement, the conscious willing of the aim is significant. Actions (in contrast to a passive, dream-like existence) are volitional movements, and handwriting belongs to this category. The question that interests us here is whether it is possible for the volitional movements to express personality. Klages answers in the affirmative. He offers the following explanation. The mind would not appear in action at all, if it were not coupled with the vitality of the person.

From here Klages proceeds to his thesis: volitional movement expresses the personality of the willing person. The volition itself is not expressive, and the aim of the volitional movement is not important in this respect either; the only thing that is of decisive importance is the individual course of the movement.

There is unity of character in all the volitional movements of any individual. Every personal movement will assume that manner of movement which is characteristic of the individual. For example, the writing movement is the result of the will to express oneself by means of a prescribed writing system. Consequently, the handwriting is a volitional movement and must necessarily carry the individual stamp of any personality.

Every state of the living body is the expression of an impulse-system; every attitude finds expression. Every movement of the living body is a vital movement (that is, impulse of modified impulse-movement), and each vital movement has two constituent parts, the impulsive and the expressive. Klages formulates the following principle of expression: "An expressive (body)-movement is the visible manifestation of the impulses and feelings which are represented in the vital movement of which it is a component part." The second principle reads: "The expression manifests the pattern of a psychic movement as to its stength, duration and direction."

In short, expression considered as an aspect of impulse-movement and, consequently, of the volitional movement, represents the essence of the personality.

The question now arises: How is it possible for the human being to perceive the expression of the soul, and how is he able to interpret this expression? The answer is that the human being's capacity for expression is by nature coordinated with his capacity for impression.

Finally, the principle of representation or "guiding image" is one of the most significant portions of Klages's science of expression. Klages formulates the principle of representation as follows: "Every volitional movement is also induced by its personal 'guiding image' (Leitbild)." This principle of the "guiding image" has proved itself very fertile, especially in graphology. With regard to the intepretation of expressive movements, according to Klages, it seems that the expressive and the representative data are usually integrated in the same direction, and that the "guiding image" usually accentuates the expressive tendency. In the artistic productions of different historic periods, cultures and races, we are able to recognize the guiding image characteristic of each of them.

Graphology

The tangible test of Klages's science of expression is his system of graphology, which he considers to be the same as the psychology of handwriting. Handwriting is a permanent and measurable record of volitional movement which can be used for comparative study at any time. Handwriting is not only an expressive volitional movement but is also formed by the personal "guiding image" (Leitbild) and is markedly influenced by the individual's sense of space. It is a rhythmic movement condition, in which each single movement reflects the entire personality, the sum total of the writer's intellectual, emotional, and physical tendencies. Handwriting is an agent of psychodiagnostics that can be used for the most varied purposes. As can be readily understood, a graphology based on Klages's philosophy of expression must naturally reject the so-called graphology of isolated signs. This latter method tries to interpret each isolated sign of writing as a specific character-trait, thus disregarding the vital basis of handwriting. According to Klages, one must be concerned with a physiognomy of functions and not with a physiognomy of organs. The real cause of an isolated detail becomes comprehensible only insofar as it is related to the living whole. Klages says that handwriting is not a separable mixture (like peas and lentils) but a compound. Every symptom bears the color of all the other symptoms with which it occurs. The criteria which Klages uses for the interpretation of handwriting are regularity and harmony, the Formniveau, spaciousness, speed and pressure, width, slant and pastosity, forms of connection and degree of connection, copiousness and character of direction, initial emphasis, overlining and distribution of the movement, spacing of the writing as a whole and related features, as well as the indications of the so-called "acquired" handwriting. I shall now proceed to a discussion of some of the fundamentals which form the basis of handwriting interpretation.

Rhythm plays a decisive part in Klages's system of graphology. He contrasts rhythm with measure in reference to "time": rhythm is similar reproduction of similar periods; measure is the mathematically exact repetition of the same periods. Rhythm is an attribute of life (soul), while measure is an attribute of the mind. The rhythmic flow of life is disturbed by the wakefulness of the mind. The conflict between rhythm (soul) and measure (mind) is manifested in the handwriting. There exists not only a rhythm in time, but also a rhythm of form, movement and distribution with which we are most concerned in graphology.

The criterion of the double meaning (plus or minus) of every graphological indication is the so-called Formniveau, a factor of greatest significance. It indicates the rhythmic reproduction of original forms in the handwriting; it means the fullness of life. The stronger the rhythm of the form, the more is original life expressed in the handwriting, the higher is the Formniveau, and vice versa. Banality, set patterns, school-copy mean just so many negations of life. Klages distinguishes five degrees of Formniveau, starting with the most original and rhythmic writing and descending into unoriginal and arhythmic or regulated writing. It is easy to see that the basis of this fundamental evaluation, which has nothing to do with intelligence, stems from Klages's general attitude.

An important point is "harmony" (Ebenmass) in handwriting, which is also a rhythmic condition. But the strength of this harmony-rhythm is based upon an evaluation of the distribution-rhythm and the movement-rhythm of the writing. We speak of a high degree of harmony if there is a rhythmic distribution of the writing impulses with no disturbances of their flow. A low degree of harmony is indicated by a lack of distribution of the writing impulses and a disturbance of the flow. The main question lies in whether or not these modes of rhythm are disturbed or undisturbed. As to the distribution-rhythm of the writing, we find that in each writing field, the word-bodies stand out against the background (the empty space) in a definite, characteristic way. Sometimes the optic impression is one of balance, sometimes one of conflict. The former reveals harmony, the latter lack of harmony and consequently, lack of distribution-rhythm. One can judge the rhythmic distribution best by considering the word-intervals only. The movement-rhythm is expressed in the writing by rhythmic fluctuation of the writing elements (pressure, width, size, slant, etc). Consequently, the harmony in a writing sample may be disturbed by an entanglement in the writing which is usually caused by the great contrasts between short and long letters and by the unrhythmic (not the irregular) proportion of writing elements.

Harmony can be called the gauge for personal excitability of feelings. It expresses the relationship of two opposite functions: psychic urge and psychic resistance. Harmony in handwriting corresponds to equanimity; a lack of harmony, to excitability.

Another important aspect of handwriting is regularity. Regularity or irregularity refers to the size, the width, and the slant of writing. While the degree of Formiveau and "harmony" is found by an evaluation of some kind of rhythm, the degree of regularity is ascertained by a measurement of the scope of oscillation in the writing features. Klages holds that the mind and its functions, logical thinking and the will, have practically no expression, meaning that they become apparent only through their efforts on the forms of life, and that the will is the regulating and blocking force. If there is regularity in the writing movement, it must be attributed to the influence of the will, the regulating principle, the nature of which is, briefly, to suppress change and mutation. Consequently, the degree of regularity will be an index to the predominance of will. Regularity is found in the handwriting of the pedantic bookworm and also in the handwriting of a strong and powerful impulse-person, who controls life with an even stronger will, such as Bismark, for example. Irregularity is found in the handwriting of the unsteady adventurer and in those of very strong will, who, nevertheless, are overpowered by passionate feelings and impulses, as for instance, in the case of Beethoven. Whatever evaluation is chosen should depend upon the Formniveau as the basis of standardization. Regularity is the expression of the material quality in handwriting (will and feeling).

The next aspect is the expression of an intellectual capacity, the degree of connectedness (another material quality). There are handwritings in which single letters stand separated from each other. This is unconnected handwriting. There are other handwritings in which each letter is connected with the following letter without interruption. This is called connected handwriting. In between the two are the so-called "equilibrated" writing in which we find an equal amount of connected and unconnected writing. (The case of an irregular change between connected and unconnected writing indicates the presence of serious disturbances.)

Writing is systematized conduct and its systematization is demonstrated in the regular stopping and starting of the pen. Connected writing can be considered an unnatural connection of natural life-factors, while disconnected writing can be considered unnatural disconnection of natural life-factors. The activity of logical connecting is extreme in cases of non-observance of the natural pauses in movement. The positive interpretation of connectedness is logical activity and a gift for synthesis and dialectic, deliberation, calculation, etc. Negatively, it is lack of new ideas — the ability of the mind to elaborate only on what is present. The positive interpretation of unconnected writing is wealth of spontaneous ideas, which often results in original discovery and intellectual initiative; or practically, in cleverness and will. One could also say that disconnected writing is, in a positive sense, the expression of intuition. The negative interpretation is the tendency to be erratic, to lack logic; practically, lack of consideration and common sense.

Another point of interest is the manner in which the principle of representation, the "guiding image," affects handwriting — and its interpretation. Certain channels of expression for the impulse for representation are the conspicuous places in the writing-field, such as the beginning of letters, words and paragraphs; this is initial emphasis, which originates in a desire for self-estimation; in certain characters, it develops into a desire for greatness. The most favorable condition is a state of equilibrium between the self-confidence of a person and his self-estimation. In writing, this is expressed by a proportionate relationship between the width and the height of the initial letters, and the rest of the writing. The positive meaning of initial emphasis is the desire for significance, its negative meaning is vanity. The initial emphasis is the graphological indication of a driving force.

It is not possible within the space of this article to present a more detailed account of Klages's system of graphology. My purpose is to show the development of some of Klages's fundamental concepts which led from his system of philosophy, through characterology and the science of expression, to his system of graphology. For a more detailed explanation, see Levinson (1938). Thanks to Klages, graphology has been used as a psychodiagnostic method in Europe for the last seven decades and has found practical application in the fields of child and vocational guidance, in cases of personality adjustment, for various business and legal purposes, and for personality studies of patients suffering from certain chronic diseases.

MAX PULVER

Born in Munich, Germany, December 6, 1889. Died in Zurich, Switzerland, June 13, 1952. Dr. Phil.

Principle work: *Symbolik der Handschrift* (1945).

The groundwork of scientific graphology having been laid by Klages, Max Pulver added the study of modern depth psychology to the interpretation of handwriting. Through his application of a psychoanalytical approach, he considerably widened the scope of handwriting analysis. In Klages's work, the symbolism of the handwriting field plays only a secondary part of his studies. However, in Pulver's studies, the symbolism of the handwriting field plays a major role which considerably broadened the scope of graphic interpretation.

The German graphological school developed relatively late and tried from the very beginning to apply the findings of contemporary scientific psychology and physiology to graphological interpretation. Pulver attempts to prove that the development of German handwriting analysis has paralleled the development of German psychology. Before Klages, phenomenology and psychoanalysis had not yet been applied to the study of handwriting. Phenomenology is the doctrine which precribes that there are no "things unto themselves"; all things are phenomena (the object appearing to the mind via sensation). Phenomenology deals at all times with the pure meaning (Sinn) of things and events. In addition, Pulver applies the psychoanalytical methods of Freud, Adler, Jung and Steckel to handwriting interpretation. He claims that only through depth psychology is the comprehension of the complex psychological layers possible. According to him, it is mainly the subconscious strata of the human being which are valuable for psychic interpretation. Graphological work presupposes two things: inner perception and introspection on the one hand, and differentiation in external observations on the other. If only the former is used, one will arrive at intuitive results. If only the latter is used, the observer will miss the correlations in the subconscious.

According to Pulver, there are three different aspects which constitute the writing movement: handwriting, brain-writing and expressive writing: in other words the mechanical, the motoric and the formative.

a) **Handwriting**: A number of schematically prescribed finger and hand movements constitute the external phase of the writing act, i.e., a rhythmic alternation of stretching and bending movements takes place. In addition to the centrifugal and centripetal movements, the basic direction of the writing from left to right demands curved strokes, which when they are sinistrogyr are called adductive and when dextrogyr are called abductive. Extension and flexion, as well as adduction and abduction movement, are prescribed by the pattern of the school copy.

b) **Brain Writing**: The word handwriting is actually misleading insofar as its form language does not depend on the hand at all but on certain parts of the cerebral cortex, from which the motoric impulses for the movement of the penpoint originate. **The handwriting, therefore, is actually brain writing.** W. Preyer was the first to establish that arm, hand and finger are not the decisive factors in forming individual handwriting peculiarities. Proof of this lies in the fact that after coordination is established through practice, foot, hand or mouth writing show characterologically the same picture as handwriting. This is also the same, when the left hand instead of the right is trained through practice to write.

c) **Expressive Writing**: The term "expressive writing" means writing as the expression of an individual personality. It is not of any importance that we write mechanically, but it is important that we write emotionally and intellectually and that our writing is at one and the same time, will and impulse expression (Klages). Only with variation in the school copy pattern and the influx of superflous accompanying movements does the individual's expressive content of handwriting become apparent. Pulver does not focus his attention principally on the mechanism of the writing act but on the meaning of the small unnecessary movements which accompany the writing act. The graphologist first ascertains the condition of the writing, by exploring and segregating in the writing, technical and psychological causes for the variations which are evident. He next determines the meaning of these writing traits and deals with the comprehension of the true being or the pith of the personality. The technical writing conditions are also very important to Pulver: the writing instrument, letter system, the style of the particular area, etc. The writing act registers itself. Inasmuch as the subconscious impulse expressions unite with the conscious strivings in the writing act, the writing reflects the totality of the human being in an unfalsified manner. Even with the help of an acquired artificial writing, a characterological disguise is impossible.

The Expressive Movement and the
Possibility of Its Interpretation

a) *Expression*

There are two things which we comprehend in the expressive movement: a person's real disposition and tendencies and his character. Actions, and still more, the action sketches, which we call expressive movements (e.g., handwriting) have a symbolic value in interpretation and perception of these basic tendencies. From the expression, a deduction of the personality (character) can be drawn.

b) *Perception of Expression*

Pulver claims that the capacity for perception of expressive functioning is common to all living things. The animal does not exteriorize it but the human being is able to do so through his ability to reflect. Meaning is not put into the life expression from without, but it exists even though we may not be able to comprehend it. To neglect the meaning of life expression means to make it mechanical and consquently to kill it. This is the decisive issue for scientific graphology. It is the basis for the difference between static and dynamic concepts, between test and psychodiagnostic method.

Pulver also developed a theory of the "composite personality" which interests us mainly in its relation to the handwriting. He considers the handwriting not only as hand or brain writing, but basically as expressive writing (very much like Klages). He stresses the expressive side of the writing movement because it is the self-registering writing act. The writer unconsciously reveals his personality and the human being is able to perceive and interpret this kind of personality expression. Pulver perceives the composite personality as a dynamic entity consisting of three layers: the constitution (the physical sphere); the intermediate part or character (the instinctive-emotional sphere); and at the top of the superstructure, the personality (the intellectual sphere) (see Fig. 1). The pit or dynamic center of the composite personality is the character which in its constant changeability is not clearly marked off against the physical and the intellectual spheres and represents the intermediator between them; influencing and forming them and being influenced and formed by them (the steering wheel of the composite personality). By its natural dynamic strength, the character is the constituent which expresses itself in a direct physical form or function, while the personality expresses itself only indirectly by giving the intentional direction or meaning to these functions.

The writing expression offers the double advantage that on the one hand it represents an objective product of the mind and is therefore an expression of the personality; on the other hand, there is an affective component in the writing expression, that is, it is also character expression. Consequently, as it contains rational and affective elements, the writing expression gives the expression of the "composite personality." The essence of the writing (Pulver's "Wesensgehalt") reflects the "composite personality" faithfully, even if according to present day research, the physiological factors appear less distinct than the characterological and intellectual factors. The mind can penetrate the writing only as much as it is able to take on some kind of shape in the movement expression. The physical can alter the writing act inasmuch as it finds it equivalent in the characterological. This then is the link between constitution, character and handwriting. **The handwriting is the fixed expression of a person's physical, emotional and intellectual tendencies and has the special advantage over other modes of expression that it is available for purposes of comparison at any time.** This is the basic premise for all scientific handwriting analysis.

The symbolism of the handwriting was Pulver's greatest emphasis and contribution. Klages had mentioned it and Pulver elaborated on it. He claims that the real or imaginary line serves as a starting point for the space orientation which we project to the writing field, the plane on which the letters are written. It is the demarcation between above and below. The human being spontaneously associates with the word "above": sky (heaven), sun, spiritual powers and light. Below the line, however, there is the counterpoint of this realm; depth, abyss, demonic power and darkness. The handwritings of our time are regulated by a generally conceived law of space expression, which zones good and evil, heaven and hell, light and shadow. In addition to the up-and-down direction, the western peoples write from **left** to **right**. Communication is directed from the Ego-moment (the present) forward into time and the future. This may seem to be a problem in metaphysics, but one has to bear in mind that Pulver tries to apply and utilize the ancient symbols which still function in the subconscious mind and influence our conscious actions as demonstrated through dreams and similar materials (the teachings of Freud and Jung). Since, according to this concept, the subconscious dominates our actions and reactions, the same should hold true for the handwriting. That being so, the symbolic interpretation of the writing picture seems to be justified and understandable.

Figure 1. Form and Content of Consciousness

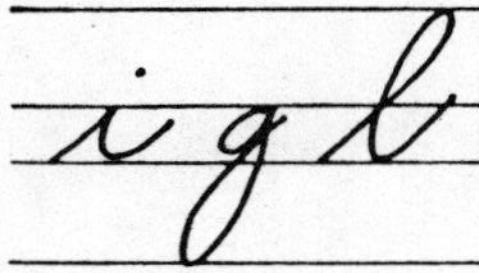

	Form	Content
a) upper zone	Intellectuality, spirituality	Ethical-religious zone
b) i-height (middle zone)	Individual day-consciousness, empirical sphere*	Sensitiveness, egotism-altruism
c) lower zone	Subconsciousness	Material, physical, erotic-sexual content

Left: Ego — and past relations of the sensitive sphere, introversion

Right: You - and future relations of the sensitive sphere, extraversion

* The imaginary or real line symbolises the threshold of consciousness

Pulver considers the handwriting as a three dimensional formation. The third dimension, depth, is the result of pressure. We thus have height, width and depth in the writing space, yielding a three-dimensional orientation of the writing field: above-below, left-right, depth (back) and front. The above-below axis is divided into three writing zones: the intellectual zone (the upper lengths), the emotional zone (the middle area) and the instinctive-materialistic zone (the underlengths). The left side of the writing field represents the Ego, the past and the female principle; the right side represents the You, the future and the male principle (see Fig. 1). These different symbolic divisions are not indicative of the true character of the writer, but in their emphasis or lack of emphasis, the tendency or lack of tendency in the writer are expressed.

Pulver stresses particularly the **multifariousness** and the **ambivalence** of the graphic expression. In contrast to Klages who used the "formniveau" as an evaluation standard which resulted in a double meaning of each graphic indication, Pulver introduces as his evaluating standard the "contents of substance" (Wesensgehalt), which he defines as the "quantity and quality of tension within an individual." For him the graphic rhythm (of Klages) is only one aspect of the process of evaluation. He considers and evaluates the graphic expression in its entirety, balancing the tensions in the different personality strata toward each other. Thus, the basis for multifarious interpretation of graphic expression was given.

For the most part, the contents of the writing are of no interest to the graphologist as they indicate little or nothing compared to the wealth of material which lies in the graphic expression. Actually, the writer does not realize that he is drawing a picture of his real self. Undisturbed by the restriction of his consciousness, he works subconsciously to draw his self-portrait. According to Pulver, the writer projects into the writing his intellectual, emotional and physical aspects, with introverted and extroverted tendencies (ego-you relationship), and this is in direct relationship to the symbolic division of the handwriting field. If expressive movement is a condensed self-portrait, it also bears formative traces (Bildkrawfte) of ancestors, as well as the inculcation of education and the influence of the environment. Every expression therefore contains elements which go beyond the subjective personal character. With reference to the fixated writing movement, the individual coins his own forms in his every variation from the school-copy. Thus, for Pulver, the meaning of the expressive movement is multifarious as the individual has his or her origin in primitive collective conditions and the hereditary constitution.

The multifariousness of the expressive symbol may well be illustrated through handwriting, e.g., the beginning of a word means the beginning of a time period and the word ending, the end of this period. The deviations of the written word represent with various modifications the phase or the time of the expression.

In addition to the multifariousness of the writing, the ambivalence of the writing is important to Pulver. Ambivalence or positive and negative factors in relation to handwriting means the presence of both good and evil. This ambivalence of the graphic expression depends on the fundamental positive and negative qualities in the human being, tensions between the most basic contradictory tendencies, attraction and repulsion. Such ambivalence permeates the multifarious graphic expression, and due to its dialectic dynamic processes, makes the manifestation of divergence in graphic expression possible. (Pulver uses here the concepts of ambivalence developed by the German psychiatrist, E. Bleuler: ". . . in the dialectic process of human development, it (the ambivalence) has a dynamically indispensable propelling and quite general role, by reason of its antithetical character. . ." Pulver demonstrates and illustrates the graphic expression of ambivalence: a) on the sexual, mythical, dynamic level; b) on the psychic emotional level; and c) on the highest level, that is the spiritual-religious level or that of anthropological existence. The infinitely various forms in which this ambivalence can be manifested on the various psychic levels, shapes the different graphic expressions and makes the dynamic interpretation of the multifarious graphic expression possible.

As a final clarification of his rather complex concepts regarding the symbolic interpretation of the graphic expression, Pulver presents a twofold description, correlating the symbolic tripartition of the handwriting field with the variations in the graphic expression. (see Fig. 1 above). He states again that collective conditions influence a priori our method of writing, the general localization, and that only from this viewpoint can symbolic handwriting interpretation be understood. It must be emphasized that in the symbolic tripartition of the handwriting field, we are not dealing with a measurement of value, but in addition to the symbolic content, with a topography (the symbolic form), a systematic direction of the different zones of consciousness. Pulver therefore makes a two-fold tripartition of the writing field (referring to the **form** and the **content** of consciousness) which, of course, can serve only schematic purposes; in reality these elements are absorbed by each other. (For an explanation of the two-fold tripartition, refer back to Figure 1.)

One might say that the participation as to **form** refers to the person as an individually formed psychophysical entity in relation to his (onto-genetic) personal development, while the second partition (as to content) refers to the person as a present transitory state in relation to his philo-genetic development. Although this two-fold tripartition of the handwriting field appears as a somewhat artificial construction, it has proved instrumental in the practical interpretation of the ambivalent multifarious graphic expression.

Space does not permit a complete demonstration of the way in which Pulver applied his symbolism to the interpretation of handwriting. Pulver was the founder of a new direction within the realm of scientific graphology upon which he had a decisive influence. Even though his theories may appear metaphysical to many of today's more rational-minded psychologists, they had a decisive influence on many grapholo-gists after him and even on some measurable systems of modern handwriting psychology, as well as on research into criminology, psycho-pathology and psychosomatic relationships.

ROBERT HEISS

Born in Munich, Germany, January 22, 1903. Died in Freiburg/Br., Germany, February 21, 1974. Psychology and Philosophy. From 1936, Professor in Cologne; from 1943 in Freiburg/Br. Founder of the Institute there for Psychology and Characterology. Dr. Phil.

Principle work: *Die Deutung der Handschrift* (1966).

Professor Dr. Robert Heiss was Director of the Institute for Psychology and Characterology at the University of Freiburg, Germany, where a considerable amount of handwriting analysis was carried out.

Taking Klages's science of expression as a basis, Heiss considers handwriting as a combination of nature and art. According to his theory, there are three most important aspects of the handwriting — the processes of **movement, space and form.** All the commonly used handwriting indicators can be arranged under these headings. Heiss considers his method new and different to previous methods. He explains that the interpretation of handwriting consists first, of comprehending the handwriting picture as an entity and then, comprehending its elements. The writing process weaves movement, form and space together resulting in three basic pictures. He attempts to illustrate his basic concepts by the development of a child's handwriting.

In looking at a handwriting sample, he asks the fundamental question: Which aspect of the writing picture is emphasized — the movement, the form, the space? Every one of these basic aspects represents different aspects of the personality. In every handwriting, the principles of expression and the principles of representation are functioning. Every one of these three aspects could carry the emphasis but sometimes the dominance is not quite clear and has to be carefully determined. It is possible that the predominant characteristics of the **space** picture are standing or falling, of the movement picture — fluent or staccato, of the form picture — positive or negative. This is just as a preliminary first impression before going into a more detailed analysis.

Heiss establishes a list of overall positive and negative possibilities for his three basic aspects: movement picture, space picture, form picture. He grades these possibilities into three degress, of which 1 and 3 are at the negative ends of his scales, while 2 is positive.

The reality of the handwritings, of course, shows all possible combinations. As is easily understandable, every part of one vertical column could occur together with any part of the other verticle columns, e.g., one writing could show richness of elements and smoothness of flow

(Column I, 2), but it could be undeveloped in its space picture (Column II, 1) and at the same time, it could show clear and original forms (Column III, 2), etc.

Table I: Positive and Negative Possibilities of the Overall Impression
(according to Heiss)

I Movement Picture	II Space Picture	III Form Picture
1. Paucity of elements inhibited in its flow.	1. Undeveloped, regulated, schematic.	1. Unformed, school-copy form.
2. Richness of elements, gliding or smooth in its flow.	2. Developed space, enlivened, (dynamized space, well-organized).	2. Clearly formed, original forms.
3. Disturbed in its elements, movement appears paralyzed, becomes rigid or uncoordinated.	3. Torn, empty, confused.	3. Form rigidity, form disintegration.

After this preliminary blueprint table, Heiss establishes three basic tables for each of his basic aspects: movement, space and form, under which he records and distributes all basic graphic indicators and also impression qualities which are commonly used by all handwriting psychologists. Each of these tables has three partitions: Undeveloped, Developed (well-defined, prominent) and Disturbed.

Table II: Basic Movement Picture Table (according to Heiss)

Undeveloped	Well Defined	Disturbed
Awkward, inhibited movement.	Easy, skilled, spontaneous movement.	Torn, whipping uncoordinated movement.
Hesitating, lame, brittle or thickly flowing.	Swinging, gliding, sure, lively in the movement flow.	Uncertain tactic in the movement flow.
Lack of smooth and free movement.	Fluid or free movement flow.	Non-uniform disturbed movement flow.
Lame, indolent or cumbersome stroke.	Firm elastic and light stroke.	Interrupted, cut-up, fringy or tremulous stroke.
Weak or hardened stiffened pressure.	Rhythmic pressure.	Unrhythmic pressure fluctuations.
Tendency toward disconnected letters, only few fluent connections.	Single movements integrated into differentiated movement aspect.	Smeariness and spotting. Cut-up, abrupt, whipping single strokes.
Prominence of single short-phased movement trends.	Agility or precision of movement shapes.	Movement elements broken in themselves or falling to pieces.

Table III: Basic Space Picture Table (according to Heiss)

Undeveloped	Well Defined	Disturbed
Space treatment according to school directives.	Individual arrangement of space with a distant space order.	Disharmonious impression of space. Torn, disorderly or overcrowded space.
Size and width according to school-copy or uncertain fluctuations, conventional proportions of size.	Size and width-balanced variations in proportion. Some prominence of the middle zone or emphasis of upper and underlengths.	Disharmonious fluctuations of size and width. Exaggerated proportions of height or extreme fluctuation.
Schoolcopy-like, rigid slant and schematic line characteristics (fluctuation and spacing) little separation of lines.	Slant fluctuations according to balanced movement. Distance between lines in proportion to the size of the writing with noticeable line fluctuation	Extreme fluctuation of slant. Disturbed line direction and fluctuation. Hooking of lines.
Indistinct or neglected treatment of margins.	Rhythmically spaced margins.	Missing margins or unharmonious fluctuations.
Schematic or unorganized space arrangement.	Rhythmic space filling or even space distribution.	Unrhythmic, disorderly arrangement of space.

Table IV: Basic Form Picture Table (according to Heiss)

Undeveloped	Developed	Disturbed
Acording to school copy.	Original, spirited and smooth or simplified essential letter forms.	Exaggerated, self-willed or rigidly schematic forms.
Imitated, uncertain and awkward forms.	Individual new formations, simplifications or new connections.	Inflated or flourished letter forms.
Inconspicuous, monotonous forms of letters.	Multifariousness and flexibility or firmness with consistently lively formation of letters.	Incomplete, broken, distorted or dissolved letter forms.
One-sidedness of letter forms.		Rigid monotony of form.
Regulated or monotonous.		Prominence of some particular form distortions or flourishes.

These tables are the backbone of Heiss's system of handwriting interpretation. The interpretation for the **movement picture** presents the emotional impetus and its development. The **space picture** represents a writer's relationship to his environment. The **form picture** indicates the coining of the personality form in its narrow sense. Heiss presents three steps for analyzing a handwriting:

1. Reception of the impression of the entire handwriting picture, which shows the personality in its structure.
2. Analysis of single elements, i.e., differential analysis to determine the meaning of the expression in the structure.

3. Combination of elements with each other and with the impression of the handwriting picture.

Heiss emphasizes the interpolation of the different graphic aspects and their relation to the dynamic entity in contrast to the interpretation of isolated signs. He formulates his concept in the following sentence: "Perceiving graphologically does not mean to grasp the word and reading picture of a handwriting, but it means to recognize individualities and shadings of a dynamic and formed entity."

In his book, **Die Deutung der Handschrift** (1966), (the Interpretation of Handwriting) the author describes in detail all the individual graphological elements, their interpretation and their relationship to his blueprint. His main theme is always that writing is a formed movement process in space. As his explanations do not vary greatly from those of his predecessors, and basically follow the general lines of graphological teaching of dynamic handwriting analysis, we shall not discuss them here. However, his somewhat different concept of rhythm, which was recently criticized by Rhoda Wieser in the **Zeitschrift für Menschenkunde**, might be of interest.

Heiss treats the concept of rhythm somewhat differently to Klages, and discusses mainly the space or distribution rhythm and the form rhythm. In addition to the exact and qualifying evaluation of handwriting factors, he considers a **qualitative** characteristic which he calls **rhythmic.** He defines rhythm as periodically repeated manifestations in the movement flow which can be conceived as graphic elements or relationships of graphic elements. This concept can be applied to the space picture and can be translated to the placement of the word bodies on the background of the writing space. We could find an overcrowded picture or a background which appears rather empty and which may even show holes, or we could have a periodic, **rhythmic** distribution of word bodies on the writing background. Heiss, quoting Klages, says that "one can receive from this type of distribution the impression either of equilibrium or of conflict." He also adds that a periodic return of the observed manifestation is decisive, as it would support the diagnosis of distribution rhythm.

Regarding the form rhythm, Heiss gives the following explanation: Wherever the movement flow and the letter formation are split apart, there is no rhythm. That could be due to over-emphasized strength or weakness of one or the other or of both. The result would be different types of disturbed forms. Only where there is an integration or a synthesis of movement and form, do we find form rhythm. Heiss prefers to call this the creative rhythm (Gestaltungsrhythmus). Instead of Klages's five-stage gradation of the "Formniveau," he prefers to determine only if the handwriting displays an unbalanced, a balanced or a disturbed creative rhythm.

Finally, as a sort of overall indicator, Heiss describes the change indicators, referring to frequency and place emphasis of a particular graphic element (Wechselmerkmale). Every graphic element can appear in a uniform way, in contrasts, especially emphasized, constantly changing, etc. He distinguishes four modifications of the change indicator which he considers important for a graphological analysis:

1) change of graphic element only in some places of little latitude;
2) change of graphic elements in some places of wide latitude;
3) continued change of graphic element of little latitude;
4) continued change of graphic element of wide latitude.

Although the list is complete, in analyzing handwriting, the following facts must be established:

1) the frequency of a graphic characteristic in the flow of the writing;
2) the constancy, the flexibility or the change of a graphic characteristic;
3) the nature, position and course of a change indicator.

Heiss considers the change indicator most important for the diagnosis of a person's behavior. From this, conclusions can be drawn as to the passive or active aspect of the personality which could possibly extend to ambivalent behavior. The more latitude of change we find in the change indicator, the more latitude of fluctuations we will find in the behavior of that particular person.

After the presentation of his graphological method, Heiss adds a chapter in which he gives a detailed description of how to make a graphological analysis which he illustrates by an assessment of the former German President, Theodor Heuss.

Strangely enough, there is not a single measurement of the handwriting mentioned in Heiss's system. However, approximately a dozen doctoral theses on graphometrics were published by his students and associates, who emphasized measurements of the handwriting and statistics.

Heiss's method had a great influence on the graphological community and is still used by a considerable number of handwriting psychologists today.

RUDOLPH POPHAL

Born in Filehne, Germany, on September 5, 1893. Died in Hamburg, Germany, 1966. From 1924, University Lecturer in Greifswald. From 1946, University Professor in Hamburg. 1954 Founded a graphological research institute. Dr. Med., Dr. Phil.

Principle work: *Die Handschrift als Gehirnschrift* (1949).

As a doctor of medicine and of philosophy, Pophal was interested in the physiological basis of the handwriting movement and in his investigations, as considerably influenced by the theories of Dr. K. Wacholder The basis of his theory was **The Muscle**:

1) Tension and Relaxation;
2) Bending and Stretching.

Tension and Relaxation form the backbone of Pophal's system regarding the different degrees of stiffening tension. The alternation of tension and relaxation together with changing the length of the muscle by bending and stretching produces **movement**: therefore, handwriting is considered to be a movement. The psychiatrist, W. Preyer, had coined the basic idea that handwriting is brain-writing, and most of the newer graphological theories, starting with Ludwig Klages, were based on this hypothesis. Pophal considered it necessary to study and present the physiology of the brain, in order to explain the basis of graphic movement. These studies are, of course, very complex and it is only possible to present the simplified basic aspects of this system. The handwriting movement is predominantly produced in varying degrees by three portions of the brain: the Pallidum, and the Striatum and the Cortex. Pophal states that these brain functions cause different types of muscular tension and he distinguishes between two different types of tension which are evident in handwriting. One is directed outward and produced by pressing the writing instrument against the paper in all varieties of shading. The application of this outward directed force releases tension and is called pressure. The second form of tension stabilizes the joints of the hand by contraction of all muscles participating in holding the pen. It is produced by static energy and Pophal calls it "stiffening tension" (Versteifungs-Spannung). Pressure is characterized by the alternation of tension and release in the up-and-down stroke, while the stiffening tension or "gripping tension" is a static form of "isotonic" muscular contraction, the polar opposite of which could be slackness.

Accordingly, the **Pallidum** causes the uncontrolled back and forth movement with practically no control and inhibiting element. The **Striatum** causes the over-controlled, possibly inhibited single movement and the functioning of the **Cortex** produces the balanced and purposeful movement. From this, it should be clear that regarding the **stiffening** of the writing movement, the effect of the Pallidum is insufficient control, the effect of the Striatum could be an overcontrol and that the effect of the Cortex could be an adequate, purposeful blending of release and control.

Pophal tries to illustrate the various degrees of stiffening tension by handwriting samples and points out supporting graphic indications which, however, cannot be found there as a rule. He concludes that the concrete diagnosis of the various stiffening tensions presents so many difficulties that it is best to treat the stiffening tension merely as an impression, especially as it is subject to so many fluctuations. The interpretation of the increased stiffening tension would be that the writer is pulling himself together, whereas the increased release can be interpreted as loss of control and lack of restraint — in various degrees, of course, In the following pages, we shall present the interpretation of the different degrees of stiffening tension.

It might be advisable to describe in detail the five levels of stiffening of the joints which Pophal found indicative of the general state of muscular tension of an individual.

Level I

Insufficient stiffening or slackness causing sloppy movement. Here the effect of the activity brain centers has the upper hand, while the restraining action of the Corpus Striatum is too weak. Activating impulses cause loose movements of the writing instrument which slips in all directions.

Level II

Some stiffening allowing relaxed repetitive movement. Here we have the perfect coordination of activating and restraining brain centers (Globus Pallidus and Corpus Striatum), typical of the easy flow of repetitive inborn movement forms.

Level III

Moderate stiffening producing well-controlled elasticity of movement and poise. This level differs from the previous level because of the added action of the cortical guidance. Single well-controlled movements are carried out by the cooperation of the three brain centers. This is the ideal of human motor behavior for here we find elasticity, but not as loose as in Level II, as well as poise and control, but not as rigid as in Level IV.

Level IV

Excessive stiffening causing tenseness, rigidity or inhibition of movement. Here there exist two possible manifestations of tenseness depending on which of the three cooperating brain centers plays the dominant role in the individual concerned. Inhibition of movement and poor line quality are caused by the over-activity of the inhibitory brain mechanisms, while regularity and rigidity will appear in the handwriting of individuals whose personality is dominated by the higher brain centers. Voluntary control or compulsive behavior may produce rigid forms and still show good line quality, i.e., homogenous smoothness of the structure of the stroke.

Level V

Extreme stiffening, causing cramps and jerky movement or near-immobilization. Here we have extreme irregularity or chopped-up forms and poorest line quality. The movements of the writer are analogous to the movement of a car attempting to brake on an icy road, or to move fast with the brakes on (see Figure 2). The most important degrees of the Stiffening Tension are, of course, the two extremes and the center (Weak, Balanced and Exceedingly Strong).

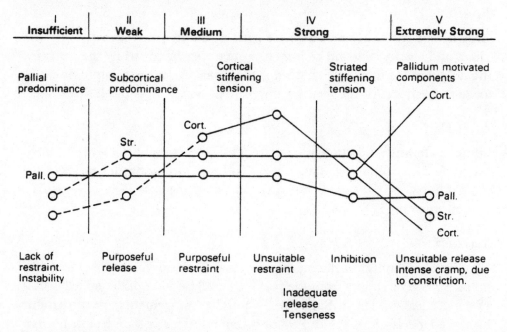

Figure 2. Participation of the Different Movement Centers in the Stiffening Tension. Gradation of the Stiffening Tension

Table V: The Stiffening Tension
(Reproduced from Pophal, 1939)

	WEAK (looseness)	MIDDLE-STRONG	STRONG (Cramped)
Writing pressure.	Little, medium or strong.	Little to medium.	Little, perhaps sporadic.
Hand position.	Medium position or "Supination".	"Pronation" to "Supination".	Medium position between Pronation and Supination to Pronation with dorsal flection and perhaps abduction of the wrist.
Finger position.	Arched	Stretched (arched).	Bent (seldom stretched).
(Pen or pencil) Grip-hold.	Not short.	Long, medium-long, short.	Medium, short & long.
Grip - Position.	Diagonal S., *Frontal S.	Sagittal and all others.	Diagonal P.**-S.Frontal S.-P.
Pen Angle.	Rather medium to small.	Small to large.	Rather large (unless long grip-hold).
Pastiness	Not exactly sharp, but still pasty.	Possibly pasty but also sharp + all transitions.	Rather sharp (if not long grip-hold).
Size of writing	Not small.	Small, large & medium.	Small
Writing speed	Medium fast, not very fast, not very slow.	Slow to medium fast.	Rather fast (intended haste). Also slow.
Slant of writing	Rather sloping.	Rather vertical.	Rather sloping (and fluctuating.
Width of writing	Wide.	Rather narrow.	Narrowness (In case of strongest stiffening wide).
Degree of connection	Rather connected (strong).	Rather connected (In case of back & forth movement).	Connected, possibly cut-up (strongest-stiffening).
Form of connection	Double curve, garland, soft angle, thread, perhaps dissolving.	Angle, arcade, garland, school-copy connections perhaps thread.	Dissolving of Forms of connection. Hasty thread.
Fullness (of contour)	Rather full.	--	Rather lean (contraction).
Upper signs	Without counter-movement or repulse (Rücktoss).	With use of counter-movement.	With single or double counter-movement (perhaps in shape of a wave).
End & beginning traits	Endings: short, long or pointed, single curved (front or back stroke).	End strokes: short or broken off or pointed. Curved or angle, front or back stroke.	Ending strokes wave-shaped (hasty thread). Perhaps pointed, possibly added front initial stroke.
Back and forth or single movement.	Medium, fast back and forth movement, slow single movement.	Back and forth movement or single movement.	Single movement, but also (not flowing) back & forth movement.
Coordination	Favored by back & forth & slow, single movement Worse with slow single movement.	Back & forth movement or single movement.	Single movement but also (not flowing) back & forth movement, improved by fast single movement. Worsened by back & forth movements.

* S=Supination
** P=Pronation

In the book, **Grundlegung der Bewegungs-Physiologischen Graphologie**, there is a table, reproduced in Table V, showing the distribution of the commonly used graphic indicators arranged under these three degrees of stiffening. In other words, this table shows the effect of the stiffening tensions on the various aspects of the handwriting movements.

The **medium degree** of stiffening tension (Level III) could be interpreted as self-control or steadiness, as self-assertion against distracting influences, a disposition for necessary inhibition and passive as well as reactive willpower, as purposeful self-discipline, steadiness and moderation and finally as power of resistance, purposefulness and concentration. These are not interpretations of pressure but of the stiffening tension which can be found in the pressure, although the stiffening of tension is diagnosed from the pressure and the stroke (see Table V).

In contrast to purposeful restraint, we have unsuitable restraint in the very strong stiffening tension. Where this no longer stems from voluntary control and discipline, such a stiffening tension is based on "weakness." Here we find lameness and emotional brittleness, due to extreme tension.

With increasing restraint and suppression of vital impulses, not only are naturalness and spontaneity lost. In the same degree, consciousness and awareness are increased and with them, egocentricity. In case of increased restraint by disposition, we can expect in addition, insecurity, embarrassment and over-sensitivity.

With increased self-assertion, there is an additional decrease of the capacity for self-devotion, and restraint as well as inhibitedness decrease the capacity for establishing contacts with others as well as possibility for self-expression and adaptability. We are no longer speaking of self-control. Every increased stiffening tension expresses increased tendencies for self-protection and expectations of possible disturbance, which finally, in the extreme cramp condition, grow into a constant preparedness for alarm and danger and into a permanent state of mobilization.

The breakdown of restraint in the cramp condition is in contrast to the inadequate restraint in the insufficient stiffening tension which we labelled instability. We mentioned the fact that the instability of the inadequate stiffening tension is of an entirely different character to the loss of control due to the extremely strong stiffening tension. In the latter, the restraining mechanisms are in action; however, the exaggerated tension (overstrain) is so great that the cramp-like stiffening tension can no longer produce any support. In the former, that is, the inadequate restraint, if there are inhibiting energies in the form of stiffening tension, they are active to such an adequate degree, that one must speak here about a weakness of resistance. We have lability in both cases but the lability of the inadequate stiffening tension is lack of restraint, while the lack of stability of the stiffening tension **results in lability in the final analysis.** Instead of the will for self-assertion of the middle and strong stiffening tension, the **inadequate stiffening tension** shows a tendency toward letting oneself go, a lack of self-assertion, and with it indicates a passive and reactive will. Instability and lack of restraint indicate, in addition, an inner lack of direction, fickleness and lack of principle.

The **purposeful lack of restraint** in the form of looseness in the stiffening tension (Level III) indicates, first of all, unrestraint, a freedom of ties. As in this case there is sufficient emotional controlling strength to serve as a guard against transgressions, we must not interpret this type of looseness as lack of all inhibitions and of all controls. We must perceive it as flexibility, naturalness and some tendency towards being yielding and impressionable. The man with weak tension is inclined to carelessness, unconcerned attitudes and euphoric moods. Even though one may not encounter problems in the emotional development, one may find a somewhat childlike nature, considerable immediateness, little general awareness and considerable naivety. The egocentric tendencies are usually reduced, and, instead, we frequently find real devotion, self-denial, altruistic tendencies and a capacity for enthusiasm. Nor should one forget here the ability and inclination for adjustment.

If we look over the interpretations of the different degrees of stiffening tension, we find that Levels I and V contain predominantly negative interpretations. Yet similar graphic indications (as well as character traits) appear in different degrees of stiffening tension. The latter could lead to diagnostic difficulties which may occur especially in the borderline areas; that is, in the adequate (Level II) and the very strong stiffening tension (Level IV.)

Being intimately related to the emotional aspect of personal experience, the degree of stiffening tension is frequently subject to considerable flunctuations. Just as we find handwritings with irregular distribution of the writing pressure, we may find considerable fluctuations regarding the stiffening tension. Therefore, we would be justified in speaking of regularity and irregularity regarding the strength of the stiffening tension.

Pophal's complete interpretation tables for the single graphic indications are so complex and long that they cannot be quoted here. The basic line is: Weak stimuli prompt the vital function, stimuli of medium strength expedite it (accelerate it), strong stimuli inhibit it and the strongest ones cancel it out.

Pophal himself said that the detailed physiological aspects of the writing movement which he studied and described may not be of great interest to the average practicing graphologist. However, of more general practical interest should be his book, **Das Strichbild** (the Texture of the Stroke), dealing with the problem of form and substance in the psychology of handwriting. Pophal distinguishes three stroke qualities: the woven stroke, the porous or granulated stroke and the brush-like stroke. The reference is to the stroke which does not carry the pressure. A magnifying glass of at least sixteen power magnification is required.

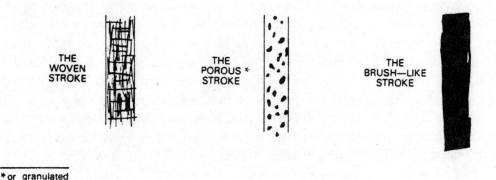

*or granulated

Figure 3. Texture of the Stroke (taken from Pophal, 1950).

Table VI is an exact translation of Pophal's detailed descriptions of the three stroke qualities and their respective interpretation.

This concludes the review of Rudolph Pophal's handwriting studies. It should be mentioned that his theories of brain physiology have been challenged by modern researchers.

Table VI: The Texture of the Stroke as Expression of Psychic Substance

(Translated and summarized by Thea S. Lewinson, 1960. From Pophal, R. Das Strichbilt: zum Form-und Stoffproblem in der Psychologie der Handschrift, Stuttgart: Georg Thieme Verlag, 1950)

1. **The Homogeneous Stroke (the woven stroke):**

    a. Mode of appearance

        Integrated structure with <u>internal differentiation</u>.
        Organically formed.
        Woven, enlivened, animated, <u>homogeneous-differentiated</u>.
        Firm, dense, coherent.
        Intimate and close coherence of the pigment particles.
        Clear, transparent, simple.
        Clean, neat.
        Quiet, even.
        Periodic (or rhythmic) exchange between lighter and darker parts.
        Conveying the impression of a plane or ribbon.

    b. Interpretation

        Inner firmness, stability.
        Even formative principle.
        Inner solidity.
        Firmness of character.
        Reliability - "soundness" (trustworthiness, faithful to own standards).
        Simplicity.
        Inner clarity and cleanliness.
        Enlivened multifariousness (many sidedness).

2. **The Granulated Stroke (the porous stroke):**

    a. Mode of appearance.

        Unintegrated structure with <u>lack of internal differentiation</u>.
        Unorganically formed.
        Not animated; mechanical, <u>unhomogeneous-undifferentiated</u>.
        Loosened, dissolved, perforated, not firm, incoherent, porous.
        Diffusion of pigment, dissolving of pigment.
        Unclear, dim, unevenly brightened.
        Granulated, mottled, spotty, washed out, burned out.
        Agitated flickering, uneven, "moldy".
        Usually with some depth penetration, possibly a "knitted" stroke.

    b. Interpretation

        Lack of inner firmness.
        Inner looseness, instability.
        Inner brittleness, lack of substance.
        "Lack of character," weakness, unreliability (not trustworthy, not faithful to his own
            standards, unprincipled).
        Excitability.
        Lack of harmony.

3. **The Amorphous, Brush-like Stroke:**

    a. Mode of Appearance

        Integrated structure without internal differentiation.
        Homogeneous-undifferentiated.
        Lifeless, dead, uniform, monotonous.
        Monochromatic, pigment diminished by melting, lack of internal architecture.
        Dim, opaque.
        Mostly conveying the impression of a plane.

    b. Interpretation

        Lack of emotional-intellectual differentiation.
        Uninterested uniformity.
        Levelling uniformity.
        Indifference, boredom.
        Lack of liveliness and of emotional content - sobriety.
        Psychic monotony.
        Simple, primitive psychic quality.

RHODA WIESER

Born August 27, 1894. Student of Ludwig Klages. Scientific Graphologist. From 1926, graphological practice in Vienna. From 1928 to 1968, sworn handwriting identification expert at the Vienna Court. From 1929 to 1933, special assistant at the Criminological Institute of the University in Vienna. Since 1969, Rhoda Wieser has lived in West Germany. Dr. rer. pol.

Principle work: *Mensch und Leistung in der Handschrift* (1960).

Rhoda Wieser developed the concept of the basic rhythm (Grundrhythmus) as a diagnostic tool. Pophal had concentrated on the pressure and the stroke itself; Rhoda Wieser also emphasized the importance of the stroke but with a different dynamic approach which had predominantly socio-ethical implications. For her, it is not the letter forms (as in periodic rhythm) that are important, but the dynamic polarity, whose essence is defined by a "growth process producing totality and transformation." The basic rhythm is a natural phenomenon which could be depicted in contrast such as: deep-flat, flabby-rigid, soft-firm, weak-hardened, strong-feeble, elastic-unelastic, free-dragging, etc. The basic rhythm as polar rhythm is an important aspect of Wieser's teachings. This is the forming movement of the strong basic rhythm in handwriting; it avoids the gliding into the picture of dissolution or of rigidity. (The latter would be the picture of death.) Therefore, no mechanical picture or routine pattern could have strong basic rhythm. Only the individual handwriting, naturally created in all details, can have strong basic rhythm. In it, one experiences the quality of the manifestation inseparable from the polar rhythm. Dynamics as quality of experience can be deduced from thin delicate writing as well as that which is strong and heavy. Basic rhythm can be found in all expressive movements. It is the quality of totality in which the human essence manifests itself. This manifestation, characterized by elasticity, was formerly called strong basic rhythm, but Wieser calls it **polar elasticity**. Therefore in the formed movement of the handwriting with a strong basic rhythm, we have the dynamic quality of the polar rhythm as well as the polar-caused elasticity manifested in the reciprocal functioning of all handwriting elements. They are two aspects of the same manifestation quality.

One could compare the stroke of a letter to the tensiveness in an elastic rubber band. A medium, balanced tension of elasticity would compare to a strong basic rhythm, while an extremely tense (over-stretched) or a very flabby characteristic (lacking all tension) would compare to the two extreme poles of weakness of basic rhythm. Figure 4 illustrates the tension characteristics of the basic rhythm.

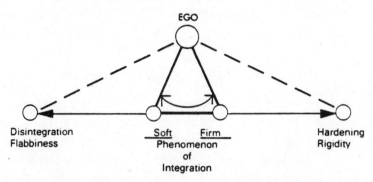

Figure 4. Tension Characteristics of the Basic Rhythm.

In her books, Wieser describes the basic research on various types of criminal handwritings from which she drew conclusions with regard to the basic rhythm. In 1928, she received from the court in Vienna more than 1000 handwriting samples of criminals for study. She was to examine them for criminality but not non-criminality and the general degree of social adjustment. Wieser considered this a one-sided approach and obtained her results by turning the negative question into a positive one. She found in these handwritings an all comprising yardstick. One needed the transitions between the two end-poles (criminal — not criminal) and she found "the red thread" (the yardstick of the basic rhythm), in her basic research work. The material was the handwritings of 700 criminals versus 300 writings of non-criminal professionals on the same educational level. The characteristic differences lay in the dynamic movement of the middle zone in the handwritings. This zone is the zone of the short letters, and it is the core of the handwritings, indicative of the entire character of the script. In the criminal handwritings, either a softening, dissolving tendency was found or a hardening and straining tendency, or both, side by side. In non-criminal handwritings, this basic tensiveness is more modified — the **stroke** itself, rather than the letter forms, were indicative.

The basic rhythm is not quantitative, but qualitative, independent of all other form characteristics. It is the phenomenological experience of the individual coining life processes in non-criminal handwritings, we find either flabbiness, dissolving or hardening to rigidity without gradual transition. In criminal writings, the basic rhythm is weak, while in non-criminal writings it is strong — both qualities as **degree of experience** and not as **quantity**.

Rhoda Wieser takes the basic pattern of Figure 4 as a blueprint for the arrangement of all commonly used graphological indicators (size, width, slant, pressure, etc.) and lists their interpretation accordingly.

The Meaning of the Basic Rhythm

The basic rhythm served as a yardstick for grading different types of criminals (on a scale from 1 to 5) and for distinguishing them from non-criminals. The greatest weakness of "basic rhythm" was found in the handwriting of murderers and and of sex-criminals. Other criminals who committed lesser crimes showed less weaknesses of "basic rhythm" in different degrees corresponding to the seriousness of their crimes.

Non-criminals hardly ever displayed weakness of "basic rhythm" and only seldom overlapped with the less severe group of "white-collar" criminals (embezzlers, etc.).

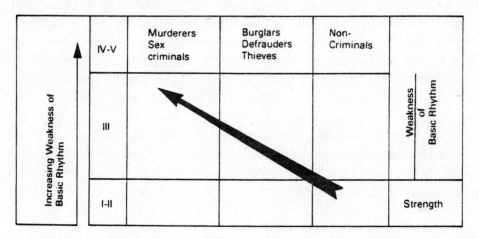

Figure 5. Basic Rhythm in Criminals and Non-Criminals.

According to Wieser, the criminal disposition could be characterized as a kind of egotism on the basis of emotional hardening (callousness) or on the basis of emotional disintegration. Both could appear at the same time. In a non-criminal disposition which is genuinely and deeply based on the inner core of the personality, there is no room for egotistic hardening or disintegration. In the emotional sphere, the unselfish relationship to the outside world manifests itself in human sympathy and a strong feeling of responsibility. It is the Ego motivated by love for its fellows. Connected with it is the basic sense of truthfulness which is absent in the criminal disposition. Also connected with it is reliability within the framework of the community. These people avoid the extremes which are found in the criminal handwriting. The graphic result is polar-elastic movement which can cover the entire scale between soft and firm without gliding to the extreme poles of hardening or disintegration (Fig. 4).

In a later work, Rhoda Wieser enlarged upon her basic theme, presenting it in greater detail, as illustrated in Figure 6. Because we perceive hardening as a binding tendency and dissolution as a releasing tendency, we reversed these two poles on the original diagram. Thus, we put "rigidity" on the left side and "dissolution" on the right side for better understanding.

Following is Wieser's detailed explanation of the philosophical-psychological system which she developed on the basis of the "polar basic rhythm."

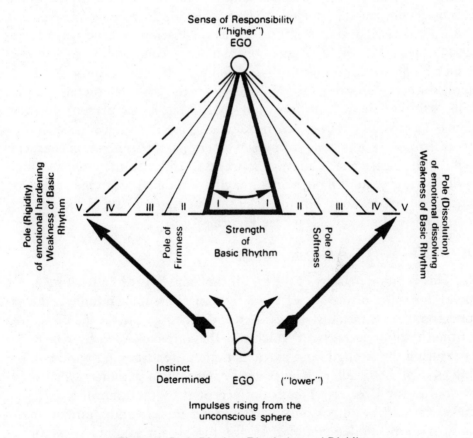

Figure 6. Basic Rhythm, Dissolution and Rigidity.

A. *Explanation of Figure 6*

We begin at the extreme poles of the horizontal line in our diagram which would be those handwritings which, as impression characters, show the pictures of extreme dissolution (extreme softening) on the right side or of the exaggerated firmness that is rigidity or hardness (both extremes could occur in one and the same handwriting at the same time). We understand both the dissolution and the rigidity as the unconscious representation of Egotism.

We can apply here the theory of the guiding image. Those people who are removed from the trends of extreme Egotisms of either kind (dissolution or rigidity), will not express pictures of dissolution or rigidity in their handwriting or any other projection. They avoid them unconsciously and produce movements and projections which correspond to their own basic psychic attitude. Otherwise, the visible expression of a person's writing activity would be completely different from the basic character of his internal attitude. This would contradict everything that has been confirmed by the experience of the guiding image. The person with a balanced internal attitude will unconsciously produce pictures and projections whose impression character corresponds to the goal which he has within himself, that of selfless self-actualization. If, therefore, softness (but not a lack of firmness) is the basic character of a psychic attitude, then the impression character of this person's forming movements will be that of a firm softness. However, if his basic character is firm, yet not lacking softness of emotions, the impression character will be firm (stretched) but also soft and flexible. In the balanced individual, the Ego and the personal imagination take part in his projection and in his expression. This means that this Ego will avoid the extreme points of our horizontal line (see Figure 6).

B. *The Yardstick of the Polar Middle*

This genuine polarity of the middle appears in the handwriting as the polar dynamics of the strong basic rhythm. The polar middle is the expression of an internally self-assured social being. This is the basic area of the rhythmic movement which was the yardstick used by Klages for measuring the strength and participation of life forces in the human being. As will be recalled, Klages used rhythm as a psychic yardstick anchored in the Cosmos. This is not accepted by the man of today, who measures and evaluates only partially and understands human values only in an incomplete manner. In order to obtain a complete picture of the human being to whom we refer in Figure 6, we have to consider the relationship between the horizontal line and the vertical line together. On the horizontal line, we find Man as a social being. However, contained in the cosmic condition of rhythm is an amalgamation of the firm and soft tendencies. The vertical line records the tension between the instinct-rooted Ego and thinking motivated by love and a will devoid of instinct (at the top of the dark-bordered triangle). We also find the instinct-based Ego (recorded below the horizontal line). A person's value is in the result of the possibility of integration between the "higher" Ego with the person's internal emotional makeup. Our diagram shows that this "higher" Ego, due to its capability for integration, carries within itself the ability to think and to will, together with a superpersonal capacity for love. Only the human being is capable of this. We speak of a thinking individual and of a willpower motivated by love. This is oriented consciously and superpersonally at the "you" and the entire world. There is no short word that describes the above in any living language in our cultural sphere. Greek Antiquity had a word which today is found only in religious connections. That word is **agape**. There is a word which means the opposite, i.e., lovelessness. It means more than lack of emotional strength and sympathy. It includes the inability to think of another person, or it could be a personal will or volition which doesn't care what happens to others or how they may be deprived. Our yardstick **(agape)** means exactly the opposite and its actualization.

Rhoda Wieser's theories about the "basic rhythm" have been the subject of great controversy, which is unlikely to be easily settled.

MUELLER – ENSKAT

Wilhelm Helmut Mueller, Dr. Phil.
Born in Berlin, Germany on September 12, 1899. Died on Berlin, Germany on December 6, 1966. Scientific graphologist, lecturer and writer. From 1936, collaborated with Alice Enskat.

Alice Enskat
Born April 18, 1897
Died April 18, 1978
Principle work: *Graphologische Diagnostik* (1973).

The Mueller-Enskat team worked together for years and published a number of books on the subject of handwriting psychology. While they did not develop any new standards of evaluation, they arranged the existing handwriting elements in a new, methodical way, in order to make the diagnosis of handwriting easier and more objective. They call their system a "structure of reference points for graphological interpretation work." They also tried to deduce psychological types from the handwriting.

In their last major work, **Graphologische Diagnostik**, they also discuss the physiological and psychological basis of handwriting, as well as the history of handwriting analysis.

They present the basic 7-point scale for their registration of handwriting elements, exemplifying it by the size of the middle zone. The smallest size is 3 on the left-hand side; the largest, 3, on the right-hand side, thus:

$$\text{Smallness} \quad \frac{3 \quad 2 \quad 1 \quad 0 \quad 1 \quad 2 \quad 3}{} \quad \text{Largeness}$$

0 is the median value; little pronounced smallness or little pronounced largeness are recorded under 1 on the left-hand side and under 1 on the right-hand side respectively and very pronounced smallness or largeness are recorded under 3 on the left-hand side or 3 on the right-hand side. This scale is applied to all the measurements and evaluations of those handwriting elements which the authors record on their basic tables, according to the size of the measurement, the emphasis or the range of deviation of the median value.

If two values of the same strength have to be recorded, at both sides of the median column, the so-called changing or shifting elements (Wechselmerkmale), are recorded by little circles while the other graphic elements are recorded by a dot. The most frequently occurring value of a graphic indication is also recorded by a circle while the other deviations are recorded by dots.

The rather complex arrangement of the handwriting elements by Mueller and Enskat consists of two main parts.

I. Graphic elements which occur in every handwriting and always are recorded. Their number is limited.

II. Graphic elements which do not occur in every handwriting and which are recorded only in particular cases. Their number is unlimited.

Under each of these headings, especially under Part I, we have a number of divisions and sub-divisions.

I. *Graphic Elements which occur in every handwriting and are always recorded.*

(1) Single handwriting elements which are partially measured, partially evaluated and are graded according to their distinctness and their range.

(a) Single graphic elements of lesser complexity.

(i) Measurable graphic elements of the finished handwriting with fixed median values (e.g., size, width, slant, etc.).

(ii) Graphic elements measurable during the writing process or evaluated from the finished handwriting (e.g., pressure, sharpness and pastiness, etc.).

(iii) Clear-cut graphic elements which can be recorded by estimating or counting (e.g., simplification-ornamentation, forms of connection, etc.).

(b) Single graphic elements of greater complexity.

(i) Graphic elements with fixed median values which can be measured from the finished handwriting (e.g., regularity-irregularity, graphic organization, etc.).

(ii) Graphic elements measurable during the writing process or evaluated from the handwriting (e.g., the degree of connection, the tempo, etc.).

(iii) Clear-cut describable graphic elements which can be deduced from the handwriting by counting or evaluation (e.g., left-right tendency, emphasis of places in the handwriting, etc.).

(c) The problem of the median values in recording the graphic elements.

(2) Overall or all-comprising graphic elements which are deduced with the aid of impression qualities or which are marked in a qualitative manner.
   (a) The stiffening tension (Pophal)
   (b) Rhythm (movement, form, distribution)
   (c) Originality
   (d) Harmony
   (e) Movement and Form

II. *Graphic Elements which do not occur in every handwriting and which are recorded only in specific cases.*
   (1) Special Features (signes fixes)
      (a) In single parts
      (b) In several parts

Under these headings, all handwriting elements are discussed in detail, drawing on the techniques of Klages, Pulver, Heiss, Pophal and others.

Mueller and Enskat's basis for the interpretation of handwriting is formulated in the following manner: The graphic factor or indicator is created by a writing process which, as movement in space and time, becomes a form. Movement, form, space and time are the highest real conditions that can be reached by the emotional trends of the writer in the writing and thus can be understood. Therefore, only the interpreter of the science of expression can use them for deduction.

The Worksheet

The worksheet is the center of the Mueller-Enskat theory. The graphic factors are arranged according to the viewpoints of interpretation. Characteristic of this work is the division into (a) the evaluative factors (the totality or all comprising indicators) and (b) the quantitative gradable factors (single factors). Only the gradable factors are plotted on the worksheet according to their emphasis in circles and dots. These plotted circles are connected by a line which illustrates the binding and releasing tendencies in various aspects of the personality as expressed by the measurable graphic factors. These findings have then to be integrated with the findings from the evaluative factors which are not represented in such a clear-cut picture. The authors illustrate their method by numerous handwriting samples and very detailed explanations. The handwriting of the internationally known German painter, Kaethe Kollwitz (Fig. 7), which is plotted and briefly analyzed here, could serve as an illustration.

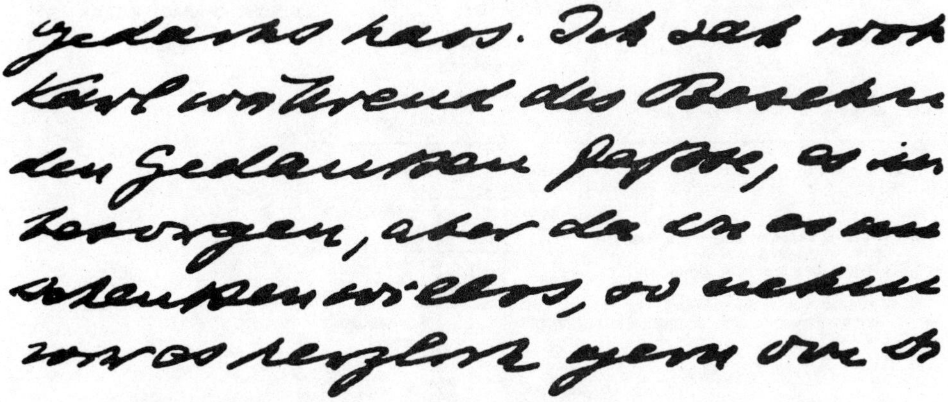

Figure 7. Handwriting of the painter Kaethe Kollwitz, at the age of 68.

The curve was plotted on a worksheet with the psychological interpretations in order to make it better understandable (see Fig. 8). Mueller and Enskat used this example in order to show how they apply their method to various psychological types and their emotional conditions. From the worksheet, it can be seen that feminine trends predominate. The handwriting is movement emphasized; the emotional disposition is more strongly developed than the rational aspects. The tendencies towards devotion and self-denial are more pronounced than any tendency towards self-centeredness. The imagination and the dependence on sympathies as well as on antipathies are more pronounced than any material concerns. Constitutionally, Mrs. Kollwitz belongs in the group of well-balanced cyclothymic personalities. According to Jung's typology, she belongs in the group of the extroverted feeling types. According to Spranger, she would belong in the group of social-ethical personalities. In all these types, the component of will is missing—the aimed active commitment, the assurance of self-confidence and last, but not least, the seriousness and the depth of her emotions which are also essential factors of her character. Apart from this, her handwriting is, in the opinion of Mueller and Enskat, an example of the fact that artistic formative talents are not expressed in the handwriting. This opinion however, is not shared by all handwriting psychologists.

Arrangement of graphic factors according to viewpoints of interpretation

A   EVALUATIVE FACTORS (totality of all comprising indicators)
    I   Relationship between Movement and Form (Artificiality, Genuineness).
    II.   Stiffening Tension (Tension, Elasticity)
    III.   Rhythm (Reproduction of Similarity and Polarity of Movement, Form & Space)
    IV   Originality (Divergences from the school-copy)
    V   Harmony (Disturbances of the flow, of the form and space handling)

B   QUANTITATIVE GRADABLE FACTORS (SINGLE FACTORS)   C. SPECIAL CHARACTERISTICS

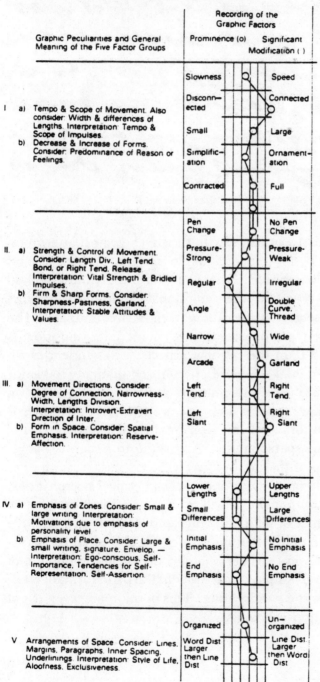

Recording of the Graphic Factors — Prominence (o) — Significant Modification ( )

Graphic Peculiarities and General Meaning of the Five Factor Groups

I   a) Tempo & Scope of Movement. Also consider: Width & differences of Lengths. Interpretation: Tempo & Scope of Impulses.
    b) Decrease & Increase of Forms. Consider: Predominance of Reason or Feelings.

Slowness — Speed
Disconnected — Connected
Small — Large
Simplification — Ornamentation
Contracted — Full

II   a) Strength & Control of Movement. Consider: Length Div., Left Tend. Bond, or Right Tend. Release Interpretation: Vital Strength & Bridled Impulses.
    b) Firm & Sharp Forms. Consider: Sharpness-Pastiness, Garland. Interpretation: Stable Attitudes & Values.

Pen Change — No Pen Change
Pressure-Strong — Pressure-Weak
Regular — Irregular
Angle — Double Curve, Thread
Narrow — Wide

III   a) Movement Directions. Consider: Degree of Connection. Narrowness-Width, Lengths Division. Interpretation: Introvert-Extravert Direction of Inter.
    b) Form in Space. Consider: Spatial Emphasis. Interpretation: Reserve-Affection.

Arcade — Garland
Left Tend. — Right Tend.
Left Slant — Right Slant

IV   a) Emphasis of Zones Consider: Small & large writing. Interpretation: Motivations due to emphasis of personality level.
    b) Emphasis of Place. Consider: Large & small writing, signature. Envelop. — Interpretation: Ego-conscious, Self-Importance. Tendencies for Self-Representation. Self-Assertion.

Lower Lengths — Upper Lengths
Small Differences — Large Differences
Initial Emphasis — No Initial Emphasis
End Emphasis — No End Emphasis

V   Arrangements of Space Consider: Lines, Margins, Paragraphs. Inner Spacing. Underlinings. Interpretation: Style of Life, Aloofness, Exclusiveness.

Organized — Unorganized
Word Dist. Larger then Line Dist — Line Dist. Larger then Word Dist

Figure 8. Mueller-Enskat Worksheet — Graph of the handwriting characteristics of Kaethe Kollwitz.

Although no longer entirely up-to-date, Mueller and Enskat's exacting and detailed publications could still be used for teaching and reference purposes. Their major contribution to graphology is the arrangement of graphic indicators on a 7-point scale. Here are the beginnings of a gradable graphological system which, after more methodical refinement, could be used for statistical studies.

CONCLUSION

Summarizing, one could say that while some of the concepts developed by the representatives of the modern graphological schools may appear vague and possibly metaphysical, they nevertheless served as a basis for the eventual development of handwriting analysis into a precise, objective psycho-diagnostic technique which may satisfy the scientific demands of modern psychology.

REFERENCES

Heiss, R. (1966). *Die Deutung der Handschrift.* Hamburg: Claassen Verlag.

Klages, L. (1932). *The Science of Character.* Translated by W.H. Johnston. Cambridge, Mass: Sci-Art Publishers.

Klages, L. (1936). *Grundelgung der Wissenschaft vom Ausdruck.* Leipzig: Johann Ambrosius Barth.

Klages, L. (1940). *Handschrift und Charakter.* Leipzig: Johann Ambrosius Barth.

Lewinson, T. Stein. (1938, March). An Introduction to the Graphology of Ludwig Klages. *Character and Personality.*

Mueller, W. & Enskat, A. (1949). *Theorie und Praxis der Graphologie.* Rudolstadt/Thueringen: Greifenverlag.

Mueller, W. & Enskat, A. (1951). *Graphologie Gestern und Heute.* Stuttgart: Altdorfer Verlag.

Mueller, W. & Enskat, A. (1973). *Graphologische Diagnostik.* Bern, Stuttgart, Wien: Hans Huber.

Pophal, R. (1939). *Grundelgung der bewegungs-physiologischen Graphologie.* Leipzig: Johann Ambrosius Barth.

Pophal, R. (1949). *Die Handschrift als Gehirnschrift.* Rudolstadt/Thueringen: Greifenverlag.

Pophal, R. (1949). *Zür Psychophysiologie der Spannungs-Erscheinungen in der Handschrift.* Rudolstadt-Thueringen: Greifenverlag.

Pophal, R. (1950). *Das Strichbild.* Stuttgart: Georg Thieme.

Pulver, M. (1934). *Treib und Verbrechen in der Handschrift.* Zurich, Leipzig: Orell Fuessli.

Pulver, M. (1945). *Symbolik der Handschrift.* Zurich: Orell Fuessli.

Pulver, M. (1949). *Intelligenz im Schriftausdruck. Zurick*: Orell Fuessli.

Wieser, R. (1938). *Der Rhythmus in der Verbrecherhandschrift*. Leipzig: Johann Ambrosius Barth.

Wieser, R. (1960). *Mensch und Leistung in der Handschrift*. München/Basel: Ernst Reinhart.

Wieser, R. (1973). *Graphologische Diagnostik*. Bern, Stuttgart, Wien: Hans Huber.

Wieser, R. (1973). *Rhythmus und Polarität in der Handschrift*. München/Basel: Ernst Reinhardt.

2

GRAPHOANALYTIC CUES[1]

JAMES C. CRUMBAUGH

Summary

THIS CHAPTER discusses graphoanalytic cues as a special dimension of graphokinesics (expressive movements made graphically) within the general framework of projected techniques of personality assessment—both (a) perceptual and (b) expressive movement. The advantages of handwriting analysis over other projective techniques are discussed. The historical background of handwriting analysis from its inception in Italy in 1622, through the development of the French atomistic and German intuitive schools, to the present compromise developed by Bunker which draws heavily from gestalt psychology and which emphasizes graphoanalysis as opposed to graphology, is reviewed. The general procedure of graphoanalysis which includes (1) the construction of a perspectograph—an analysis of the first 100 upstrokes that appear in a sample of writing, (2) the completion of a worksheet listing primary and evaluated traits and (3) interpretation of the data into a unified, meaningful gestalt which yields a valid picture of the personality of the writer is surveyed. Samples of some of the traits revealed by the perspectograph—e.g., emotional responsiveness, approach to achievement, levels of determination—are presented and discussed in some detail. The question of validation studies are cited. Recommendations both for the development of the graphoanalytic art and science and for its applicability as an additional diagnostic tool are included.

Introduction

Graphoanalytic cues are based on a particular system of graphology or handwriting analysis, which in turn is a particular dimension of graphokinesics or expressive movements made graphically. Interpretation of all forms of graphokinesics for the purpose of assessing the personality and character of the subject is based on the fundamental concept in clinical psychiatry and psychology that personality is expressed by or "projected" into all of the individual's responses to the environment. The person may respond in either of two ways: (1) cortically, by perception or interpretation of an ambiguous stimulus (as in the case of the Rorschach inkblots), or (2) behaviorally, by a motor reaction (as in the case of such expressive movements as projective drawing or handwriting).

Projective techniques of the perceptual type include (1) the Rorschach, Holtzman, and other inkblot tests; (2) the Murray Thematic Apperception Test (TAT); (3) the Shneidman Make a Picture and Story Test (a variant of the TAT); (4) the Twitchell-Allen Three Dimensional Apperception Test; and (5) the tautophone test (ambiguous recorded sounds which can be unstructured like inkblots or more definitive like the apperception tests) — to name but a few. Most projective methods have been of the perceptual type, and most of these have involved visual perception.

The chief expressive movement types of projectives are the various forms of projective drawing or writing: (1) the Goodenough (1926) Draw-a-Person Test and the Buck (1948) House-Tree-Person Test; (2) the Mira (1940) Myokinetic Test (which requires a blindfolded subject to draw different types of lines free-hand in various planes with both hands alternately); and (3) handwriting analysis. Of these, handwriting analysis offers the advantage of being more easily measurable, while at the same time allowing the seasoned analyst to drop elaborate details of measurement and to make overall (global) interpretations based on a subjective fusing of the relationships between the data trends.

"Sign" interpretations (tying specific personality traits to exact details or signs in inkblots, drawings, or handwriting) have never validated well for any projective techniques, and it is often said that the validity is always in the clinician and not in his tools. Global validation has consistently been superior among these techniques, which means that what is actually valid is the experience of the clinician in putting together in a totally unanalyzable way the overall picture of personality yielded by the complex interaction of all of the signs. Since the meaning of the sign changes as it interacts with other signs, a sign cannot be interpreted in a constant manner from subject to subject.

As mentioned, handwriting analysis permits the experienced clinician to make global interpretations and also offers the learner and less expert practitioner adequate quantification to depend on until "holistic" expertise is developed. (The Rorschach also offers this, but most projective methods are inadequate in this respect.) Handwriting analysis has further advantages: (1) the sample of writing can be taken by a clerk without expenditure of professional time. (2) It can be taken without the subject's knowing what it is for. (3) Samples can be obtained from most subjects over a span of many years (since most people have something which they have written by hand at most key periods of life), thus making possible a longitudinal study of personality. This usually cannot be done by other techniques of evaluation, since test data are usually not available from the earlier life stages.

BACKGROUND AND CURRENT STATUS

The first organized attempt to analyze handwriting was probably that of Camillo Baldi, an Italian scholar and physician. While a professor at the University of Bologna in 1622, he published a book, **Treatise on a Method to Recognize the Nature and Quality of a Writer from His Letters.** The next published work was by Johann Kasper Lavater (1741-1801), a Swiss scholar of personality at the University of Zurich. These early publications interested many intellectuals but had little following as a possible method of personality analysis. The reason for neglect was simple; very few people could read and write.

As education became more widespread in the nineteenth century, handwriting analysis rapidly gathered interest. It was practiced more as an art than a science, but often with amazing intuitive skill, by such assorted figures of the history of this period as Goethe, Poe, the Brownings, Leibniz, Balzac, Dickens, and many others. It is said that Gainsborough achieved the lifelike quality of his portraits by having before him, while painting, a handwriting specimen of his subject. He felt that the handwriting enabled him to capture the essence of the subject's personality.

In France, Abbé Jean Hippolyte Michon, published in Paris in 1875 the most scholarly work on handwriting up to that time. Entitled **The Practical System of Graphology**, Michon's work coined the generic term for handwriting analysis. He tirelessly studied hundreds of graphic signs which were supposed to indicate specific personality traits, and his system became known as "the school of fixed signs."

In the late nineteenth century, a disciple of Michon, Crépieux-Jamin, expanded his master's studies and modified to some degree the rigid one-to-one relationship that Michon assumed to exist between handwriting strokes and personality traits. But the basic theory of "isolated signs" remained dominant in French schools of handwriting analysis.

Near the turn of the century, Crépieux-Jamin interested the great French psychologist Alfred Binet (who originated the first intelligence tests) in handwriting analysis as a technique for testing personality. Binet's experiments indicated that handwriting experts could distinguish successful from unsuccessful persons by their writing with an accuracy or 61 to 92 percent. This was very remarkable in view of the crude methods of the day. Binet was also able to determine (to a considerable degree) the intelligence and honesty of writers, but not their age or sex. These findings have been verified in the graphoanalytic system of handwriting analysis.

In Germany there were also serious students of handwriting during the last half of the nineteenth century. William Preyer at the University of Berlin demonstrated an essential similarity between handwriting, foot writing, teeth writing, opposite-hand writing, and even crook-of-the-elbow writing; and he noted that "all writing is brain writing." Later, psychiatrist Georg Meyer showed important differences between spontaneous writing and drawn or copy writing.

The biggest name in German handwriting analysis was for some years Ludwig Klages. He coined the term **expressive movement** to refer to all motor activities performed habitually and automatically without conscious thought: walking, talking, gesturing, facially responding, and especially handwriting. But while Klages's influence was strong for a time in Germany, it did not spread, because his system was esoteric and subjective, intuitive in the extreme, complex and mixed with an intricate personal philosophy that made it incomprehensible, and of dubious authenticity to serious scholars.

Graphoanalysis, founded by M.N. Bunker in 1929, has been called a protest against the atomistic one-to-one "sign" graphology that typified the French school, and also against the broad, sweeping, intuitive graphology of the German school. This middle-of-the-road compromise position drew heavily from the then new Gestalt school of psychology, which insisted that people must be studied as dynamic wholes and that these wholes are more than the sum of their atomistic parts. Bunker based his method of personality evaluation through handwriting on this fundamental Gestalt concept, thus considering how the interplay of related traits produces an overal effect that is different from that of any single trait; and this holistic or global personality pattern may be produced by a variety of single-trait combinations, all of which must be learned by experience.

Following Bunker's death in 1961, V. Peter Ferrara of Chicago assumed the leadership. Holding a master's degree in psychology, Ferrara emphasized sound validation research to support the concepts of graphoanalysis and to modify those that did not prove valid.

Graphoanalysis now has certified practitioners in all states of the union and in most countries of the world. It has a wide variety of practical applications. The chief areas of use are (1) in business and industry (Rast, 1966; Fullmer, 1971), where graphoanalysts assist personnel specialists in job applicant selection based on specific aptitudes, in job placement and promotion, and in the determination of character in credit risks; (2) in education (International Graphoanalysis Society, 1975), where graphoanalysts help vocational counselors determine areas of aptitude and help teachers determine the patterns of personality that cause either the student to have difficulty in school or the school to have trouble with the student; (3) in mental health clinics and hospitals (Watanuki, 1963; Root, 1966), where graphoanalysts help psychiatrists and psychologists understand the personality structure, traits, and psychodynamics of patients (it should be noted that graphoanalysts do **not** offer diagnoses of either mental or physical illnesses and they do not do therapy); and (4) in forensic or questioned-document work, where graphoanalysts serve as expert witnesses in authenticating legal instruments (International Graphoanalysis Society, 1975).

CRITICAL DISCUSSION

General Areas of Concern

The general procedure of graphoanalysis is based on the following steps: First, a **perspectograph** — an analysis of the first hundred **upstrokes** that appear in the sample of writing — is constructed. This sample, incidentally, should be a full page or more of spontaneous writing made with a ball-point pen or pencil on unruled paper, without the subject's knowing that it is for analysis. The result yields the percentage of each of seven different degrees of slant to be found in the writing, from far forward to markedly backward, marked and measured by a specially constructed gauge. In general, far-forward writing is found in extremely emotional persons, while backward writing indicates emotional constraint and blockage. This characteristic becomes important in determining the way in which many traits found in one's writing will affect one's behavior. The percentage of each slant span is plotted on a bar graph for reference as other traits are revealed. The interpretation of slant is demonstrated in Figure 1: 1a shows back slant and its meaning; 1b shows vertical slant and its significance; 1c represents forward slant and its interpretation.

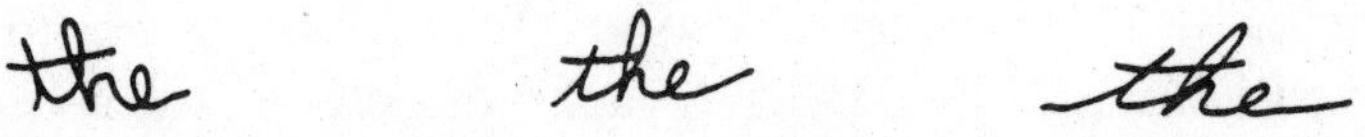

Figure 1. Levels of Emotional Responsiveness. (a) Withdrawal (b) Objectiveness (c) Intense Responsiveness

The second general step in constructing a graphoanalysis is completion of a special worksheet listing around one hundred "primary" personality traits and some fifty "evaluated" traits. A primary trait is one that can be determined from a single-stroke formation. For example, temper is indicated by t-bars made to the right of the t-stem. An evaluated trait is one that must be inferred from two or more other traits. For example, timidity is a product of lack of self-confidence, shyness, self-consciousness, and clannishness. Both primary and evaluated traits are rated as to intensity in the sample on a three-point scale in which "X" is slight, "XX" is moderate, and "XXX" is strong.

The worksheet is divided into trait groups, which serve to delineate the personality. Among these groupings are:

1. Emotions, revealed by slant and depth of writing, as shown in Figure 1.

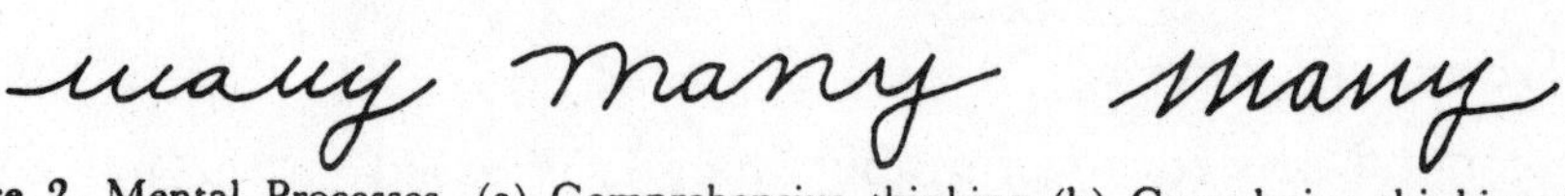

Figure 2. Mental Processes. (a) Comprehensive thinking (b) Cumulative thinking (c) Exploratory or investigative thinking

2. Mental processes, revealed by such traits as comprehensive, cumulative and exploratory thinking, as demonstrated in Figure 2. The sharp points of **m** and **n** in 2a show comprehension: the rounded tops of the loops of the same letters in 2b show logical thinking, the wedges of **m** and **n** in 2c show investigative thinking. Mental processes are intensified by traits like conservatism, generosity, op-

timism, loyalty, positiveness, broad-mindedness, and tenacity; they
are reduced by such traits as impulsiveness, pessimism, prejudice,
and narrow-mindedness.

3. Social behavior (supported by such specific traits as diplomacy,
   frankness, humor, optimism, poise, and self-reliance; negated by
   such traits as clannishness, selectivity, selfishness, and impatience),
   as illustrated in Figure 3. Note the tight loops of the **m** and the **n** in
   3a, which indicate repression, and the spread loops in 3b, which
   show the opposite.

Figure 3. Social Responsiveness. (a) Repression (b) Uninhibition

Fears and defenses, and the degree and type of adjustment, are
indicated by such traits as caution, bluff, dignity, decisiveness, pride,
tenacity, and persistence. Special aptitudes are evaluated in the fields
of business (indicated by such traits as diplomacy, decisiveness, determination, and initiative), science (shown by traits like creativity,
imagination, and analytical thinking), mechanics (shown in traits of
manual dexterity, precision, rhythm, and the like), and other areas.
Further illustrations of stroke interpretations in the determination of
personality traits are shown in Figures 4 through 10[2].

Figure 4. Approach to Achievement. (a) Lack of self-confidence (b) Strong willpower

Figure 5. Levels of Social Appeal. (a) Simplicity, modesty (b) Ostentation

Figure 6. Levels of Honesty. (a) Frankness (b) Self-deception or rationalization (c) Intentional deception

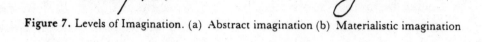

Figure 7. Levels of Imagination. (a) Abstract imagination (b) Materialistic imagination

Figure 8. Attitude toward Life. (a) Depression, pessimism (b) Optimism

Figure 9. Levels of Determination. (a) Strong determination (b) Weak determination

Figure 10. Levels of Attention. (a) Close attention to details (b) Inattention

The low t-bar in Figure 4a reveals a lack of self-confidence, while the high t-bar of 4b indicates an opposite trait of strong willpower. Figure 5a shows simplicity or modesty in the small **a** of **Ann**, while 5b reveals ostentation in the large a. Figure 6a shows frankness in the closed **a** of **and**; 6b shows self-deception in the initial loop of **a**; and 6c shows purposive or intentional deceit in the double loop of **a**. Figure 7a demonstrates abstract imagination in the large upper loop of the letter l, while 7b reveals materialistic imagination in the large lower loop of the letter g. Figure 8a portrays depression or pessimism in the downward droop of the word **many**, while 8b indicates optimism in the upward trend of the word. Figure 9a shows strong determination in the bold downstroke of **y**, while 9b shows weak determination in the short light downstroke of this letter. Figure 10a reveals close attention to details in the closely dotted **i**, while 10b portrays inattention in the high and removed dot of the **i**. (Graphoanalytic definitions of traits are often different from the definitions most commonly employed among mental health disciplines, although personality theorists differ so much among themselves that few uniform definitions are possible.)

These cues will not be "sure fire" for any individual, but if the reader will check a given cue against the personalities of a dozen or so people who show it in their writing and whom he knows well, he will find that most of these people also show the trait represented by the cue. Of course, in a given case the cue meaning may be modified by overriding counter cues, and the true interpretation on balance requires broad clinical experience.

When the worksheet has been completed, the true skill of the graphoanalyst is tested by his ability to put all of these data together into a unified, meaningful Gestalt, or total pattern, which yields a valid picture of the personality of the writer. Graphoanalysis, like the Rorschach or any other good projective technique, thus becomes not a cut-and-dried mechanical process but, rather, a dynamic means of assessment which can be learned only through broadly based experience. The fundamentals and basic procedures can be taught in school and the neophyte must depend on them until he or she gradually accumulates the experience necessary to make adequate clinical judgments based on intuitive feelings about the meaning of the various patterns of traits. Here again is verification of the adage that the validity of a projective technique is in the clinician and not in the instruments. The beginner can, upon mastery of the instrument of graphoanalysis, offer considerable helpful information about the writer's personality and style of dealing with life situations, but only years of practice will make him a master of the art.

The gross description of the graphoanalytic technique given previously is a "bare-bones" outline of the total procedure. The many variations of each handwriting stroke and the probable meaning of each variation is studied. After mastering these elements, the student is coached and given practice in putting together the tremendous mass of data into a personality picture that shows the trait interactions and the overall effect of these interactions in producing the individual's unique personal Gestalt.

Comparative Philosophies and Theories

The theory of handwriting analysis rests on solid ground as a projective technique of the expressive movement type, but it has historically been plagued by the label of a pseudo-science because the early psychologists reacted negatively to the intuitive and loose systems of early graphology. Psychologists have typically written in elementary textbooks that handwriting **should** logically reveal personality (that it has good "face validity"—it looks as if it should work) but that the systems just do not validate. In more recent years, many tests have reexamined the evidence, particularly that for graphoanalysis, and have concluded otherwise (e.g., Ruch, 1967). Within the last ten years more validating research has appeared and will be presented in the next section.

Because of the poor early scientific start of handwriting analysis, the majority of psychologists turned to other projective techniques of expressive movement (like projective drawing). Projective drawings have long been a part of the armamentarium of every clinical psychologist, even though they have validated very poorly (Murstein, 1965). But with more and improved studies of validation of handwriting analysis, a number of psychiatrists (and other physicians) and psychologists have begun to take training in graphoanalysis.

Elaboration on Critical Points

The question of validation continues to be raised by critics, and these critics are primarily psychologists. Only a minority have seen the advantages and have taken the training. Perhaps this is understandable in view of the fact that the training required to become expert in handwriting analysis is at least as great as that reqired to master the Rorschach. (It should be noted that all this applies primarily to America; in Germany many universities have required training in graphology as a part of the work for a Ph.D. in psychology.)

The studies listed in the section on references in the present chapter seem to be the most effective in demonstrating a scientific basis for the assumption that handwriting can be as valid in personality assessment as the other major projective techniques. As demonstrated in the studies of Eysenck (1945), Wolfson (1949), Weinberg, Fluckiger, and Tripp (1962), and Crumbaugh and Stockholm (1977), "global" or "holistic" validation has proved to be the most effective approach. As with the other projective techniques, "atomistic" or "molecular" or isolated "sign" validation has not worked out very well, which means, as noted earlier, that in all clinical assessment procedures the validity is primarily in the clinician rather than in the technique. Only experience blended with good intuitive judgement makes for valid assessment by any instrument. Further substantial validation evidence has been offered by Fluckiger, Tripp, and Weinberg (1961), Mann (1961), Naegler (1958), and Thomas (1964).

Personal Views and Recommendations

The present state of graphoanalytic art and science warrants its practical employment by well-trained graphoanalysts in a variety of working situations, though neither graphoanalysis nor any other single assessment technique should ever be used alone in making any important life decision. For example, neither handwriting nor any other psychological test of personality should determine whether one enters a certain occupation, gets credit, and so forth. Tests must be combined with clinical, educational, demographic, and all other reasonable sources of data. The validation of graphoanalysis is neither better nor worse than that of most other projective techniques. While all projectives leave something to be desired in adequate "hard-core" validation, no experienced clinician doubts that any one of them may constitute a useful tool in the hands of one who believes in it, studies it deeply, and gains broad experience in the relationships between the responses it elicits and various patterns of behavior and personality traits.

APPLICATION TO PARTICULAR VARIABLES

Even the infant shows personality tendencies in graphic movements, and these tendencies do not disappear in old age. While handwriting reflects the motor failure of advanced age, neither age nor sex can be assessed by handwriting. Education (beyond basic literacy) and socio-economic status are not factors in analysis. Vocation is also not a factor, although vocational aptitudes and interests are reflected in handwriting. Ethnic and racial factors have no bearing on the ability of graphoanalysis to determine character and personality.

As has been noted, neither mental nor physical disease can be diagnosed by graphoanalysis, although handwriting does often give information that helps the physician make a better estimate of the cause of symptoms. IQ is never determined by the graphoanalyst, although one can estimate the level of intellectual efficiency. Graphoanalysts can help those professionals who are charged with responsibility for almost all types of disorders — though they do not in any case assume this professional responsibility themselves — by offering a picture of personality patterns that gives very helpful clues. These clues can often point up the presence of underlying organic factors in the etiology of psychiatric disorders.

REFERENCES

Buck, J. N. (1948). The House-Tree-Person Test. *Journal of Clinical Psychology, 4,* 151-158.

Crumbaugh, J. C. and Stockholm, E. (1977) Validation of graphoanalysis by "global" or "holistic" method. *Perceptual and Motor Skills, 44,* 403-410.

Eysenck, H. J. (1945). Graphological analysis and psychiatry: an experimental study. *British Journal of Psychology, 35,* 70-81.

Fluckiger, F. A., Tripp, C. A., and Weinberg, G. H. (1961). A review of experimental research in graphology, 1933-1960. *Perceptual and Motor Skills, 12,* 67-90 (Monograph Supplement 1-V12).

Fullmer, T. P. (1971). The use of graphoanalysis in personnel selection. *Best's Review, 72,* (2).

Goodenough, F. L. (1926). *Measurement of intelligence by drawings.* Yonkers, N.Y.: World Book.

International Graphoanalysis Society. (1975). *Field reports from IGAS students and graduates: The many varied and successful uses of graphoanalysis.* Catalogue No. G623 0475. Chicago: International Graphoanalysis Society.

Mann, W. R. (1961). *A continuation of the search for objective graphological hypotheses.* Unpublished doctoral dissertation, University of Ottawa.

Mira, E. (1940). Myokinetic psychodiagnosis: A new technique for exploring the cognitive trends of personality. *Proceedings of the Royal Society of Medicine, 33,* 173-194.

Murstein, B. I. (Ed.) (1965). *Handbook of projective techniques.* New York: Basic Books.

Naegler, R. C. (1958). *A validation study of personality assessment through graphoanalysis.* Catalogue No. 309. Chicago: International Graphoanalysis Society.

Rast, G. H. (1966). The value of handwriting analysis in bank work. *Burroughs Clearing House, 50,* 40-41 ff.

Root, V. T. (1966, July). Graphoanalysis—an aid in solving human relations problems. *Hospital Topics Magazine.*

Ruch, R. L. (1967). *Psychology and Life.* (7th ed.) Glenview, Ill.: Scott, Foresman.

Thomas, D. L. (1964). *Validity of graphoanalysis in the assessment of Personality Characteristics.* Unpublished master's thesis, Colorado State University.

Watanuki, H. H. (1963). Graphoanalysis: A tested tool in clinical counseling. *Journal of Graphoanalysis, 3* (12), 11, 13.

Weinberg, G. H., Fluckiger, F. A., and Tripp, C. A. (1962). The application of a new matching technique. *Journal of Projective Techniques, 26,* 221-224.

Wolfson, R. (1949). *A study of handwriting analysis.* Ann Arbor, Mich.: Edwards Brothers.

NOTES

1. This chapter is an abridged version of an article orginally published in the *Encyclopaedia of Clinical Assessment,* Jossey-Bass, 1980, 919-929.
2. Constructed by Teresa Croteau-Crumbaugh, MGA, Master Graphologist.

3

THE USE OF HANDWRITING ANALYSIS AS
A PSYCHODIAGNOSTIC TECHNIQUE[1]

THEA STEIN LEWINSON

Summary

THIS CHAPTER introduces the Lewinson-Zubin method of handwriting assessment, the only dynamic, exactly scaled handwriting assessment technique to combine the measurable and evaluative aspects of handwriting, and present them in one common denominator—i.e., the **Contraction-Balance-Release** scale. This technique produces calculations which can readily be used for statistical purposes. The grouping of 21 basic handwriting factors under four major components (Form, Vertical, Horizontal, Depth) is explained, together with the application of 7-point scale based on Contraction-Balance-Release. The plotting of graphs, their interpretation, and calculation of the "productivity" or "effectiveness" quotient are demonstrated. In addition, a "pathology" or "tension" index is calculated from the scale indicating the degree of **stress** under which a person labors. As an illustration of the use of the Lewinson-Zubin method in mental disorders, a sample case of psychopathological development is presented.

INTRODUCTION

During the past decade, few publications (Wolfson, 1949, 1951) have appeared in America on the psychodiagnostic technique of handwriting analysis and its potentialities for useful application. During the same period, this technique has gained an increasingly prominent place in the field of psychological testing in Europe, where a stringent official licensing system is enforced in order to protect professional practice in this field. Among the very considerable European literature (Wintermantel,

1957) which has appeared on the subject of handwriting analysis, research studies in various areas of psychodiagnostic application have also notably increased, in which American standards of statistical validation have been adopted (Mueller, 1957; Gruenewald, 1959a, 1959b; Wallner, 1959; Zuberbier, 1960).

It now seems appropriate to present in concise, summary fashion the fundamental principles, techniques and potentialities of handwriting analysis so that American psychologists who are interested may have an up-to-date source in English to which they can refer. Handwriting is in more than one respect an **indirect** psychodiagnostic tool. Not only does the subject frequently not know that he is being tested, but he also does not know which aspects of the test material are to be evaluated. Furthermore, the examiner does not require the presence of the subject at a particular time in a prepared test situation. Such factors give handwriting analysis a strategic advantage in some aspects of personnel selection, and sometimes in preliminary testing for psychotherapeutic consultations. Another potential advantage is that handwriting material from earlier periods of a person's life is often available, and its evaluation can be of great importance in cases involving developmental, criminal and psychopathological problems when psychological background information is needed and not available in any other way. Actually handwriting analysis is virtually unique in that it is the only available diagnostic method which can be used in a **retroactive** sense.

Regarding the method of handwriting analysis, it should be pointed out that the techniques of measurement and evaluation are objective and repeatable, while the techniques of interpretation are based on a fairly well outlined theory of personality, the techniques themselves being quite teachable by traditional methods of clinical instruction.

HANDWRITING ANALYSIS: ITS BACKGROUND AND THEORY

Handwriting analysis, as it is used in its present form as a psychodiagnostic technique, is an outgrowth of the science of expression by Ludwig Klages in Germany. Klages (1936, 1940) claimed that every human movement had to be considered as an expressive movement from which the distinctive personality makeup of its author could be deduced. He developed a reference system of principles for interpreting the expressive aspects of human dynamics, and he demonstrated this system in its application to handwriting, after explaining and proving that the latter is the only permanently **recorded** expressive movement.[2] As handwriting material lends itself to certain measurements and evaluations, yardsticks and comparative rating scales could be established for psychodiagnostic purposes.

In the development and interpretation of this technique, Klages and his followers (Saudek, 1926; Pulver, 1931; and others) fused three approaches, the dynamic, the symbolic, and the phenomenological, in close alignment to psychoanalytic concepts. Dynamically, handwriting is considered to be a series of movements which involve an interplay between "contracting and releasing tendencies." These are revealed by the manner in which the writer modifies the penmanship he has learned in grade school. A writer may predominantly contract writing movements to the point of cramp and rigidity; he may predominantly release them to the point of complete expansiveness and disintegration; or he may evenly balance and blend contracting and releasing tendencies in a harmonious rhythmic manner.

In addition to the dynamics which permeate writing in all its aspects of letter formation, the "space symbolic" interpretation of the writing field (the paper) plays a considerable part. As prescribed by prevailing western school copies, we execute up-going and down-going movements (between the top and the bottom of the writing field), i.e., between "above" and "below" which correspond symbolically to the "intellectual-theoretical" and the "physical materialistic" components of personality in their various ramifications. In addition, we write from left to right. The hand moves away from our body toward the outside. Symbolically speaking, the writing moves from the Ego to the You, the private-personal sphere to the environmental-social sphere. A third dimension is not so obvious: the depth-front dimension. In executing writing movements, we exert pressure in varying degrees which penetrates more or less into the area behind the writing plane. The impressions can easily be felt on the back of a sheet of paper on which writing under strong pressure has taken place, and one can picture the writer as having pressed through and into the dimension behind the paper. The "counterpoint" to this depth sphere is the **front** of the paper. In interrupting writing movements within letters or between letters, the writer has to lift his pen from the paper and move in front of the paper until he puts the pen down again for the next stroke. These interruptions of the writing lines represent the "counterpoint front tendency" to the depth-tending movement, with their symbolic parallels of instinctual subconscious drives and super-ego inclinations.

In addition to the **dynamic** and **dimensional** aspects of handwriting, there is also the **formal** aspect. The letters written are formed lines which every person modifies according to his own personal style in greater or lesser degree, and these modifications lend themselves to various kinds of phenomenological interpretation.

EXPLANATION OF SOME OF THE TECHNICAL TERMS

In handwriting analysis, we distinguish three **letter zones**: the **upper zone**, the **middle zone** and the **lower zone**. Such letters as i, e, m, n, etc., consist of a middle zone only. The extensions of the letters above the middle zone, as in l, b, h, etc., are called the **upper lengths**, and the zone in which they occur in called the upper zone. The extensions below the middle zone, as in g, y, etc., are called the **under lengths** and the zone in which they occur is called the lower zone. (Figure 1, A.)

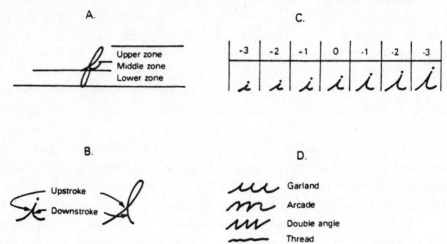

Figure 1. Illustration of (A) Zones, (B) Strokes, (C) Contraction-Release Characteristics for Height of the Middle Zone, and (D) Connecting Forms.

Strokes which are drawn from the bottom toward the top of the writing field are called the **upstrokes**. The strokes which are drawn from the top of the writing field towards its bottom are called the downstrokes. (Figure 1, B.)

The connection between two letters or between two strokes within the same letter is called the **connecting form**. It consists of an upstroke leading from the preceeding writing element followed by an upstroke leading to the next writing element. These connecting forms are in the middle zone of the letters. There are three fundamental types of form used in connecting letters in cursive script: The **Garland** has the shape of an open bowl as in the small **u** of the American school copy. The **Arcade** is a reversed garland which has the shape of an architectural arcade. This form is found in the small **m** and **n** of the American schoolcopy. The **Double Angle, N,** consists of a connection whose upper and lower turning points are made in the shape of an angle producing a zigzag effect. These three fundamental forms of connection can be found in many different modifications and combinations, even to the point of complete dissolution in the shape of the **Thread** which lacks any clear-cut form. (Figure 1, D.)

Figure 1, C illustrates the balanced, intermediate, and extreme aspects of contraction-release with respect to the Height of the Middle Zone. (Figure 1, C.)

THE SYSTEM[3]

We can now formulate the basic definition of handwriting with respect to expressive movement: handwriting is a **formed line** which extends through **three dimensions** (vertical, horizontal and depth) which are connected by a dynamic relationship (contraction, balance, release). There are 21 primary elements of writing movement, and these are arranged under four major components (Form, Vertical, Horizontal, Depth) in the following manner:

I. **Form Component**: (formed line)
   (a) Ornamentation — simplification of form.
   (b) Contraction — amplification of the contour of form.
   (c) Contraction — amplification of the connecting form.
   (d) Thinness — broadness of the stroke.
   (e) Sharpness — pastiness of the stroke borders.
   (f) Tension — flabbiness of the stroke.

II. **Vertical Component**
   (g) Height of the middle zone.
   (h) Proportion of upper, middle and lower zone.
   (i) Direction of the line.

(k) Fluctuation of the line.

(l) Space between lines.

III. **Horizontal Component**

(m) Space between the letters.

(n) Breadth of the letters.

(o) Direction of the slant.

(p) Fluctuation of the slant.

(q) Left-right tendency.

(r) Distance between words.

(s) Breadth of the margins.

IV. **Depth Component**

(t) Increase — decrease of pressure.

(u) Control of pressure.

(v) Degree of connection.

As the dynamics, i.e., the contracting and releasing tendencies, permeate every aspect of the writing movement, each of the 21 graphic elements is graded on a 7-point scale (Contraction: $+3$, $+2$, $+1$: Balance: 0: Release: -1, -2, -3). (See Table I.)

To facilitate scoring, to take into acount the **extent** to which any element is present, and to assist in compiling over-all scores for the major components and elements, a plotting form has been devised which expedites evaluation of a specimen considerably. The plotting form is shown in Figure 2. The individual boxes of the plotting form are divided into four portions which indicate the degree of intensity of the plotted handwriting element. Each fourth of a box represents one unit in the gradation: little, moderate, intensified, predominate. In other words one quarter (1/4) of a box (little) equals 1 (unit); one half (1/2) of a box (moderate) equals 2 (units); three quarters (3/4) of a box (intensified) equals 3 (units); and four quarters (4/4) of a box (predominant) equals 4 (units).

For making a graphological analysis, **spontaneously** written material of one or several pages, in ink, is required. A representative number[4] of letters in the handwriting sample is subjected to all the measurements and evaluations indicated above and plotted according to their various intensities on the plotting sheet. For each component (form, vertical, horizontal, depth) the 7 vertical columns are added, the sums entered on line "Total" and converted into percentage scales (lines ΣI, ΣII, ΣIII, ΣIV.) In addition, the 7 vertical columns of all four components

Table I

	BEND +3	+2	+1	BALANCE 0	-1	RELEASE -2	-3
I. FORM COMPONENT							
a / a'. Ornamentation of Form	Queer Form	1) Distorted Form 2) Flourished Form	Schoolcopy or Conventional Form / Atypical	Individual Essential Form	Neglected Form	1) Equivocal (neglected) Form 2) Symbolic Forms	Decadent Forms / Simplification of Form
b / b'. Contraction of Form Contour	Extremely Contracted (Rigid) Contour	Exactly Detailed Contour	Exactly Outlined Contour	Normal Contour	Ballooned Contour	Equivocal (Amplified) Contour	Uncontrolled Enlarged Contour / Amplification of Form Contour
c / c'. Contraction of Connecting Form	Split: 1) Arcade-Garland 2) Angle Thread	Artificial: 1) Looped Arcade 2) Looped Garland 3) Supported Angle	Conventional: 1) Schoolcopy Form 2) Repeated Arcade or angle 3) Peaked Arcade 4) Deeply Saddled Garland	Essential: Alternating Fundamental Connecting Forms	Widened: 1) Repeated Garland 2) Amplified Arcade, Garland, Angle	Dissolving: Formless: 1) Double Curve 2) Thready Garland, Arcade, Angle	Formless: 1) Thread 2) Different Indistinct Forms / Amplification of Connecting Form
d / d'. Contraction of Width of Stroke	Less than 0.10 mm	From 0.10 to 0.19 mm	From 0.20 to 0.28 mm	From 0.29 to 0.31 mm	From 0.32 to 0.49 mm	From 0.50 to 0.60 mm	More than 0.60 mm / Amplification of Width of Stroke
e / e'. Sharpness of Stroke Borders	Both Borders Sharp and Isolated	Both Borders Sharp	External B. Sharp & Internal B. Pasty	Both Borders Slightly Pasty	Internal B. Sharp & Internal B. Pasty	Both Borders Pasty	Smeariness / Pastiness of Stroke Borders
f / f'. Contraction of Curvature of Stroke	1) Atactic Disturb. 2) Tremor 3) Interrupted Stroke	Considerably Tense Stroke	Tense Stroke	Elastic Stroke	Flabby Stroke	Considerably Flabby Stroke	Mechanical (Lifeless) Stroke / Amplification of Curvature of Stroke
II. VERTICAL COMPONENT							
g / g'. Height of Middle Zone	Less than 0.75 mm	0.76 to 1.49 mm	1.50 to 2.75 mm	2.76 to 3.25 mm	3.26 to 4.50 mm	4.51 to 6.00 mm	More than 6.00 mm / Height of Middle Zone
h / h'. Proportion of Upper, Middle, Lower Zones	Lower to Middle: More than 4:1	Lower to Middle: 3:1 to 4:1	1) Lower to Middle: 2:1 to 3:1 2) Displacements 3) Upper to Middle: Less than 2:1	2:1:2	1) Upper to Middle: 2:1 to 3:1 2) Displacements 3) Lower to Middle: Less than 2:1	Upper to Middle: 3:1 to 4:1	Upper to Middle: More than 4:1 / Proportion of Upper, Middle, Lower Zones
i / i'. Direction of Lines	Descending Line: Angle of more than -3°	Descending Line: Angle of -2° to -3°	1) Descending Line: Angle of 2 to -2° 2) Concave Line	Horizontal Line: Angle of 0	1) Ascending Line: Angle of 0 to 2° 2) Convex Line	Ascending Line: Angle of 0 to 3°	Ascending Line: Angle of more than 3° / Direction of Lines
k / k'. Fluctuation of Lines	Lack of Fluctuation (0 to 1/2)	Considerable Suppressed Fluctuation (1/2 to 1)	Suppressed Fluctuation: (3/2 to 2)	Slight (normal) Fluctuation: (2)	Increased Fluctuation: (2 to 5/2)	Considerably Increased Fluctuation: (5/2 to 3)	Extremely increased Fluctuation (More than 3) / Fluctuation of lines
l / l'. Space between Lines	Space to Middle Zone: More than 3:1	Space to Middle Zone: 3:1 to 2:1	Space to Middle Zone: 2:1 to 1:1	Space to Middle Zone: 1:1	Space to Middle Zone: Less than 1:1 (Not touching)	Touching of Lower and Upper Lengths	Hooking of Lower and Upper Lengths / Space between Lines

Table I (Continued)

	+3	BOND +2	BALANCE +1	0	-1	RELEASE -2	-3	
III. HORIZONTAL COMPONENT								
			Space compared to Height					
m Space between Letters	No Space (Touching)	1:2 to 1:3	1:1 to 1:2	1:1	1:1 to 3/2:1	3/2:1 to 2:1	More than 2:1	**m'** Space between Letters
			Breadth Compared to Height					
n Breadth of Letters	0 (Covered Letter)	1:2 to 1:3	1:1 to 1:2	1:1	1:1 to 3/2:1	3/2:1 to 2:1	More than 2:1	**n'** Space between Letters
o Direction of Slant	More than 120°	105° to 120°	96° to 104°	85° to 95°	84° to 60°	59° to 30°	Less than 30°	**o'** Direction of Slant
p Fluctuation of Slant (Parallelism)	More than 90%	75% to 90%	60% to 75%	45% to 60%	30% to 45%	15% to 30%	Less than 15%	**p'** Fluctuation of Slant (Parallelism)
q Left-Right Tendency	Curls	1) Added Left Ending 2) Added Left-Tending Loops 3) Broken Letters	1) Right Tending Strokes Omitted 2) Right-Left Tending Strokes like Schoolcopy	Normal Right-Left Tendency According to Essential Letterform	Omitted Left Tending Strokes	Emphasized Right Tending Strokes (Left Turned into Right)	Dissolving Forms due to Overemphasized Right Tendency	**q'** Left-Right Tendency
			Distance of Words Compared to Space Between Letters					
r Distance of Words	More than 4:1	3:1 to 4:1	2:1 to 3:1	2:1	2:1 to 1:1	1:1 to 1:2	0 No Distance between words	**r'** Distance of Words
s Restriction of Writing Area (Margins)	1) Left Margin: a) No Margin b) More than 4:1 2) Right Margin More than 4:1	1) Left Margin: a) 1:4 to 1:3 b) 4:1 to 3:1 2) Right Margin: 4:1 to 3:1	1) Left Margin: a) 1:2 to 1:3 b) 3:1 to 2:1 2) Right Margin: 3:1 to 2:1	Left and/or Right Margin: 2:1	1) Left Margin: 1:1 to 2:1 2) Right Margin: a) 1:1 to 1:2 b) 2:1 to 1:1	Right Margin: 1:2 to 1:3	No Right Margin	**s'** Expansion of Writing Area (Margins)
IV. DEPTH COMPONENT								
			Pressure Stroke Compared with Stroke					
t Increase of Pressure	More than 4:1	3:1 to 4:1	2:1 to 3:1	2:1	2:1 to 3/2:1	3/2:1 to 1:1	Lack of Pressure	**t'** Decrease of Pressure
u Control of Pressure	Displaced Pressure in Upper Zone	Displaced Pressure in Middle Zone	Displace Pressure in Lower Zone	1) Even Pressure in Down Stroke 2) Gradually Increasing & Decreasing Pressure within Letter Form	Uneven Pressure within a Pressure Stroke (Increasing or Decreasing)	Light Pressure-Pointed Endings	Heavy Pressure-Pointed Endings	**u'** Control of Pressure
v Degree of Connection	No Connection	One Connection within 2 Joints	1) First Letter Disconnected in Words of 3 or 4 Joints 2) Last Letter Disconnected after 3 or 4 Joints	1) Upper Signs Connected with Following Letter 2) One Disconnection after 3 or 4 Joints	Five Joints are Connected	Six to Seven Joints are Connected	1) More than Seven Joints are connected 2) Words are Connected	**v'** Degree of Connection

are added together (line "Composite Total") and converted into a percentage scale (ΣV). The figures of ΣI, ΣII, ΣIII, ΣIV, ΣV are graphed separately. Examples of such graphs are shown in Figure 2 below.

		BOND			BALANCE	RELEASE				
		+3	+2	+1	0	−1	−2	−3		
FORM COMPONENT	I								I'	FORM COMPONENT
	a								a'	
	b								b'	
	c								c'	
	d								d'	
	e								e'	
	f								f'	
Total										
	I									
VERTICAL COMPONENT	II								II'	VERTICAL COMPONENT
	g								g'	
	h								h'	
	i								i'	
	k								k'	
	l								l'	
Total										
	II									
HORIZONTAL COMPONENT	III								III'	HORIZONTAL COMPONENT
	m								m'	
	n								n'	
	o								o'	
	p								p'	
	q								q'	
	r								r'	
	s								s'	
Total										
	III									
DEPTH COMPONENT	IV								IV'	DEPTH COMPONENT
	t								t'	
	u								u'	
	v								v'	
Total										
	IV									
COMPOSITE	V								V'	COMPOSITE
Total										
	V									

The Plotting Form

Figure 2. The Plotting Form.

THE INTERPRETATION (LEWINSON AND ZUBIN, 1942)

The basic theory underlying handwriting interpretation is that the type of movement which produced the handwriting is a projection of the personality of the writer. Consequently the specific aspects of handwriting such as form, height, breadth, pressure, etc., are presumed to reflect various personality attributes within each individual's overall personality, the latter viewed dynamically as a constellation of interacting characteristics. The basic interpretation of the four major components corresponds to four basic personality spheres: each of the primary elements has its respective meaning within the general conceptual framework.

I. **Form Component**: The integrative factor of the personality, the form in which the other component correlates are integrated in the individual's functioning.
   (a) The modification of the essential form — mode of performance.
   (b) Contour of form — degree of creativeness.
   (c) The form of connection — mode of contact.
   (d) The width of stroke — hardness.
   (e) Border of stroke — instinctual control.
   (f) Curvature of stroke — coordination.

II. **Vertical Component**: The rational organization within the individual (i.e., the relationship between the intellectual, the emotional and instinctual tendencies).
   (g) The height of the middle zone — self importance.
   (h) The relative height of upper, middle and lower zones — level of aspiration.
   (i) The direction of lines — mood level.
   (k) The fluctuation of the line — fluctuation in mood level.
   (l) The distance between lines — sense of proportion.

III. **Horizontal Component**: The emotional-social sphere (i.e., the relationship between the individual and his environment).
   (m) The space between letters — reciprocity between individual and his environment.
   (n) The breadth of the letters — self-confidence.
   (o) The direction of the slant — attitude towards environment.
   (p) The fluctuation of slant — variability in attitude towards environment.
   (q) The left-right tendency — introversion-extraversion.

(r) Distance between words.

(s) Treatment of margins — degree of contact with environment.

IV. **Depth Component**: The instinctual sphere (i.e., the utilization of the individual's instinctual drives).

(t) The degree of pressure — available energy.

(u) The control of pressure — utilization of energy.

(v) The degree of connection — analysis-synthesis ability.

V. **The Composite**: The integrated picture of the over-all personality structure.

The second fundamental aspect (the dynamic aspect) of the graphic picture is the contraction-release scale which permeates the four basic components and consequently the composite. When the contracting and releasing tendencies in a person's movements are evenly or rhythmically balanced, it is presumed that they are the expression of a balanced and adjusted personality. Consequently, the contraction-balance-release scale of the handwriting should reflect the degree of balance of the writer. This point was tested and demonstrated in a earlier study of well-adjusted and mentally disturbed persons (Lewinson and Zubin, 1942). If a person exhibits a considerable tendency toward contraction in his handwriting, his personality too is said to be contracted. That is to say, he is hemmed in by his rational control and does not attain a desirable rhythmic balance. On the other hand, if his writing is very released, he is thought to be lacking in mental control to such an extent that his emotions carry him away. We thus see that predominant contraction corresponds to detrimental inhibitory control while predominant release corresponds to detrimental loosening of control. Only a rhythmically balanced control will permit an individual to make the best possible adjustment.

Corresponding to Step $+3$, extreme contraction, we have complete disorganization of the personality (or of a particular personality aspect) due to inhibitory trends. Corresponding to step $+2$, we have distortion, but not complete disorganization, while $+1$ corresponds to mechanization and stereotypy in the personality. On the other end of the scale, -3 represents complete dissolution of the personality (or of a particular personality aspect) through complete loss of control. The second stage, -2, represents distortion due to lack of control and a considerable degree of impulsiveness, and step -1 indicates a loosely structured personality lacking in control and therefore having some accentuation of impulsiveness. It will be noted that the central point in the contraction-release scale corresponds to an "ideal" personality. Each individual is characterized in part by the degree to which he attains the characteristics of the ideal personality:

The seven steps of the contraction-release scale permeate all 21 graphic factors of the four basic components, and their specific interpretation will vary with the factor and component in question.

The final graphs, based on the plotting form, illustrate the dynamic constellation in the various aspects of the personality:

    I Form — formative integration;
    II Vertical — rational organization;
    III Horizontal — emotional-social sphere;
    IV Depth — instinctual sphere;
    V In the personality composite.

(For examples of such graphs showing the contraction-bond-release curves, see Figure 4, below.)

The more the graphs approach the normal distribution curve, the better balanced and adjusted is the writer. The more divergent the graph, the more disturbed is he. Lewinson and Zubin (1942) found that the graphs of extremely disturbed psychotic patients showed almost a reversal of the normal distribution curve with a dip in the middle (at the 0-point) and an emphasis of one or both extreme ends ($+3$ and/or -3).

In addition a **productivity** or **effectiveness** quotient has been developed which has proved most useful in some studies as yet unpublished. The number of points (or units) under the 0 column (the point of integrated dynamic strength) was divided by the number of points under the 6 columns ($+3$, $+2$, $+1$, -1, -2, -3) which represent the dynamic strength utilized in varying degree as contraction or release. This division was made for each of the four components (Form, Vertical, Horizontal, Depth) and also for the Composite Graph. The resulting quotients appear as decimal figures, as the numerator (the sum of units related to the integrated strength) is always smaller than the divisor (the sum of units related to the utilized strength). The decimal figures indicating the productivity or effectiveness quotient denote the person's degree of effectiveness in the separate component and composite areas respectively. The following scale has been tentatively established, based on the analysis of nearly 600 cases:

Below- 0.10 Pathological — Inferior
0.11 - 0.20 Low Average to Average
0.21 - 0.30 High Average to Outstanding
0.31 - 0.40 Outstanding to Superior
0.41 - 0.50 Superior (Genius)

CASE ILLUSTRATION

It is generally worthwhile to illustrate an unfamiliar method by presenting an actual case and showing what kind of evaluation is possible, using the method. The subject selected for presentation here later became schizophrenic, requiring hospitalization. At the time she wrote the sample shown in Figure 3, she was attending high school. For purposes of research, the investigators concerned were interested in knowing what she was like during her premorbid period. From the subject's family, they obtained the handwriting sample shown in Figure 3 (which had been written ten years before) and submitted it to me for evaluation. As it turned out, the subject was already showing signs of disturbance (although I knew nothing of her earlier history) and in fact, as I learned later, was withdrawn from school the following year because of behavioral problems and deteriorating academic performance. Figure 4 shows the five basic graphs whose rationale was described earlier and the integrated evaluation of the writer's personality and psychological status at that time.

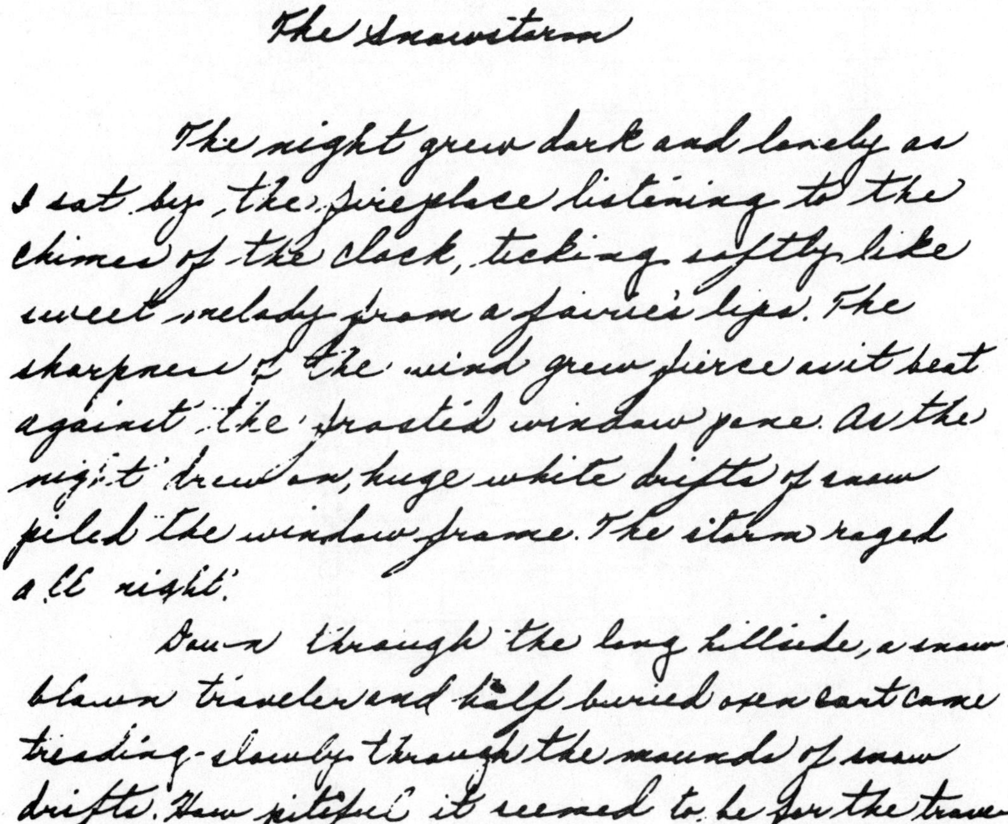
The Snowstorm

The night grew dark and lonely as I sat by the fireplace listening to the chimes of the clock, ticking softly like sweet melody from a fairie's lips. The sharpness of the wind grew fierce avit beat against the frosted window pane. As the night drew on, huge white drifts of snow piled the window frame. The storm raged all night.

Down through the long hillside, a snow-blown traveler and half buried oxen cart came treading slowly through the mounds of snow drifts. How pitiful it seemed to be for the trave-

Figure 3. Handwriting Sample of Female Subject, Aged 16, Who Subsequently was Hospitalized as Schizophrenic.

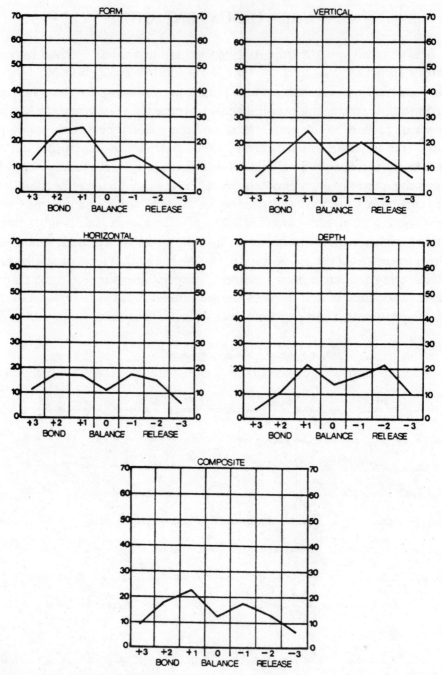

Figure 4. Contraction-Bond-Release Curves for the Major Components, Based on the Handwriting Sample Shown in Figure 3.

RUTH, AGE 16

Intellectual-Practical Capacities

The writer possesses a higher than average intelligence, but she may at times convey the impression that she is not particularly bright. She has tried and failed to assimilate the material she has read. She has difficulty in coping with intellectual and practical demands placed upon her. She seems to compete desperately, but cannot make the grade. In handling concrete facts, she may be inaccurate and make mistakes, while in dealing with more abstract concepts, she tends to become vague and confused. Either she becomes too absorbed in material she is handling and is too subjective about it, or she is completely detached and rather unrealistic in her approach to it. She can hardly express her fantasies and imagination in understandable and acceptable form. Some of the images in her mind are distorted and strange, and she may not care to bring them out in the open. She is a fairly good observer, attends to details which interest her and tries to relate them in broader perspectives to which they belong. Her analytical faculties are not very strong. Either she accepts things the way they are presented to her, or she shapes them in a subjective way. Scientific work should be very difficult for her. She has some synthesizing abilities, and can combine two different facts and ideas quite skillfully. However, at times, she may carry this tendency too far and combine unrelated items in a manner that distorts their meaning. She forces herself to think clearly and logically, along prescribed lines, but she cannot help it when her thoughts begin to wander and get entangled and confused. She is quite critical, but not in an objective, individualized manner. She evaluates by set conventional standards, to which she may add her subjective emotional connotation. She possesses a certain ease and fluency in expressing herself, which is somewhat hampered by her general underlying disturbance. She can be quite eloquent at times. Her presentations may have a nice flair and touch, and at the same time, she cannot keep up a consistent level of adequate performance. She has some aesthetic inclinations, and should have feeling for color, form and sound. She may try her hand at some creative work of rather private character, but most of her activities in the artistic field should be predominantly of a reproductive and imitative nature. Her sense of proportion is not strongly developed. She can do calculations on a low, uncomplicated level. She would like to spend money freely, but apparently has been taught to restrain herself. Thus, she can manage with the means at her disposal. She has no particular organizing abilities and would have difficulty in dealing with the over-all picture of a situation or a project. In the execution of tasks, she tries to be accurate, conscientious and reliable but there are inaccuracies, mistakes and unclear presentations. When she tries to correct herself, she sometimes increases the faultiness of her performance. She seems to be more disturbed by internal than by external interferences. She seems constantly to lose the thread of what she is doing. However, she forces herself to keep going. She is neat and orderly and tries to give her work a pleasant external appearance. By nature, she has a precisely-functioning memory, but at the time of the writing, it was subject to the same disturbances as her ability for concentration.

Emotional-Social Sphere

Emotionally, the writer is torn in opposite directions, resulting in strong tensions, with which she does not have enough strength to cope. As a result, there are strong contrasting and contradictory tendencies, which find their manifestations in her mental as well as in her social functioning. She is highly ego-centered and introverted to the point of personal detachment. At the same time, she makes a great effort to fit into her environmental setting, to the point of complete identification and absorption. She has strong tendencies toward personal isolation, while, on the other hand, she cannot stand being alone and is dependent on the support and protection which those in her environment can provide for her. She has created a private reality of her own which is not in tune with surrounding reality. The discrepancy does not reach the level of full awareness, as she tries to cover up and hide it. She is suffering from feelings of inferiority and insufficiency, is dissatisfied with herself and at time projects this dissatisfaction onto objects and people around her. She can be irritable, argumentative and quarrelsome—trends which unexpectedly may alternate with strong attempts at compliance, sweetness and conformity. She can be reticent and reserved, and then become affectionate and sentimental. While she tries to control her feelings and impulses as much as possible, she occasionally may be completely carried away by them. She is suffering from a nervous restlessness, feeling not quite comfortable in her own skin. At times she feels as if she is losing the ground under her feet. She is very high-strung and has great difficulty in relaxing. She is suffering from considerable anxieties, which she tries to repress, but which seem to haunt her with vague and obscure images. She is hypersensitive and is not able to assimilate properly experiences of strong emotional impact. She has strong idiosyncracies. She is quite excitable and a small incident may work her up to a pitch of over-stimulation. While, in general, she tries to cover up her emotional immaturity with a sophisticated external appearance more in line with her age, she can at times act and react like a baby. She is strongly tied to her traditional background in spite of some rational attempts at emancipation. She is spiritually bound by an ideological system (most likely of religious character) with its inherent fundamental ethical principles, which she tries to follow quite meticulously. However, she has to cover up her inner difficulties and support her pretence of full-hearted participation in the activities of her environmental setting. As a self protective mechanism, she makes herself believe that things are different from what they actually are, and she tries to make others believe the same. She is most subjective, particularly when emotional issues are concerned, and has little insight either into her own or into other people's psychic problems.

Instinctual-Physical Sphere

Her instinctual-physical sphere, though not strong, is the best balanced area, but it is not fully integrated into her personality. Her originally adequate psychophysical resources are considerably drained by her emotional tensions, leaving insufficient energy to properly support her general functioning. There is even the possibility of an underlying organic disorder, which may manifest itself intermittently, aggravating her emotional distress. She functions and navigates on the surface barely adequately and seems still to cover up her underlying disturbance, which may break through at any time and destroy her makeshift adjustment.

REFERENCES

Allport, G. W. & Vernon, P. E. (1933). *Studies in expressive movements.* New York: MacMillan.

Gruenewald, G. (1959a). Über Auswirkungen von Belastungs-und Überforderungs - Reaktionen auf die Schreibmotorik bei Hirnverletzten und Gesunden. *Archiv f. Psychiatrie und Zeitschrift f.d. ges. Neurologie, 199*, 235-247.

Gruenewald, G. (1959b). Über den Einfluss von Drogen auf die Schreibpsychomotorik. *Archiv f. Psychiatrie und Zeitschrift f.d. ges. Neurologie, 198*, 687-704.

Klages, L. (1936). *Grundlegung der Wissenschaft vom Audsdruck.* Leipzig: Barth.

Klages, L. (1940). *Handschrift and Charakter.* Leipzig: Barth.

Lewinson, Thea Stein. (1956). Graphische Darstellung der Handschriftlichen Dynamik. *Ausdruckskunde, 3* (4 & 5).

Lewinson, Thea Stein & Zubin, J. (1942). *Handwriting analysis.* New York: King's Crown Press.

Mueller, W. H. (1957). Über die Objektivität von Anmutungsqualitäten in der Handschrift. *Psychologische Beiträge,* 3, (3).

Pulver, M. (1931). *Symbolik der Handschrift.* Zurich & Leipzig: Füssli.

Saudek, R. (1926). *The psychology of handwriting.* New York: George H. Doran.

Wallner, T. (1959). Das System der Handschriftvariablen. *Zeitschrift für Menschenkunde, 4.*

Wintermantel, F. (1957). *Bibliographia Graphologica.* Stuttgart: Ruehle-Diebener Verlag KG.

Wolfson, R. (1949). *A study in handwriting analysis.* Ann Arbor: Edwards Bros.

Wolfson, R. (1951). Graphology. In: H. H. Anderson and Gladys L. Anderson (Eds.), *An introduction to projective techniques.* New York: Prentice Hall.

Zuberbier, E. (1960). Über die Einwirkung von Stimmungsfaktoren auf Sprech und Schreibweise. *Psychologische Beiträge, 4,* (2).

NOTES

1. This chapter is an abridged version of an article originally published in: *Journal of Projective Techniques,* 1961, *25,* 315-329.
2. This theory was tested in the U.S.A. by Allport and Vernon in their *Studies in Expressive Movements* (1933).
3. The system described here is a modification and simplification of the scales used in *Handwriting Analysis* by Lewinson and Zubin (1942). Its main advantage is that only one-fourth of the time is needed for plotting and drawing the graphs. In this form, the system is presented for the first time in the English language. Also see Lewinson (1956).
4. It is advisable to use as a basis for measurement one or two words (depending on their length) of the following areas of the submitted handwriting specimen: beginning of the first line, the middle of the middle line and the end of the last full line. In case a specimen is large, a word of another line may be added. Also, in case the selected words should not have any upper or under lengths or any form of connection, or should not include any emphasis or peculiarities occurring in the body of the writing, an additional word or two much be included which contains the missing elements.

Editor's Note (1)

THE ECLECTIC APPROACH

Many graphologists of the 1980s apply an eclectic approach to their practical work. By "eclectic" we mean proper use of elements from various schools and their integration in the final reports on the individuals under examination.

The typial eclecticist will "borrow" from Klages and Wieser the concepts of "Formniveau" and "Grundrhythmus" (general level) of the handwriting, as the starting point and baseline for further interpretations. Sign graphology (see Michon and Crépieux-Jamin), which was prominent in European graphology of the 19th century, never died; our eclecticist still employs certain one-to-one interpretations of specific graphological indicators and personality characteristics, even though he does so much less intensively and with more reservations that he would have done a hundred years ago. Pulver's symbolism is also alive and well. Handwriting is viewed by the eclecticist as an expressive movement reflecting, by a symbolic process, inner conflicts and motivations — much in the same way as the psychodiagnostic principles underlying the Draw-a-Person and Bender-Gestalt tests. Health problems are inferred from handwriting disturbances, following some of the ideas of the physician, Pophal. There are other schools, of course. Common sense and intuition also have a part to play.

Practitioners differ from each other in the weight they ascribe to each of the aforementioned schools. Their preference depends on the experience they have accumulated, on their personal taste and on the view of their mentor, the graphologist who trained them. Yet in spite of the fact that graphologists differ from one another, not very many, today, could be considered fanatic believers in any of the old schools. The majority will adopt some compromise which, in their view, incorporates the best of all worlds.

Editor's Note (2)

THE IMPLICATIONS OF THE UNDER-DEVELOPED STATE OF GRAPHOLOGICAL RESEARCH

As a generalization of what was presented in Part I of this book, one may legitimately conclude that by and large, the formalization of theories of graphology is of poor quality. Some of the weaknesses are as follows: terminology is not standardized and even **within** a specific school, terms are not clearly defined; detailed operational definitions are not provided; no clear differentiation is made between assumptions, hypotheses, and conclusions; the methodology for the testing of hypotheses is not fully laid down. In short, existing theories in graphology are not well-shaped. Even believers in practical aspects of graphology will admit that. But what does that imply? Some scholars argue that it is not possible to build solidly if the foundations are unsound. In other words, they lay the blame for the mediocre practical results on the shaky theoretical frame, and they conclude that because of this situation, there is no future for graphology — either as a scientific domain or as an applied technique. On the other hand, one could defend a completely contrasting view, according to which, the mediocre results achieved by graphologists are not **due** to the shaky theoretical foundation; rather, any significant results obtained are achieved **in spite of it!** Accepting this view enables us to arrive at a more optimistic forecast: if and when a sound theory is formulated, greatly improved practical results in personnel selection, personality diagnosis, etc., can be expected. Which one of these two opposing views is more accurate? Once again, the decision will be left to the reader.

PART II

DEVELOPMENTAL AND SITUATIONAL EFFECTS ON HANDWRITING

4

THE HANDWRITING OF CHILDREN AND ADOLESCENTS

URSULA AVE-LALLEMANT

Summary

THE CHAPTER surveys the graphological study of children's handwriting, from early childhood to adolescence, over the last half century. Particular attention is paid to the largely neglected area of adolescent handwriting. Differences and similarities between the treatment of children's graphology in the French, German and English-speaking countries are noted, and criticism of the various methodologies is offered.

Introduction

Graphology, the study of handwriting, especially as an expression of the writer's character, developed independently in the French, German and English-speaking countries. As yet, open critical disagreement between the schools is rare, as each school is barely acquainted with the theories of the others. This is particularly true with regard to the graphological study of children's handwriting and that of adolescents. In this area, research lagged behind research into adult handwriting. This chapter examines research carried out in all three schools (scarce as it is), tracing the development of the child's handwriting, from the pre-school age to adolescence.

THE PRE-SCHOOL CHILD

A child scribbles and draws spontaneously from a very early age. In order to write, the child has first to learn the letter shapes, and master the psychomotoric skills necessary for this complex behavior. It should thus be possible to plot the course of development, from scribbling to writing. This would make it possible to determine at what age children, in general, should commence school. It is advisable to carry out a test about a year before a particular child starts school, in order to establish a basis from which to chart his/her development, and to use it as an aid in making the decision regarding school entrance. As an example, a star-wave test is shown here (Figs. 1-3). The task is to depict stars over waves of water. This requires organization and movement in an areal composition. Figures 1-3 show the graphical products of three children.

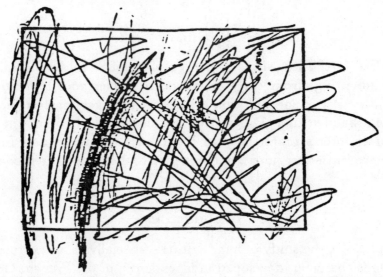

Figure 1. Until the age of three, the child is only stimulated to scribble. Here we see how he already expresses his own individual character.

Figure 2. Between the ages of 3-4, the child grasps the border as a frame and understands the task; stars and waves are incorporated into his scribbles.

Figure 3. Between the ages of 4-5 the child is able to carry out the task. This shows that he is able to conceive, imagine and produce. The child should be able to carry out the task one year before starting school.

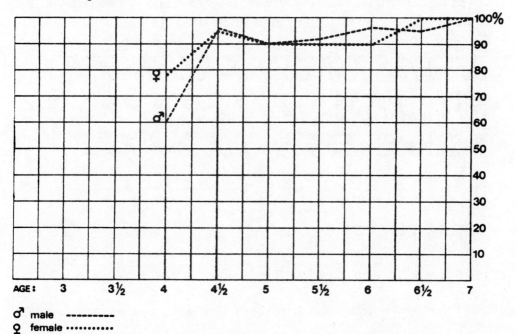

♂ male   ----------
♀ female ···········

Figure 4. The star-wave test as ability-test in preschool-age. Results of survey carried out in Israel in 1983. Male: N 413; female: N 484; total: N 897. Graph in %:
(Corresponding surveys were then carried out in 5 countries.)

At 5 years of age, 90% of children from European countries manage to carry out this task (compare the Israeli findings in Fig. 4). We may conclude that a child who is unable to carry out the star-wave test is not ripe for school, although a child does not prove his readiness for school merely by completing the test. It should be pointed out that by administering the star-wave test to pre-school age children, future disturbances and peculiarities of personality can be recognized, as they can be at a later stage, from handwriting. (For more details about this test, see Ave-Lallemant, 1984.)

THE SCHOOL-AGE CHILD

The school-age child will now take his or her first steps in learning to write. This entails, first of all, mastering the mechanics or writing. Learning the writing framework, the arsenal of letters, which have to be copied calligraphically, the child is given a basis which becomes important during later progressions. This is the reason why experienced educators demand that attention be paid to correct writing, right from the start.

The first attempts at writing already show the child's personal style of expression. This may be seen even in single letters (Fig. 5).

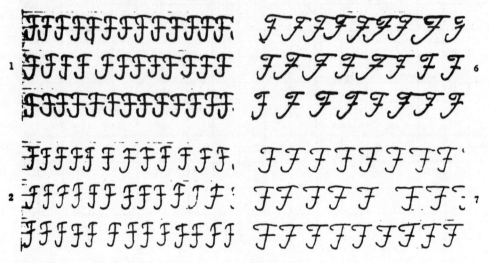

Figure 5. First school year (3/4 of the original size). Taken from Ave-Lallemant (1970), partial reproduction.

Scientific research into children's handwriting has been motivated by various interests. Bang Vinh (1959) studied the handwriting of children and adolescents aged 7 to 18. He was interested in the study of the developing human being, in its broadest sense. Others can see physiological or anatomical elements in the writing activity. We, however, are interested in the graphological study of children's writing. If we survey the present state of this field of research, we can discern three trends, which originally developed in the French, German and Anglo-American schools. We shall examine these more closely.

In France, the leading book on the graphological study of children's writing is **La Connaissance de l'enfant par l'écriture** (Knowledge of the child through handwriting) by Jacqueline Peugeot (1979), which followed the tradition of Gobineau and Ajuriaguerra, while using the terminology and symbols of Michon Crépieux-Jamin and his successors.

The work of Gobineau and Ajuriaguerra will be easier understood if their methodology is explained.

In 1954, Helene Gobineau, together with the psychologist Perron, published the results of a comprehensive study, which included children's handwriting. Both children's writing (till the age of 14) and adult writing were examined for specific signs. Samples taken from the children's writing were marked E (for "enfantine" — childish); those taken from the adult scripts received the sign A (for "autonome" — autonomous). An occurrence of E signs in the writing of adults was taken as the appearance of childish features. The occurrence of E signs decreases with age and the occurrence of A signs increases.

The syndrome E encompasses all the typical hallmarks of the awkward writing of the child: shaky lines, unevenness, breakages, patchings. As the inexperienced child easily finds himself under pressure to display progress, we also find under the sign E, the expression of a reaction to over-demands: twisting, narrowness, uneven spacial pictures. The sign E does not primarily signify a childish personality, but is, first and foremost, an expression of the child's lack of experience of the forms and signs requested, and of inhibition and insecurity, when the child feels himself unable to meet the demands made upon him. When the frequency of these signs diminishes over the years, it is not only because the child gradually improves his mastery of the craft of writing, but because his personality is maturing.

In 1964, Ajuriaguerra et al., produced 2 volumes on children's handwriting, concentrating on the writing of 6-11 year olds. They defined three different age groups as "the three great stages of growth": (1) the pre-calligraphic stage; (2) the childish calligraphic stage; (3) the post-calligraphic stage. In other words, they prefer a stages-model of development, rather than a continuous model. Their research continued that of Gobineau and Perron. The factor E was examined separately for boys and girls, until the children reached calligraphic maturity.

The authors further investigated the reasons for problems in mastering calligraphic writing. The concept of "disgraphy" received a central place in their work and later on, had a great impact on the traditional sphere of graphology. It is recognized now that there are variations in the motoric and intellectual reasons for disgraphy. Disgraphy research opened the door to a new sphere in the reteaching of writing—graphotherapy. Childish handwriting is one form of disgraphy.

Ajuriaguerra distinguished between writing which displays the characteristics of F and M. E denotes handwriting which includes childish characteristics. F signifies form and arrangement typical of childish handwriting. M signifies graphic malformation typical of problematic adults as well as disturbed children. Here are some examples for F and M:

F8   a in 2 parts
F12   gluings
F13   uneven spaces between the lines
F15   descendant lines taken up again
M17   on the whole dirty
M21   tremblings
M22   staggering contours
M25   broken lines
M28   words dancing on the line

Later, Gobineau and Ajuriaguerra noted all the singularities of children's handwriting.

We now enter the era of classical graphology. It was Jacqueline Peugeot who presented this synthesis to the reader in her book **La Connaissance de l'enfant par l'écriture.** Peugeot deliberately retained the terminology of classical French graphology. Her work integrates both lines of thought and the result is an independent graphology of children's handwriting.

Peugeot uses Ajuriaguerra's table of signs for the individual diagnosis of children's writing. She explains it, giving the example of a 9.2 year-old child. After introducing the handwriting (Fig. 6), she compiles a table (Fig. 7) which includes all the important F and M signs. The results are then summed up. Thus, the rate of development can be drawn and, from it, retardation might be deduced. In the case shown, a minimal retardation exists and is reflected in the handwriting.

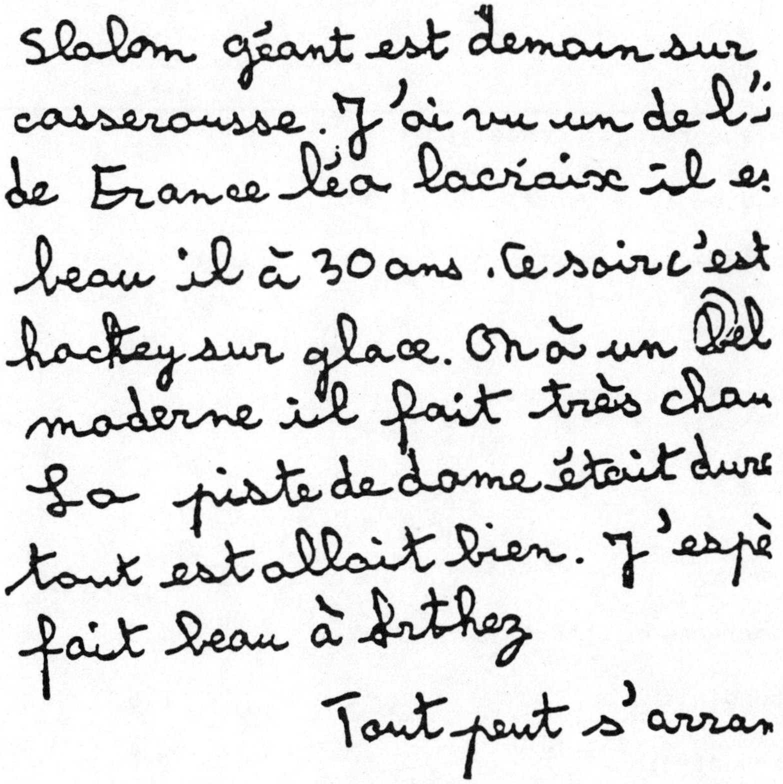

Figure 6. From Peugeot (1979), p. 95.

Item		Present	Coefficient of balance	Total
F items				
F1	surface writing	1	2	2
F2	swollen thick writing	0.5	1	0.5
F4	large writing	0.5	2	1
F5	m and n according to schooling	0.5	2	1
F6	t lines according to schooling	0.5	2	1

Figure 7. Peugeot's table of F and M signs (1979).

Figure 7 (*continued*)

Item	Present	Coefficient of balance	Total
F7 p according to schooling 1		?	1
F9 d,g,q, in 2 parts	0.5	2	1
F11 solderings	1	3	3
F12 glueings	1	1	1
F13 uneven area between the lines	0.5	3	1.5
Total EF			13

M items

Item	Present	Coefficient of balance	Total
M16 corrected letters	0.5	1.5	1.5
M18 bendings	0.5	0.5	0.5
M19 indentations	0.5	3	1.5
M20 bad curves on the upper loops	1	2	2
M23 breakages	1	2	2
M26 wavering lines	1	1	1
M29 irregularities in dimension	0.5	3	1.5
M30 irregularities in direction	1	1	1
Total EM			11

Total EF + EM = 24

Peugeot explains and interprets writing samples with their F and M signs without grading them. Interestingly, character descriptions as contained in Peugeot's book of 1979, could also have originated from the

German graphologist Minna Becker (1949). This shows how close graphologists are to each other, in spite of differences of country or time, when their subject is the handwriting of children.

In Germany, classical children's graphology received its theoretical basis in 1926, when Minna Becker published the book **Graphologie der Kinderschrift** (Graphology of Children's Writing). In order to do justice to her work, one has to remember that it was written by an amateur, self-taught graphologist. Statistical analyses are almost entirely missing from the book. "Qualities scales" are graded without mentioning the writing signs which typify them.

Minna Becker dealt with three areas: character disposition, intellectual predisposition and character analysis. She aimed at interpreting graphological expressions so as to determine the best education for the child, whose predisposition should be understood and respected. The graphologist is the advisor of the educator. He is not the educator. It is not his concern to evaluate the child's character, but to facilitate the understanding of that character, which develops from early character disposition, and to predict possible alterations for the future.

Minna Becker is, even today, seen in Germany as the "Mother of Children's Graphology," although very few have followed her lead.

German textbooks on the graphological study of children's handwriting are numerous. A major connection between them seems to be that each author mentions Klages at some point or other. However Ludwig Klages's table system cannot be used for the analysis of children's handwriting because of its static approach. The child's personality, as expressed through writing is still developing towards full maturity. Klages's polaric system, with its **formniveau** (form level), is inextricably tied to a static way of interpretation, which could not be directly used on children's writing, as the form level of a child could not have reached its peak. Still, there are several books which attempt to apply Klages's sytem to children's handwriting. One such is **Die Graphologie der Schulerhandschrift** (The Graphology of Pupils' Handwriting) by Bauer and Mann (1933). However, just to use one example, whereas Klages set arcade writing on the negative side, deducing from it such characteristics as lack of openness, insincerity, untruthfulness, distrust, superficiality, formality, pretentiousness—most of these only concern adult writing, and cannot be applied to children.

Wittlich (1940) also utilized the Klages theory. He substituted "particular rhythm" for formniveau as a key for interpretation. Lack of particular rhythm is identified with hysterical tendencies, and with a gift for dissimulation. Once again, this is a mistake when applied to children.

Richard Kienzle (1937, 1949) suggested that when evaluating a pupil, interpretation of his or her handwriting should be included. In his books, he associated himself with the system of Klages — the two-way interpretation of all writing signs — which Klages used to note height of letters, differences in length, proportions above and below the line, width/narrowness, position of writing, level of connection, roundness/ slimness, disturbances of rhythm, etc. Kienzle described these signs as "slowly developing and strengthening signs, which may be used in the interpretation of the child's writing only with care, as the child gradually matures."

The most widely-read book on the graphological study of childrens' writing in German after the Second World War is probably that of Erich and Lotte Schelenz (1958). This work surveys the course of writing development, the history of graphology and the start of children's graphology. In the main part of the book, the authors describe their own practical experience. Scribbles, handwriting samples from first grade to last grade pupils, and also handwriting samples from vocational schools, are included. The book deals comprehensively with quesions which are of interest to every educator — maturation, puberty and dissimulation as expressed in handwriting, lefthanded writing, intelligence, writing and drawing tests are discussed. Then, inevitably, come the sign groups from the work of Klages — size, speed, width, etc.

Much has been said about the childish lie. It has been attributed to the most diverse reasons — the desire to show off, fear, fantasy, even a kind of make-belief. In spite of the importance of this phenomenon, the Schelenz chapter, "The Lie in the Writing-Picture of the Adolescent," is a regrettable lapse into the "awkward age" of graphology, and one of the book's weaknesses.

The 1960s saw a wave of criticism of graphology in Germany. Until then, the work of Klages had been widely accepted. Now, however, existing graphological literature was considered "unscientific" by the younger generation of psychologists, who call themselves "graphometricians." The word "graphometry" was not new: Crépieux-Jamin had used it in proposing a way to measure the inclination of the writing angle and even Gobineau called her statistical method by this name. Graphometry was suggested as the basis for future work in the diagnosis of handwriting. This was no longer to be called graphology, but "the psychology of writing." A whole group of graphometricians appeared, most of them from the school of Robert Heiss in Freiburg. Lockowandt proposed a program for the future development of the graphological study of children's handwriting, to be established on a graphometric basis, and suggested discarding the methods used until now in adult graphology. Lockowandt chooses as a model, a study by A. L. Gesell (1906) which fulfills Lockowandt's requirement that a very high number of handwriting samples be used (N-4, 361 pupils) and which pursues a question of general interest — intelligence. The handwriting phenomenon to which Gesell refers is indeed not the quality of the handwriting, as Lockowandt infers, but the accuracy of the calligraphic handwriting. The quality of the handwriting may be seen in its agility or even, as Klages understand it, in its spirituality. Accuracy of performance might, for a child, mean copying the school standard of the handwriting with the highest degree of perfection. This writing phenomenon Gesell attempted to correlate with the intelligence of the child. The correlation proved to be positive.

The work of Gesell obviously could not have been carried out without modern statistical methods. Although Lockowandt acknowledges Gesell's work, he explains it with recourse to modern signs. "Girls normally write better than boys ($chi^2 = 62.0$; df$=1$; P$<0.1\%$). Pupils with high and low motoric agility differ in respect of the quality of handwriting ($chi^2 = 62.0$; df$=1$; P$<0.1\%$). Pupils with high and low motoric agility differ in respect of the quality of handwriting ($chi^2 = 200.7$; df$=1$; P$<0.1\%$) and pupils with high and low writing agility differ regarding handwriting signs ($chi^2 = 197.5$; df$=2$; P$<0.1\%$)."

Lockowandt, however, criticizes the fact that from the graphometric standpoint, the determination is missing from Gesell's work of the sign "Quality of the handwriting" and the choice and recording of criteria. Obviously the "quality" of the handwriting is to a high degree left to a subjective judgement, where Ajuriaguerra, for example, would certainly employ different criteria to those of Klages. Accuracy, however, is unequivocal, because it shows the exactness with which the school standard was copied. The objection is, in fact, of a different kind. Exactness of handwriting, as compared to a given model in the first year, is nothing but a test of performance; good writing displays a high correlation rate with good school results.

Lockowandt also rejects the idea of applying the method of analysis used for adult writing, on that of children by what he calls a "transplantation of method." Children's graphology should develop a method of its own. Graphometrics should be the common basis for adult and children's handwriting analysis.

THE PUBESCENT CHILD

In the past, it was considered advisable to judge the handwriting of the pubescent child with extreme caution. Suzanne Delachaux (1955) however, deals with handwriting in childhood, puberty and adolescence, without clearly differentiating between these phases. She notes that most adolescents have broken writing during their puberty crisis. She then gives samples from subjects up to the age of puberty. Bernhard Wittlich wrote a monograph on the theme of the puberty crisis as expressed in the writing picture. In this essay, he called attention to the graphologically ascertained acceleration in the puberty crisis—the marks of crisis now appear as early as age 11-12, whereas formerly, they did not appear until round about age 14. He further pointed out that when puberty signs do not appear in the child's writing, it is an indication that the physical and/or emotional development is not proceeding normally.

A systematic study of writing signs in puberty was first undertaken by the author of this chapter in the course of her research into the writing of adolescents, and was published in 1970. In this study, the unelastic line emerged as a decisive sign of crisis. The central sign established was a "dynamic/elastic formline." Its development clearly shows the puberty crisis as the formline decreases. (See Fig. 8.).

The recorded curve in 1,096 handwriting samples taken from female secondary school pupils clearly demonstrates that the writing decay conforms to a phase-typical set of rules. This shows that puberty is a separate phase of writing development. The curve shows the strongest manifestation of the unelastic line at the age of 12. 70 of the schoolgirls display this trait. The percentage then decreases and levels off at 25. In the senior classes at secondary school, we again find an increase in manifestations of this phenomenon, and this may be connected with the heavy demands made on pupils in the highest grade, comparable to the burden placed on 10 year-olds, which stems from the change from primary to secondary school. There are therefore two possible reason for the unelastic line: one is the endogenous reasons (biopsychic puberty); the other might be an external reason (excessive academic demands). The 1970 survey established further signs typical of puberty, such as narrowness, doughiness, retouching and meandering. Meandering writing is seen especially with girls; retouching occurs particularly with boys. In her book, "Pubertätskrise und Handschrift," (Puberty crises and handwriting) (1983), the author of this chapter presents the puberty signs in detail.

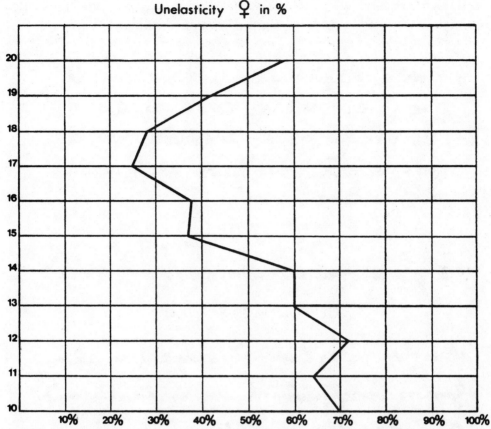

Figure 8. Unelasticity. Course of curve of the unelastic line. Taken from 1,096 writing samples of female secondary school pupils. All the samples that display inelasticity are shown, without taking into account the level of prominence, converted into percentages for the age-groups from 10-20.

Let us now consider three approaches to handwriting at the age of puberty. We may use three handwriting samples of 14 year-olds (Figs. 9-11). The first is that of a girl, taken from Peugeot (1979), the second is from Dubouchet (1967) and the third is taken from "Pubertätskrise und Handschrift," by the author of this chapter. As the titles of these works show, the samples are attributed by three different authors to three different stages of development. They agree with one another on the decisive graphical phenomenon. All three samples show unelastic, doughy lines. In all three, the microstructure, the inner part of the body of the word, is out of control. The first sample (Fig. 9) shows covering-lines, rolling, a left-angled position, a tendency to meander, etc. In the second sample (Fig. 10) we find, together with the pronounced unelastic line, end barriers. In the third sample (Fig. 11), we see unelastic connections—the words waver on the lines and endings are torn off.

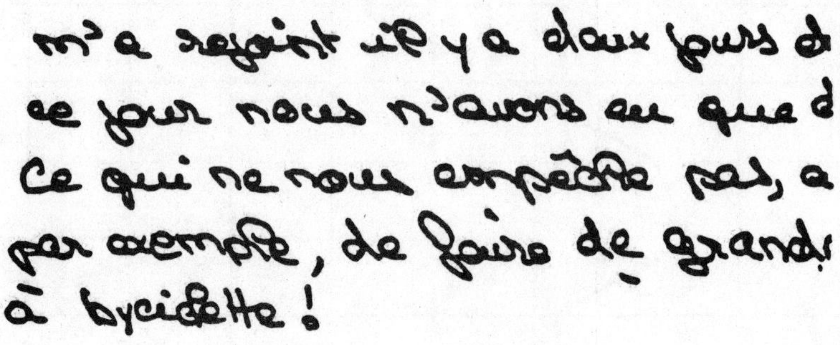

Figure 9. From Peugeot (1979).

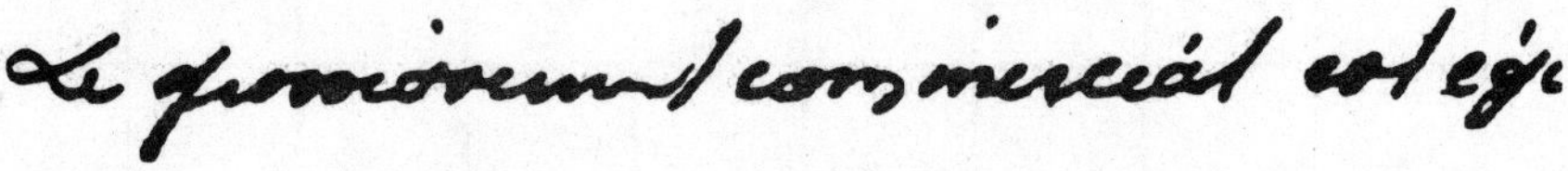

Figure 10. From Dubouchet (1967).

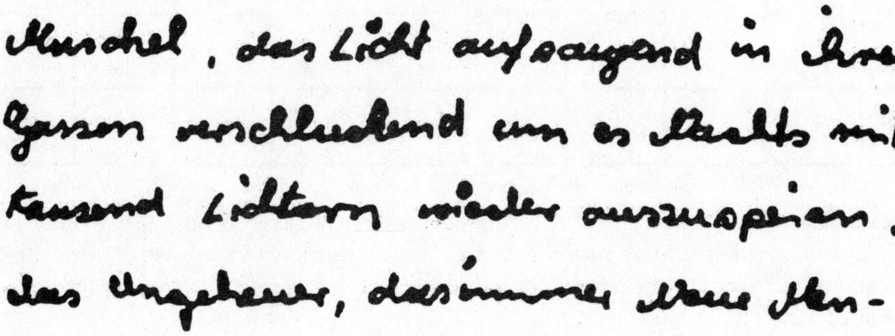

Figure 11. From Ave-Lallemant (1983).

It would be interesting to compare those handwriting samples which were described as "disgraphic" by the French school. Do they display typical puberty signs? Here, a joint Franco-German research project would be of value, even for the study of the psychology of development.

THE ADOLESCENT

The adolescent phase has seldom been made the subject of special observation. Either it was included in general observation of pupils' handwriting, or—more frequently—it was considered as adult writing.

The handwriting of the adolescent was often judged by the same qualitative norms as the writing of the mature person. These norms were not suited to the adolescent, as, after puberty, a rather surprising individual form of writing appears. The adolescent is generally much too easily seen as a "finished object." There was, however, an additional reason to overlook the singularity of expression in adolescent handwriting. The child's writing is already dependent on the culture of his country and on his education (writing style is taught). Naturally, his handwriting in later life is even more closely linked to the culture of his country, and, with the adolescent, roll-writing, for instance, is even more accentuated. It is for this reason that it is recommended to deal with typical adolescent handwriting through the study of inter-cultural and intra-cultural differences.

In general, one may say that although the child's writing does not yet have the full force of expression as that of the adult, it nevertheless reaches a certain uniformity. The adolescent's writing is full of expression, but also of versatility. It must therefore be judged in accordance with its context.

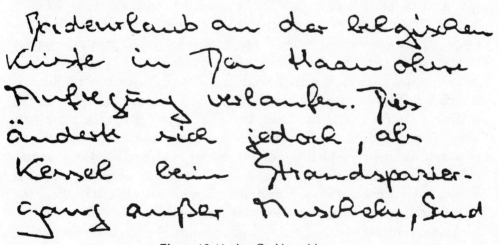

Figure 12. 'Acting-Out' in writing.

Let us now take a closer look at the writing of the adolescent. The metamorphosis from child to adult occurs between the ages of 15-17. It is then that the adolescent starts to stand on his own feet. His handwriting shows that he has demands upon others and upon himself. He has ambitions, and these are legitimate at this phase of his life. Here is the start of the search for his own identity. Being and being seen become confused and this is expressed in the adolescent's handwriting, in which we can see how the young person wants others to see him. Fig. 12 is a good example. From it, we can deduce that this adolescent girl wants to appear energetic and secure and is concerned with the impression she is making. The writing shows demonstratively oversized capital letters, pronounced, jagged underlengths, overblown upperlengths and a slightly flat middle zone. It is possible to build a picture of these writings; they have a certain unreality about them and are a type of acting out.

In the author's 1970 survey of adolescent handwriting, she noted the appearance of hyperkinesis and left-angled bends (especially with girls), and breaks (especially with boys). The result of a second survey, as yet unpublished, of writing samples in the same group, confirmed and complemented these findings. The latter was a statistical survey, carried out in 1976 on 2,311 secondary school pupils (1,217 males and 1,094 females) in a medium-sized German town. Roll-writing was noted and the $\mathcal{T}$ was strikingly obvious, confirming the earlier observations of its appearance at 14, with girls and 16, with boys. The appearance of "adolescent" indicators reached its peak in very late adolescence—at the age of 16-18 for girls and 18-19 for boys—after which a decline set in.

It is clear that the crisis of puberty is followed by the crisis of adolescence. There is a sudden increase of roll-writing round about the age of 14-16; at this age, the unelasticity of the writing-line has not yet faded away. The long-lasting narrowness in the writing, caused by inhibition, is striking. There is even an increase in the incidence of breaks in the writing, until the age of 18. These are most often seen in the handwriting of 18 year olds in their last year of school and are a sign of nervousness and insecurity, which is not surprising, as their age leads one to infer that they had to repeat one class. When one considers that it is during adolescence that we find the highest suicide rate, then the urgency of investigating this life-phase becomes obvious.

The investigation carried out by the Societé Francaise de Graphologie, the results of which were published in 1980 (La Graphologie), also made a valuable contribution to the study of handwriting in adolescence. The handwriting of pupils aged 17-20 from European countries, was studied vis-a-vis their performance in school and their social behavior, as judged by their teachers. Two French specialists collaborated on the study of the writing of adolescents—Arlette Lombard and Madeleine de Noblens (1983). Of the writing syndromes which were noted in this connection, inhibition should be mentioned as an example. The results show that both the social behavior and the school performance of those whose handwriting showed inhibition, were similarly inhibited. (The sample consisted of 236 males and 375 females.) The high percentage of weak performers who write arhythmically, hints at the way in which such a survey could be of assistance to psychologists. On the one hand, there might be a strong emotional disturbance because of personal or family reasons, which lower the level of the scholastic performance. On the other hand, the bad scholastic performance may be — and probably is — a further cause for the pupil's anxiety.

In the German contribution to the French investigation, made by the author of this chapter (cf. **La Graphologie**, no. 158 and Zeitschrift für Menschenkunde, 1980/3), the evaluation of the teachers regarding the pupils' social behavior was standardized. In addition, the teachers were asked to apply four grades (very good to weak) to school performance. Finally, a limited number of writing syndromes, which were connected with the experience of the adolescents under investigation, were chosen and graded 1-5. These three improvements made it possible to place each writing syndrome side by side with the grade stemming from the teacher's evaluation and thus to check its specific meaning. To do this, a computer was used, thereby permitting very detailed analysis. If the handwriting and the performance in school are studied in relation to one another, we find a high co-existence rate between handwriting with an above-average levelled arrangement and a very good school performance, while a similarly high co-existence rate appears between handwriting whose levelled arrangement is below average (i.e., disturbed), and a weak school performance. However, it should be noted that "school performance" in this case relates to the mastering of tasks in 13 subjects in the final years of secondary school, and that the handwriting was analyzed as a symbol of emotional expression, rather than with regard for its calligraphic accuracy. If we follow tradition and interpret the arrangement of the writing picture as an expression of emotional balance, the practitioner may find a clue here as to the individual treatment required by the adolescent.

Fig. 13 shows the phenomenon known as "simplicity." It makes its appearance with the growing maturity of the pupil and is thought of as an ability for abstract thinking. Fig. 14 shows the joining of letters in the script. This appears gradually and is interpreted as an ability for combination. These phenomena show a very clear connection between handwriting syndromes and scholastic performance. This subject will be more fully explained in a book by the author of this chapter entitled **Leistungsversagen und Handschrift** to be published shortly.

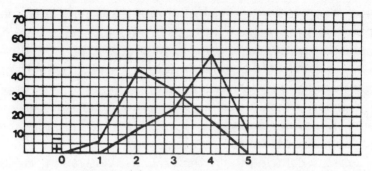

Figure 13. Simplicity and performance.

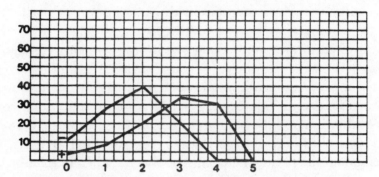

Figure 14. Combination ability and performance.

The Life-Style of Handwriting Development

If we now take a comprehensive view of the development of the young person's handwriting, from infancy to the end of adolescence, we can chart a course of development, starting with the problematic character of the pre-school years and the first troubles in school, followed by emotional disturbances connected with the move from primary to secondary school. Next, the first disturbances of puberty are shown, and can already be noted in the writing-picture of the 12 year old. These may continue for several years, especially in a rich, structured personality. Finally—usually around the age of 15—the crisis of adolescence brings about a further change in the writing-picture. Childhood and adolescence are phases of identification. At first, it is mostly the parents who determine the child's experiences. At puberty, we find a natural detachment; parental support diminishes and there is, as yet, no replacement. Then the adolescent commences the search for his own identity, and the more pluralistic the society in which he lives, the longer this phase is likely to last. Only in his early 20s does he really find himself. Only now does his handwriting become truly autonomic. Even so, it continues to develop for the rest of his life, as new experiences change his attitude toward himself.

Conclusion

In this chapter, we have presented a systematic historic sketch of graphology as it stands today, insofar as it relates to the handwriting of the child and the adolescent. No attempt was made to encompass all the existing literature. Only the leading authors were considered. It became clear, however, that a wide gulf exists between the work of the German, French and Anglo-American schools. It is the author's hope that by working together, ignoring the language barrier, it may be possible to further enrich research into this area of graphology.

REFERENCES

Ajuriaguerra, J. et al. (1964). *L'Ecriture de l'enfant. Vol. I. L'Evolution de l'écriture et ses difficultés.* Neuchatel.

Ajuriaguerra, J. et al. (1964). *L'Ecriture de l'enfant. Vol. II. La rééducation de l'écriture.* Neuchatel.

Ave-Lallemant, U. (1970). *Graphologie des Jugendlichen Vol. I. Längsschnitteanalyse.* München/Basel.

Ave-Lallemant, U. (1973). Die Längschnittanalyse der Jugendhandschrift und ihre Ergebnisse für die Schriftpsychologie. *Zeitschrift für Menschenkunde,* 1973 (1-2).

Ave-Lallemant, U. (1973). Graphologische Forschungsergebnisse der Jugendkrise. *Zeitschrift für Menschenkunde,* 1973 (4).

Ave-Lallemant, U. (1979). *Der Sterne-Wellen-Test.* Munchen/Basel.

Ave-Lallemant, U. (1981). *Le test des étoiles et des vagues.* Paris.

Ave-Lallemant, U. (1984). *The Star-Wave Test.* München: Ernst Reinhardt.

Ave-Lallemant, U. (1980). Ergebnisse einer europäischen Enquete über die Sozialisation Jugendlicher. *Zeitschreift für Menschenkunde,* 1980, (3).

Ave-Lallemant, U. (1982). Die Jugendhandschrift als Argernis oder Chance der Graphologie. *Zeitschrift für Menschenkunde, 1982,* (4).

Ave-Lallemant, U. (1982). *Notsignale in Schülerschriften.* München/Basel.

Ave-Lallemant, U. (1983). *Pubertätskrise und Handschrift.* München/Basel.

Bang, Vinh. (1959). *Evolution de l'écriture de l'enfant a l'adulte.* Neuchâtel.

Bauer, S. & Mann, O. (1933). *Die Graphologie der Schülerhandschrift.* Leipzig.

Becker, M. (1949). *Graphologie der Kinderschrift.* (3rd ed.). Hamburg.

Delachaux, S. (1955). *Ecritures d'enfants.* Neuchâtel.

Dubouchet, J. (1967). *L'Ecriture des adolescentes.* Paris.

Gesell, A. L. (1906). Accuracy in handwriting as related to school intelligence and sex. *American Journal of Psychology.*

Gobineau, H. & Perron, R. (1954). *Génétique de l'écriture et étude de la personalité.* Neuchâtel.

La Graphologie (1980). *158, 159.* Paris.

Kienzle, R. (1937). *Vom Ausdrucksgehalt der Schülerhandschrift.* Stuttgart.

Kienzle, R. (1949). *Graphologie der Schülerschrift und Schülerzeichnung.* Tübingen.

Kienzle, R. (1951). *Schülerbeobachtung und Schülerbeurteilung* (3rd ed.) Esslingen.

Lockowandt, O. (1970). Die Kinderhandschrift—ihre diagnostischen Möglichkeiten und Grenzen. *Zietschrift für Menschenkunde. 1970,* (1-2).

Lombard, A. & De Noblens, M. (1983). La Graphologie de l'adolescente. Pierre Faideau (Ed.). *La Graphologie.* Paris.

Olivaux, R. (1971). *Rééducation de l'écriture.* Paris.

Peugeot, J. (1979). *La Connaissance de l'enfant par l'écriture.* Toulouse.

Peugeot, J. Rééducation de l'écriture et graphotherapie. Pierre Faideau (Ed.). *La Graphologie.* Paris.

Schelenz, E. & L. (1958). *Pädagogische Graphologie.* München.

Wittlich, B. (1940). *Handschrift und Erziehung.* Leipzig/Berlin.

Wittlich, B. (1957). Krisenhafte Pubertät im Schriftbild. *Schule und Psychologie 1957,* (11). München/Basel.

5

SCHOLASTIC DIFFICULTIES IN HANDWRITING: AN EXPLORATORY CONTRAST-GROUP STUDY

MARTIN WIRTHENSOHN

Summary

IN THIS STUDY a large number of handwriting characteristics were investigated through a comparative group design in connection with scholastic difficulties. Two groups were formed from the handwriting samples of about 500 young people (17-19 years of age): one consisting of those whose school careers indicated that they had scholastic difficulties (repetitions, repeated changes of school-types) and a second group in whom the corresponding indicators were not present. Then a random selection of 20 handwriting samples was taken from each group. These handwriting samples were then assessed graphologically by the author.

The evaluations of the handwriting underwent bivariate and multivariate analysis. With the discriminant analysis and with the inclusion of 13 handwriting characters, 97.5% of the 40 cases could be assigned to the correct group. However, using exclusively the characteristic "over-organization of space," 65% of the cases were classified correctly.

Suggestions are made for the practice-oriented transposition of the study results and consequences for further studies are discussed.

Introduction[1]

Up until now efforts have been made in various studies to demonstrate the correlation between certain aspects of scholastic success, or failure, and handwriting. These investigations embodied the hope that graphology could provide diagnostic support in order to be able to recognize scholastic difficulties at an early stage and to take appropriate corrective measures.

One of the earliest studies in this field was published in 1906 by Gesell, who studied the connection between scholastic intelligence and handwriting. More recently, Ave-Lallemant (1970, 1973, 1979, 1982a, 1982b), Legruen (1960a, 1960b, 1961, 1965, 1969), Lockowandt (1970, 1972), Oinonen (1961) and Wallner (1965), among others, have dealt with this subject. However, in spite of the relatively large number of studies, only a few empirical investigations are available.

Oinonen, in her study of 7-9 year old children, found a "factor of poor handwriting," comprising certain variable characteristics which, when sufficiently pronounced, are in her opinion symptomatic of psychic disorders or of an abnormal personality. These characteristics are:

- blots (smudging)
- improvement of letters by writing over
- unevenness of writing pressure
- deviations from the straight line
- errors of form
- change of angle of slope

In an earlier work (1922), Legruen had already listed the following characteristics which impair the legibility of children's handwriting:

- lack of isolation of words and lines (unclarity)
- insufficient height
- excessive width or narrowness
- excessive slant
- too little connecting of letters
- disproportion in the linear division

Lockowandt (1972) attempted to validate the various characteristics described by Oinonen and Legruen. For this purpose, 594 young people aged between 10 and 17 years were divided into two groups of good and of poor performers in the Pauli test. Female students then classified the handwriting of these young people according to the presence or absence of the characteristics described by Oinonen and Legruen. The scores for each handwriting sample were totalled and a biserial correlation calculated with the item, "performance in the Pauli test." The results are contradictory. While in the 10-13 age group the correlation coefficients are significant, both per year and for the whole age-range, this is only partially true for the 13-17 age group: here the results are significant only with regard to the whole age-range, but not when the different ages, in years, are classified separately.

These results seem to suggest that at different ages, different characteristics are of more significance than others. However, the relevance of the characteristics may itself be questionable. Lockowandt suggests that an exploratory comparative-group study be carried out, embracing further handwriting characteristics.

In a recently published work, Ave-Lallemant (1982a) presents 14 danger signals of diagnostic relevance. These are:

- Disordered use of space
- Confusion of space
- Overorganization of space
- Meandering or "boxing"
- End blocking
- Covering strokes
- Retouching
- Narrowness
- Slackening of movement
- Stiffening of movement
- Hyperkinesis
- Inelasticity of the shaping stroke
- Fuzzy, indistinct strokes
- Breaks in the stroke

She discusses these danger signals on the basis of handwriting samples of young people aged between 7 and 19 years, from 12 different countries, and points out that many danger signals may appear only temporarily, while others are to be found over a longer period. Besides the age factor, other individual factors also seem to be responsible for this. Ave-Lallemant particularly stresses that although the presence of danger signals in the handwriting always means that the young person concerned is in need of help, their absence does not necessarily mean that he or she is emotionally balanced. Together with the characteristics described by Oinonen and Legruen, there is thus a whole series of variables in handwriting which it can be assumed are appropriate as indications of scholastic difficulties. It therefore appeared to be of particular interest to investigate to what extent these handwriting variables differ between the various groups of school-children.

METHOD

Within the framework of a longitudinal study[2] of the scholastic and occupational careers of young people in Zurich, I was given the opportunity to investigate certain aspects of the subject. As this was a secondary analysis, the design of the study was largely already established and a number of inadequacies had to be contended with.

Sample and Criterion

The random sample population for this longitudinal study, from which the comparative groups formed here were taken, comprised a total of 1,565 young people who constitute a representative selection for the Canton of Zurich. About one-third of these young people had made use of the opportunity to enter their remarks and comments on the study in their questionnaires. Two groups were formed: one consisting of those whose school careers indicated that they had scholastic difficulties, and a second group consisting of those in whom the corresponding indicators were not present. Young people whose parents were divorced or separated were excluded. A random selection of 20 samples of handwriting was then taken from each group. These handwriting samples were then assessed graphologically by the author, without his being aware of the group from which each was taken, or of the sex of the individual or the type of school he or she attended.

At the time when the questionnaires were completed most of the subjects were 17 years of age: a few were already 18.

The criteria for the formation of the groups are related to the three-year period the upper school phase (age: 13-15 years). Scholastic difficulties were indicated by two criteria which defined allocation to the experimental groups:

1) Repetitions during the three-year upper-school phase.
2) Attendance at a different type of school in each of the three upper-school-phase years.

The control group consists of young people who attended the same type of school for three years, without repetitions. Their objective scholastic career during the upper school phase thus contains in the sense of the operationalization no signs indicative of scholastic difficulties. The events which are considered as indicators for scholastic difficulties may have occurred up to four years earlier. The experimental group includes eight individuals who attended three different types of school during the upper school phase and twelve who repeated a period of schooling (one in "Realschule," six in "Sekundarschule" and 5 in "Gymnasium"). In the control group, five attended "Realschule" and fifteen "Sekundarschule." In both the experimental group and the control group there were 7 boys and 13 girls.

It should be emphasized that the operationalization of scholastic difficulties applied here is one of many possibilities. The fact that a pupil remained in a certain type of school throughout the whole upper-school phase does not necessarily mean that he or she had no scholastic difficulties. These may be expressed in many ways — for example, in scholastic performance (grades) or disturbed social contacts. It is also possible for the emphasis to be placed on self-appraisal by the pupils or assessment by the parents.

Handwriting Characteristics

For the purpose of an exploratory procedure it seemed important not to restrict the study to only a few specific features, but to investigate a large number of handwriting characteristics. The handwriting features presented by Mueller and Enskat (1973) formed the basis of this extensive list, with the addition of the variables proposed by Legruen (1922), Oinonen (1961) and Ave-Lallemant (1982a), which are listed above. Handwriting characteristics considered in the analysis included the following (No. of score values in brackets):

1) Arch-like/Garland-like (7)
2) Downward extensions longer than upward extensions/Upward extensions longer than downward (7)
3) Initial emphasis/Initial underemphasis (7)
4) Space between words — small/large (7)
5) Unevenness of pressure — not present/pronounced (4)
6) Deviations from the straight line — not present/present (2)
7) Inelasticity of the forming stroke — not present/very pronounced
8) Breaks in the stroke — not present/very pronounced (6)
9) Number of the danger signals defined by Ave-Lallemant appearing
10) Number of the variables defined by Legruen appearing
11) Number of the variables defined by Oinonen appearing

A full list of the handwriting characteristics considered can be obtained from the author.

The values 9, 10, and 11 are total values which indicate how many of the characteristics defined by the authors concerned occur in a particular handwriting or are indicative, in their intensity, of scholastic difficulties.

RESULTS

The handwriting characteristics were first investigated at the bivariate level, in that biserial correlations, F-tests and t-tests were calculated between the handwriting characteristics and the "group affiliation" variables (control group, trial group). Depending on whether or not the F-test indicated differences in scatter, the test was calculated for homogeneous or inhomogeneous variances. As may be seen, the characteristic of "over-organization of space," with $r_{bis} = -.54$, shows the highest correlation with the group direction, in that the subjects of the experimental group write in a more organized way. The mean-value and scatter tests are equally significant. The experimental group shows a more marked scatter. As comparison shows, this is true for all cases in which the scatter test gives a significant result. The handwriting samples of the experimental group also show more scatter in the variables "Leftward tendency/Rightward tendency," "Disorder of space," "Confusion of space," "Width of left margin," "Differences in length" and "meagreness/fullness" than those of the control group. As in no case was a greater scatter found in the control group, one can speak here of a uniform picture. At least at the group level the handwriting of the young people with scholastic difficulties shows a wider range of variation in regard to the scatter than the writing of those who, in the sense of our operational definition, passed through the school system without difficulties.

Mean correlations can be established for the characteristics "width of left margin" ($-.45$), "regularity/irregularity" ($-.44$), "slowness/haste" ($.42$) and for "peculiarity" ($-.38$). The direction of the correlations indicates that the handwritings of the experimental group show a wider right-hand margin than those of the control group and are written more regularly, with more rightward tendency and faster, and are characterized by a higher level of individual peculiarity. For these characteristics the t-test is also significant, at the 5% level.

Characteristic for the handwriting of the experimental group are a higher level of disorder of space, a larger number of the danger signals are defined by Ave-Lallemant, greater confusion of space, lighter writing pressure and larger spaces between words. The totals of the characteristics as defined by Legruen and Oinonen show no statistically significant differences between the two groups. On the other hand, all the characteristics of Ave-Lallemant concerning the writing space appear in Table I and the total number of the characteristics defined by her show statistically significant differences between the two groups. This seems to indicate that of the three authors, it is the variables defined by Ave-Lallemant which are of greatest significance, at least on the basis of the bivariate analysis.

Bivariate analyses are, however, of only limited significance for graphological practice, being based on the unrealistic assumption of a connection between a handwriting characteristic and a particular feature of personality or character. No graphologist would work in that way. More important are multivariate procedures, which allow one to find, from a larger set of variables, a "best" sub-set for answering a particular question. In the present case the discriminant analysis is applied, a procedure which to the best of the author's knowledge, has been used in graphological practice only by Paul-Mengelberg (1983).

Discriminant analysis is a multivariate procedure by which it is possible to determine, stepwise, from a large number of variables, those which best separate the members of the experimental group with regard to a particular criterion, in this case, scholastic difficulties. In addition, a discriminant function is calculated which assigns a point-score to each experimental group member. This point-score is calculated from the weighted degree of intensity of those variables which are entered into the discriminant function, and a constant. The stepwise procedure is complete when none of the remaining variables improves the separation of the groups. In a subsequent classification step, on the basis of the point-score calculated for each experimental group member, the calculated affiliation of the individuals to the groups can be compared with the real situation.

In order to ascertain which set of variables permits the best separation between the control group and the experimental group, the handwriting characteristics were thus submitted to a discriminant analysis in a second assessment step. The results of these assessments are summarized in Table II.

TABLE I: Results of the bivariate analyses

Variable	r_{bis}	Sign.	Significance of difference in mean values*	Significance of difference in scatter**	Remarks
Over-organization of space	-.54	ss	ss	ss	TG writes with more over-organization
					TG shows more scatter
Width of right margin	-.45	ss	s	—	TG shows wider right margin
Regularity/irregularity	.44	ss	s	—	TG writes more regularly
Leftward tendency/rightward tendency	-.44	ss	s	ss	TG writes with more rightward tendency
					TG shows more scatter
Haste/slowness	.42	ss	s	—	TG writes more hastily
Peculiarity	-.38	s	s	—	TG shows more peculiarity
Disordered use of space	-.34	s	—	ss	TG show more disordered use of space
					TG shows more scatter
No. of alarm signals	-.34	s	—	—	TG shows more alarm signals
Confustion of space	.30	s	—	ss	TG shows more confusion of space
					TG shows more scatter
Writing Pressure	-.30	s	—	—	TG shows lighter writing pressure
Space between words	-.28	s	—	—	TG shows more space between words
Width of left margin	—	—	—	—	TG shows more scatter
Difference in length	—	—	—	—	TG shows more scatter
Fullness/meagreness	—	—	—	—	TG shows more scatter

ss = Significance level 1%
s = Significance level 5%

* determined by t-test
** determined by F-test

TG = Test Group

TABLE II: Results of the discriminant analysis

Step	Variable considered	Group mean values (Discriminant function)	% of correctly classified individuals
1	Over-organization of space	± .47	65.0%
2	Slowness / Haste	± .79	82.5%
3	Retouching	± .88	87.5%
4	Disordered use of space	± .96	85.0%
5	Simplification / Complication	± 1.00	90.0%
6	Leftward / Rightward tendency	± 1.09	90.0%
7	Covering strokes	± 1.13	92.5%
8	Left-slanting / Right-slanting	± 1.20	87.5%
9	Space between letters	± 1.25	87.5%
10	Arch-like / Garland like	± 1.29	90.0%
11	Regularity / Irregularity	± 1.33	90.0%
12	Structuredness / Unstructuredness	± 1.41	92.5%
13	Smallness / Largeness	± 1.47	97.5%

We see that on its own, the characteristic "over-organization of space" gives the best separation. On the basis of this variable alone, 65% of the 40 cases can be assigned to the correct group. However, the two groups still lie relatively close to one another. The mean group value of the control group is $-.47$, and that of the trial group $+.47$. When in addition to "over-organization of space," "slowness/haste" is also considered, the percentage of correctly classified individuals increases to 82.5% and the group mean values diverge to $\pm.79\%$. With each further characteristic that is included, the separation of the groups continues to improve, although the proportion of correct classifications remains static in some cases, or even decreases. The position of the two groups when seven characteristics are considered is illustrated in Fig. 1. At this stage of the assessment, the proportion of correct classifications is 92.5%. As may be seen, on the basis of the discriminant score, two cases from the control group are wrongly assigned to the experimental group, and one case from the experimental group wrongly assigned to the control group (Figs. 2-4). Comparison of these handwriting samples shows that it would certainly not have been easy, even for experienced graphologists, to forecast correctly to which group they belonged.

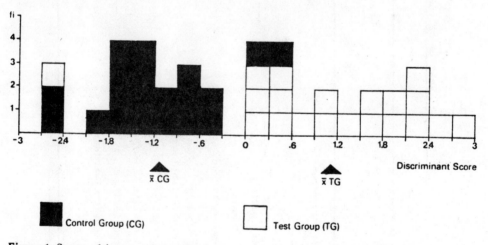

Figure 1. Status of the control group and test group with inclusion of 7 handwriting characteristics.

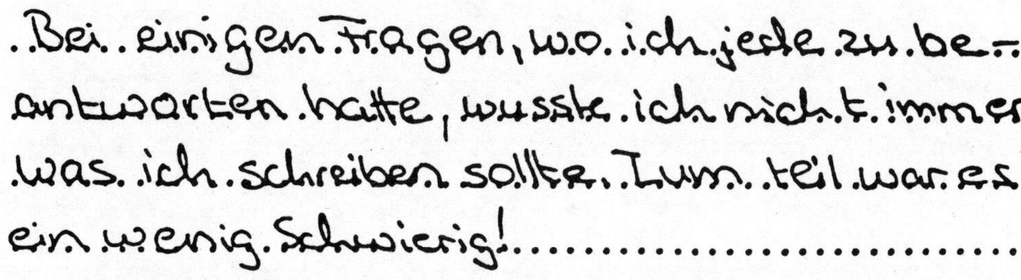
.Bei..einigen.Fragen,wo..ich.jede.zu.be-:
antworten.hatte,wusste.ich.nicht.t.immer
.was.ich.schreiben.sollte..Zum.teil.war.es
ein.wenig.Schwierig!

Figure 2. Handwriting which was wrongly classified in the control group.

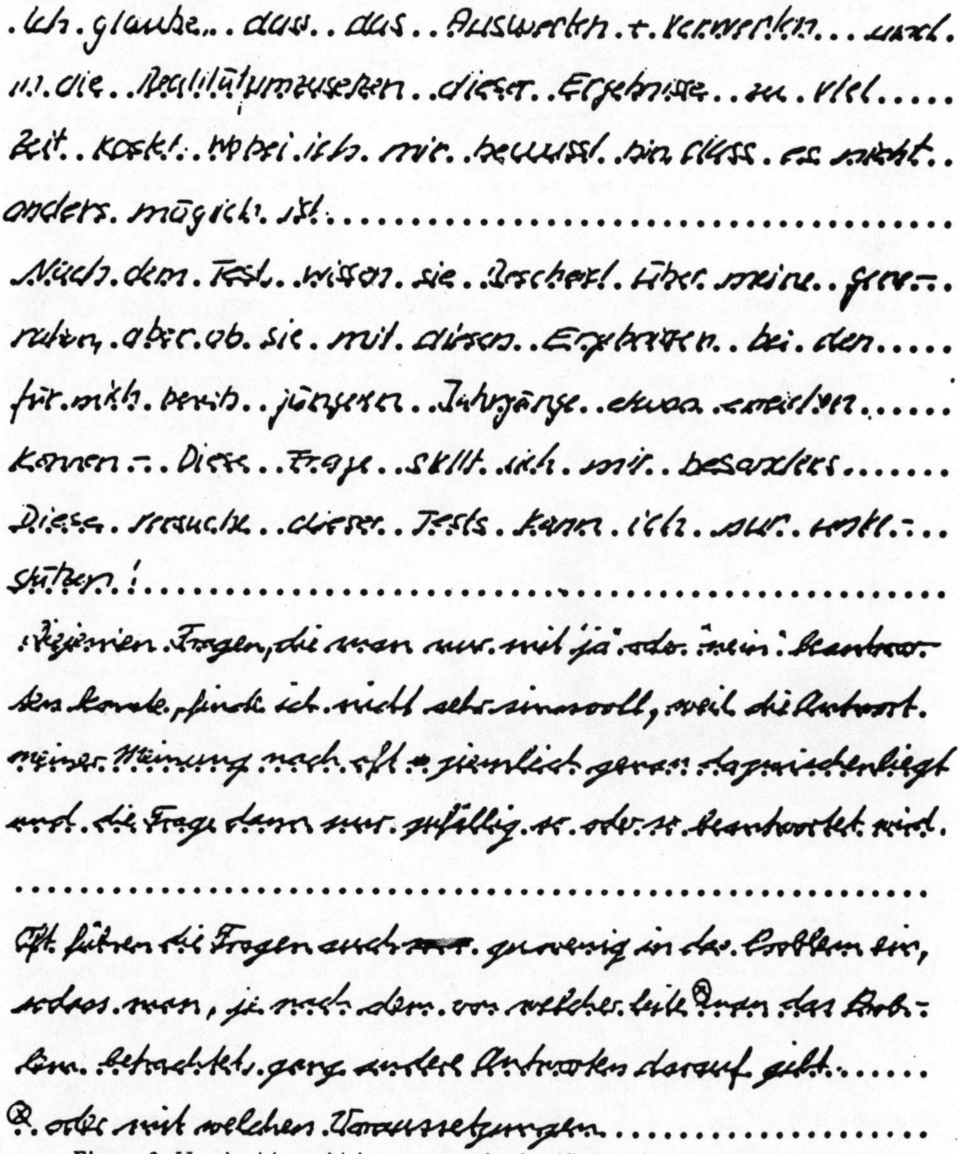

Figure 3. Handwriting which was wrongly classified in the experimental group.

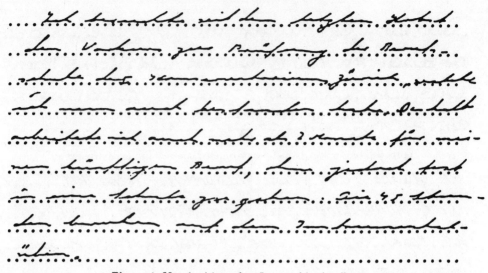

Figure 4. Handwriting of a 17 year old schoolboy.

With the inclusion of a further six variables, 97.5% of the cases are classified correctly, the group mean values being ± 1.47. Fig. 5 illustrates the position of the groups when all the 13 characteristics listed in Table II are considered. Only the handwriting reproduced in Figure 2 appears wrongly in the control group.

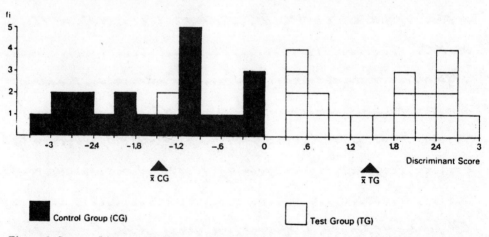

Figure 5. Status of the control group and test groups with inclusion of 13 handwriting characteristics.

It will by now be clear that an important advantage of the discriminant analysis lies in the fact that the individual handwriting samples and experimental group members do not become "lost" in the analysis, but that after each assessment step, the handwriting samples can be compared, on the basis of the calculated values of the discriminant function, with the position which each one assumes on the separation function.

Finally I would like to mention a further important aspect of the discriminant analysis which is of relevance in graphological practice. Using the weighting factors of the individual variables and the constants of the discriminant function, the discriminant score can be calculated for further handwriting samples not included in the investigation and the position of his new writing on the discriminant function determined. However, it has to be ensured that the handwriting variables show the same degrees of intensity as in the experiment and also that the same codes are assigned to the degrees of intensity. The discriminant scores are calculated according to the following formula:

$$D_i = k + d_{i1} z_{i1} + d_{i2} z_{i2} + \ldots d_{ip} z_{ip},$$

where D_i represents the discriminant score of the person i, k the constant, d_{i1} the weighting factor of the first variables (non-standardized) and z_{i1} the corresponding degree of intensity of the first variables in the person i. The weighting factors and the constants for the first seven and for all 13 handwriting characteristics are given in Table III.

TABLE III: Non-standardized discriminant function co-efficients
based on 7 and 13 handwriting characteristics

Variable	Coefficients (7 characteristics)	Co-efficients (13 characteristics)
Over-organization of space	.881	.776
Slowness / Haste	.717	.812
Retouching	.815	1.130
Disordered use of space	.416	.498
Simplification / Complication	.945	1.545
Leftward / Rightward tendency	.635	.754
Covering strokes	.177	.348
Left-slanting / Right-slanting		-.370
Space between letters		.748
Arch-like / Garland-like		-.623
Regularity / Irregularity		-.752
Structuredness / Unstructuredness		.811
Smallness / Largeness		.399
Constants	-10.890	-11.649

The classification procedure will not be discussed by means of an example. The discriminant score for a handwriting sample from the experiment (Figure 4) is to be calculated. The seven handwriting characteristics which proved to be important in the discriminant analysis (see Table II) form the basis for this calculation. The characteristics, "slowness/haste," "simplification/complication" and "leftward/rightward tendency" were classified in the experiment according to a seven-code scale, by which Code 1 was assigned to a markedly slow, or very simplified or very leftward written handwriting, while Code 7 was applied to writing with the most pronounced characteristics at the other end of the scale. Code 4 was given for normal intensity of the particular handwriting characteristic. The characteristics according to Ave-Lallemant are classified by means of a six-code scale. Code 0 indicates that the particular characteristic is not present in the handwriting being studied, while Codes 1-5 indicate the intensity of the characteristic, Code 5 representing the most pronounced manifestation. The various characteristics of this particular handwriting are coded as follows:

Over-organization of space	3
Slowness/haste	6
Retouching	0
Disordered use of space	0
Simplification/complication	1
Leftward/rightward tendency	7
Covering strokes	4

I thus classified the handwriting as moderately over-organized, and written rather quickly. The writing is very simplified and at the same time also shows a marked rightward tendency. Covering strokes are rather pronounced. On the basis of the codes assigned to the various characteristics of this writing, the equation for the calculation of the discriminant score is as follows (weighting factors and constant taken from Table III):

$$D = (-10.89) + (.881*3) + (.717*6) + .945 + (.635*7) + (.177*4).$$

D thus equals 2.153. It can be seen from Fig. 1 that a handwriting with this value lies within the range of the trial group and is in fact clearly above the mean value for the young people of this group. As the handwriting comes from the experimental group, we know that the writer does in fact belong to the group of young people who have had difficulties at school.

The importance of the procedure presented here is the fact that it can be used to study further samples of handwriting in order to clarify probable scholastic difficulties. However, further studies should be carried out to confirm the results presented here, before its definite use can be considered.

DISCUSSION

This study has shown that a relatively small number of handwriting characteristics is sufficient to differentiate young people with scholastic difficulties, in the sense of the operational definition used, from a control group without these indicators. As long as only bivariate comparisons are performed, differences in the mean values are, however, only to be observed in a few of the handwriting characteristics. In the bivariate comparison it was also shown that the handwritings of the experimental group diverge more markedly than those of the control group. However, this result applies only at the group level and not to the individual handwritings.

In both bivariate and multivariate analyses, the variables relating to the writing space have emerged as particularly relevant. It thus seems that in regard to scholastic difficulties, the manner in which the writing space is treated is of considerable significance. Here particular attention should be paid to the characteristic, over-organization of space, but also to disorder of space.

A further aspect of scholastic difficulties concerns the cognitive component. Although the young people of the experimental group write more hastily, some of the handwritings show a considerable lack of concentration. The characteristic, simplification/complication, is also relevant in this connection. Among the handwritings of the experimental group there are some which are simplified to the point of unsubstantiality. This form of haste and simplification must also be understood as a danger signal.

A similar phenomenon, which may refer to the social components of scholastic difficulties, is to be observed in regard to the characteristic, leftward/rightward tendency. The handwritings of the experimental group show a moderate to pronounced rightwards tendency in a surprisingly large proportion of cases. This is an indication that not all young people with scholastic difficulties withdraw (characteristic: space between words) and that many seek contact with other people who might be able to help them. The tendency of the young people of the experimental group on the one hand to withdraw and on the other to seek contacts is also underlined by the great scatter observed in the findings concerning the characteristic, leftward/rightward tendency.

Finally, it still remains to be pointed out that the writing of the experimental group subjects shows noticeably more covering strokes and more frequent retouching, two of the danger signals mentioned by Ave-Lallemant. Taking into consideration the other handwriting characteristics defined by Ave-Lallemant which have emerged as relevant in this study, the results obtained can be considered as at least a partial confirmation of the danger signals described by this author. That the characteristics defined by Oinonen and Legruen are not capable of discriminating between the two groups cannot be considered as a final verdict after this one study. Further investigations with other, secondary criteria would have to be carried out, which would possibly substantiate the results of this study.

Due to the time lapse of up to four years between the appearance of scholastic problems and the sampling of the handwriting, variables of handwriting of a relatively lasting nature have been recognized as significant. This could also mean that scholastic difficulties have to be viewed in connection with a global concept of difficulties, even if these are age-related. It also seems evident that possible difficulties are not necessarily connected with school. It may be that they merely manifest themselves there—for example, in performance, behavior and sociability. It would also be desirable to perform studies which consider scholastic difficulties on a somewhat broader basis and possibly also even to define them operationally differently from the method used in this study. (The problems of operational definition have already been mentioned.) With such studies it would in time be possible to establish which handwriting characteristics are important in this connection, in spite of differences in operational definition and different types of secondary criteria in the studies.

The handwriting samples discussed here were assessed by only one person, namely the author. It would be desirable for several specialists in graphology to perform the handwriting assessments. Various studies of this type have in fact shown only relatively slight differences between the assessments of handwriting by individual graphologists. An experimental procedure with multiple assessment would therefore be appropriate, because only in this way can the reliability of the assessments be checked.

The results of the study should also not be overestimated as they are based on only 40 scripts. It would of course be better to work with 100 or more subjects. Certainly, a replication study is required before the specific weights and equations could be crystallized.

In conclusion, I would like to come back once again to the discriminant analysis, which I consider to be a very suitable procedure for making multivariate assessments within the framework of studies based on comparative-group design. It can also be used for studies comprising more than two comparative groups, when there are several discriminant functions. In my opinion, the particular advantages of the discriminant analysis are the informative value of the results and the possibility of using them for diagnostic purposes. With sufficiently accurate understanding of the relevant handwriting variables one could also consider using the findings for prognostic purposes. With serial investigations, it would then be possible, under certain circumstances, to provide help, in good time, for young people who are particularly at risk and in this way to spare them many scholastic problems.

Once again, it should be stated that this investigation is only a pilot study, and no definite conclusion should be drawn before a large-scale replication is performed.

REFERENCES

Ave-Lallemant, U. (1970). Graphologie des Jugendlichen. Band 1: Längsschnittanalyse. München: Reinhardt-Verlag.

Ave-Lallemant, U. (1973). Die Längsschnittanalyse der Jugendhandschrift und ihre Ergebnisse für die Schriftpsychologie. *Zeitschrift für Menschenkunde, 37(1-2)*, 78-104.

Ave-Lallemant, U. (1979). Die Psychologie der Kinderschrift. *Angewandte Graphologie und Charakterkunde, 27(1)*, 16-31.

Ave-Lallemant, U. (1982a). Notsignale in Schülerschriften. München: Reinhardt-Verlag.

Ave-Lallemant, U. (1982b). Die Jugendhandschrift als Aergernis oder Chance der Graphologie *Zeitschrift für Menschenkunde, 46*, 4, 397-410.

Gesell, A. L. (1906). Accuracy in handwriting, as related to school intelligence and sex. *American Journal of Psychology, 17*, 394-405.

Legruen, A. (1922). Die Schülerschrift in zeitgemässer Beurteilung. Wien-Leipzig.

Legruen, A. (1960a). Eine Reifungs-Skala für Schülerschriften. *Zeitschrift für Menschenkunde, 24*, 261-281.

Legruen, A. (1960b). Aufsatzschreiben und Schrift. *Schule und Psychologie, 7*, 145-153.

Legruen, A. (1961). Schriftgruppen in einer Mädchenklasse. *Zeitschrift für Menschenkunde, 25,* 141-144.

Legruen, A. (1965). Ein Schrift-"Bazillus" befällt eine Mädchenklasse. *Zeitschrift für Menschenkunde, 29,* 66-68.

Legruen, A. (1969). Studie über die Schriften einer Schülergruppe. *Zeitschrift für Menschenkunde, 33,* 145-152.

Lockowandt, O. (1970). Die Kinderhandschrift — ihre diagnostischen Möglichkeiten und Grenzen. *Zeitschrift für Menschenkunde, 34,* 301-326.

Lockowandt, O. (1972). Empirische Utersuchungen zur Validatät der Kinderhandschrift. *Zeitschrift für Menschenkunde, 36,* 293-311.

Mueller, W. H., Enskat, A. (1973). *Graphologische Diagnostik. 2. Auflage.* Bern: Huber.

Oinonen, P. (1961). Poor handwriting as a psychological problem. *Acta academiae paedagicicae Jyväskylämisis. 21,* Jyvaskyla.

Paul-Mengelberg, M. (1983). Zür Handschrift des bildnerischen Menschen. *Zeitschrift für Menschenkunde, 47,* 16-56.

Wallner, T. (1966). Zusammenhänge zwischen Prognosedaten, Handschriftenvariablen und Ausbildungsergebnissen. *Zeitschrift für Menschenkunde, 30,* 380-387.

NOTES

1. I would like, here, to thank Mrs. A. Honegger most sincerely for her suggestions and help.
2. This study was carried out by the Educational Department of the Education Authority of the Canton of Zurich in collaboration with the Institute of Applied Psychology, University of Zurich.

6

THE GENAIN QUADRUPLETS AT AGE 51: REPORT OF HANDWRITING ASSESSMENT[1]

THEA STEIN LEWINSON

Summary

A SET OF monozygotic female quadruplets developed schizophrenia at age 26 and were treated at the National Institute of Mental Health for several years. Using graphic material of these unusual subjects, this study demonstrates how handwriting, statistically in graph forms, expresses the developmental stages before (at age 16), during the acute phase of the disease (age 26 to 28) and 25 years later (age 51) when they functioned outside a hospital setting in various degrees of competency.

To make the results of the handwriting assessments based on the most recent scripts of the Genain Quadruplets more understandable, it seems advisable to give a short introduction to the techniques and interpretations of handwriting psychology, with special reference to the Lewinson-Zubin scales (1942).

Handwriting is considered an expressive movement which can be analyzed and interpreted according to the principles of the science of expression (see e.g.: Allport & Vernon, 1933). The advantage of handwriting is that it is the only recorded expressive movement which can be used for research and comparison at any time, independently of when and where it was written. This aspect is particularly important in the case of the Genain quadruplets. We were able to graph their handwriting when they were twenty-eight years old at the time of their first hospitalization, and at the age of fifty-one when they were recalled for a follow-up study.

Handwriting is a **formed line** extending through three dimensions: up-down (the vertical), left-right (the horizontal) and back-front, i.e.,

119

the pressure which goes behind the paper versus the disconnections in the writing when the pen is lifted from the paper (depth). As handwriting is a **movement,** it has dynamic aspects. These are represented by **contracting, balance,** and **releasing** tendencies. For these dynamic characteristics, a 7-point scale was developed: Contraction (or Bond): $+3, +2, +1$; Balance: 0; Release: $-1, -2, -3$. All handwriting elements (form, height, width, breadth, depth) are distributed among the four dimensions: form, vertical, horizontal and depth, and then ranked on the 7-point scale of Bond, Balance, Release.

These basic ratings result in four tables which serve as a standard model for the measurement and evaluation of a particular writing. The measurements and evaluations are entered on a plotting sheet corresponding to the blueprint of the standard tables, from which we obtain our figures and calculations. The results are marked on a corresponding graph, resulting in curves showing modifications of the normal distribution curve, as basis for the psychological interpretation. This is only a short summary of the rather complex technique developed by Dr. David Rosenthal (1963).

Interpretation of the five individual components may be summarized as follows:

I. The Form Component is the integrative factor of the personality, the form in which the other component correlates are integrated in the individual's functioning (approximately the level of performance.)

II. The Vertical Component is the rational organization within the individual, i.e., the relationship between the intellectual, the emotional, and instinctual tendencies.

III. The Horizontal Component is the emotional-social sphere, i.e., the relationship between the individual and his environment.

IV. The Depth Component represents the instinctual sphere, i.e., the utilization of the individual's instinctual drives and his psychophysical energies in general.

V. The Composite or the Total of the four components provides an integrated picture of the overall personality structure and adjustment.

Using our calculations on the plotting sheet, we obtain a productivity or efficiency quotient expressed in decimals. From our data base of more than one thousand cases, the following scale has been established:

Below- 0.10 Pathological-Inferior
0.11 - 0.20 Low Average to Average
0.21 - 0.30 High Average to Outstanding
0.31 - 0.40 Outstanding to Superior
0.41 - 0.50 Superior (Genius)

Dr. Rosenthal's Pathology Index (1963) derived from the final line of calculations on the plotting sheet can range from 35 to 180. This is a sort of a tension index with the figures between 90 and 100 still possibly in the healthy range. Above that, the higher the index, the greater the pathology.

For the present handwriting study of the quadruplets at age fifty-one, we used the above techniques. Based on the resulting curves, the Efficiency Quotients of the different personality aspects were calculated and the respective Pathology Indices were established. Following this, a table was drawn up, listing the Efficiency Quotients for all personality aspects and composites, deduced from each woman's handwriting at the ages of sixteen to seventeen years, twenty-eight years, and fifty-one years (see Table I).

The same comparison was registered on a separate table for the Pathology Index (see Table II). As an over-all conclusion regarding their efficiency and pathology, all four women continued pretty much in the same sequence through the years. Sarah was the most efficient and the least disturbed, Edna being second, Wilma third, and Helen fourth. It may be useful to interpret the table of the Efficiency Quotients in greater detail, especially in the light of the most recent graphed results from the handwritings at age fifty-one.

At the age of fifty-one, Edna performs fairly well on an average level, whatever she may have learned (Form quotient 0.17), while her rational organization is on a low average level, possibly interfering at times with the quality of her performance. The vertical quotient of 0.13 indicated a slight imbalance. Compared to her sisters, her emotional social sphere functioning is on a slightly better than average level (Horizontal quotient of 0.17). She seems to have deeper feelings and is possibly more involved than the others. In the instinctual-physical sphere, her resources are adequate, but she does not seem particularly strong (depth of 0.17). Her over-all personality (total 0.16) indicates a medium level of efficiency and adjustment, probably somewhat lowered by her inadequately integrated rational organization.

TABLE I

EFFICIENCY QUOTIENTS, DEDUCED FROM GRAPHIC COMPONENTS

Subjects	Formal Form Aspects			Vertical Rational Organization			Horizontal Emotional-Social Aspects		
Age (yr.)	16-17	28	51	16-17	28	51	16-17	28	51
Edna	0.16	0.13	0.17	0.16	0.14	0.13	0.17	0.12	0.17
Wilma	0.16	0.13	0.15	0.18	0.13	0.13	0.14	0.09	0.11
Sarah	0.15	0.15	0.15	0.22	0.17	0.19	0.11	0.12	0.14
Helen	0.15	0.15	0.14	0.15	0.09	0.13	0.13	0.09	0.12

	Depth Instinctual Aspects			Total Over-all Personality Picture		
Edna	0.17	0.13	0.17	0.16	0.13	0.16
Wilma	0.21	0.17	0.18	0.17	0.12	0.14
Sarah	0.19	0.19	0.20	0.16	0.15	0.17
Helen	0.17	0.16	0.16	0.15	0.12	0.13

TABLE II

PATHOLOGY INDICES DURING PREMORBID, MORBID AND POSTMORBID CONDITIONS

	Edna	Wilma	Sarah	Helen
Age 16-17	109	101	93	137
Age 28	148	177	101	179
Age 51	99	146	99	156

The handwriting suggests a not particularly bright, but well-meaning individual who, under supervision, will try to execute more or less mechanical jobs which she has learned, in a conscientious and exacting manner. She lacks initiative and mental independence, and would get confused when confronted with an assignment or a situation which does not correspond to her customary frame of reference. While emotionally not quite mature, she nevertheless relates well to people and apparently manages a fairly satisfactory social adjustment within her limited sphere. Summarizing, Edna is a psychologically not very strong individual of medium efficiency who needs support and proper guidelines for her best possible functioning.

Wilma at fifty-one functions at a barely average level of performance (form aspect of 0.15). Her rational organization between intellectual, emotional, and instinctual tendencies is not too well coordinated (vertical 0.13). Her emotional-social adjustment is on a very low average level (horizontal 0.11); however, instinctually, she is the second strongest of the girls after Sarah (depth 0.18), while her total personality adjustment comes only to a low average (total 0.14).

Wilma possesses some manual skill and probably can perform some practical type of work in the line of her aptitude. She has some difficulty in thinking clearly and in concentrating properly on a mental task. Nevertheless, she tries hard to carry out assigned work conscientiously. She is less realistic than Edna but not fully conscious of her limitations. Subjective in her attitude and judgment and very sensitive, she is emotionally rather withdrawn and somewhat self-protective. She may live partly in a private world of her own. Instinctively, she is comparatively stronger than she may appear. She has then some support for her activities and also is able to compensate for some of her shortcomings. The integration of her personality is in the low average range, so she needs considerable support and guidance in her striving for a satisfactory adjustment.

Sarah is the best integrated and best adjusted of the four sisters. While her performance level is just average (0.15), her rational organization is near high average (0.19). In the emotional-social sphere her score is just average (0.14); however, it is higher than on previous tests. Her instinctual sphere is also near high average (0.20) and provides her with two personality aspects to compensate for existing weaknesses. The total—the over-all personality picture—is 0.17—the highest of all four sisters.

Sarah is able to think fairly clearly and follow more complex instructions. Although still conflicted emotionally and immature for her age, she has improved and often compensates rationally and instinctually for shortcomings: she is always willing to learn and to improve. Her good level of psycho-physical energies supports her endeavors quite satisfactorily. There is even the danger that at times, she may overdo and be hyperactive. Although subject to mood fluctuations, she makes strong, partially successful efforts to achieve a satisfactory adjustment, even under difficult conditions.

Helen was always the weakest and most vulnerable of the quadruplets. Although some of her efficiency quotients show a slight improvement, her adjustment is only marginal. At fifty-one, her performance level is of low average (0.14); her rational organization is of even lower average (0.13) and her emotional-social sphere shows a still lower efficiency quotient (0.12). Her instinctual resources are just above average (0.16) which means not very much strength in this area. Her over-all personality picture (0.13) is also low average (the lowest of all four sisters). This suggests that she may need a lot of support, guidance, and protection.

Helen does not seem to be particularly bright or capable. She may be able to perform concrete mechanical tasks when they are exactly spelled out for her. Under those conditions, she will try to do her best and perform in a neat and orderly fashion. She is slow to learn new material and has not much grasp of abstract concepts. She is somewhat divertible and talkative and not very well able to discern the vital points in a problem or a situation. She does not form her own opinions and will try to repeat what she has heard from those in her environment. Emotionally immature, she has more or less remained a little girl. She needs a well structured and safe environment for adequate functioning and performing adequately on her particular level. She needs encouragement and praise for whatever work she is able to perform.

All four women still strongly identify with the images and concepts of their childhood, and still try to conform to them as best they can, each in her own way.

For the previous comments, the longitudinal data was summarized in Tables I and II. Table II shows the Pathology Indices, with the content of the first two assessments taken from Rosenthal's tables (p. 235). These are supplemented by the Pathology Indices of the subjects at age fifty-one. Table II shows that from the beginning, Sarah apparently was the healthiest and that there has been a considerable improvement in

Edna. Wilma's pathological development from comparative health as a young girl of sixteen to a very strong disturbance at age twenty-eight (pathology index of 177) is partially depicted in the graphs of previous handwriting material. She shows considerable improvement now at age fifty-one, with an index of 146 which nevertheless still indicates disturbances and tensions. Helen apparently has never been a very healthy or stable individual as the pathology index of 137 indicates at age sixteen. With a pathology index of 179, at age twenty-eight she was undoubtedly the sickest of them all. In spite of the marginal adjustment she may have made, Helen's mental health must still be considered precarious with a pathology index of 156.

REFERENCES

Allport, G. W., and Vernon, P. E. (1933). *Studies in Expressive Movement.* New York: Macmillan.

Stein-Lewinson, T. (1961). The use of handwriting analysis as a psychodiagnostic technique. *Journal of Projective Techniques, 25,* 315-329.

Stein-Lewinson, T., and Zubin, J. (1942). *Handwriting Analysis.* New York: King's Crown Press.

Rosenthal, D. (Ed.). (1963). *The Genain Quadruplets.* New York: Basic Books.

NOTES

1. This chapter is an adaptation of an article published in *Perceptual and Motor Skills, 56,* 171-176.

7

HANDWRITING ANALYSIS OF
HOLOCAUST SURVIVORS[1]

HAVA RATZON

Summary

IN THIS CHAPTER, the author reports on a project which examined the presumed existence of delayed-action psychological damage in Holocaust survivors by using a psychodiagnostic battery, consisting of four different tests:

A. Bender-Gestalt
B. Rorschach
C. Draw-a-Person
D. Handwriting Analysis (psycho-graphology)

The test material was gathered during the years 1961-1975.

The Experimental Group consisted of Holocaust survivors — people who went through the Holocaust in concentration camps, labour camps or ghettos, or who lived as partisans or in hiding from the Nazis (the "Holocaust" group).

Two control groups were chosen for comparison:

1) People who suffered some persecution by the Nazi regime, but who immigrated to Israel before World War II (the "Nazi-persecuted" group);
2) A group of psychiatric patients who had no personal connection whatsoever with the Holocaust (the "Psychiatric" group).

In addition, a sub-group was singled out from the experimental group, consisting of Holocaust survivors who had suffered organic brain damage ("Holocaust with O. B. D.").

The different groups were matched as to age, sex and education. The total number of participants in this study was 184.

The Psycho-Graphological Test was carried out on 184 handwriting samples, transmitted to the graphologist in one package, without any arrangement or classification. The graphologist analyzed and classified the sample, before receiving any details or information whatsoever about the four research groups. After the data had been scored and matched, the following results were obtained:

1) The test consistently showed that the Holocaust group displayed the lowest level of psychological competence:

2) The secondary, brain-damaged survivors' group (Holocaust with O. B. D.) scored lowest, within the Holocaust group;

3) In third place were those persecuted by the Nazi regime before World War II;

4) The control group of psychiatric patients without experience of the Nazis showed relatively the highest level of psychological functioning.

Most of the differences between the groups were statistically significant.

THE PSYCHO-GRAPHOLOGICAL EXAMINATION

The Research Topic

The topic of the research project was the examination of the Holocaust survivors' reality testing, their integrative forces and their "ego-strength" in comparison with other groups.

The graphologist was asked to describe the socio-communicative functions and competence of the Holocaust group in comparison with the Nazi-persecuted and the Psychiatric control groups, by the psycho-graphological analysis of 184 handwriting samples, using tested and reliable methods.

The assignment included the detection and classification of possible disturbances and/or signs of enhanced stress situations or fear symptoms, which could influence social attitudes or behavior.

The Examination Method

In the framework of the research project, it was not possible for the graphologist to transmit individual, detailed and inclusive analyses of the personalities of the 184 subjects. The specific, structured and limited design of the project dictated terms and methods to guarantee maximum exactitude, reliability and validity of statistical comparison.

The Technique Chosen for the Project

This technique deals with disturbances which appear in handwriting in such a quantitative and qualitative measure as to indicate pathological elements affecting the writer's personality. The topic has been extensively investigated in graphological research, so that today, reliable methods can be used for the description and classification of certain signs of disturbance in handwriting.

Wittlich (1968, 1971), devised a technique for assembling a series of "Contrast Syndromes" detectable in handwriting samples — a procedure whereby personality conflicts can be described. These are combinations of graphic signs, which were found to be the expression of conflictual drives and of disharmonious and unbalanced behavior patterns. Wittlich classified these contrast syndromes into three groups, according to the three accepted dimensions of handwriting:

a) Movement (rhythm)
b) Form
c) Space arrangement

This method was chosen because it guaranteed the highest possible level of valid screening results.

The data, statistically arranged and computerized, validated the choice of method, showing a fixed order of symptoms, which appeared repeatedly in a graded sequence of personality features, ranging from "highly disturbed" to "least disturbed." The final results of the test battery show a high correlation between the results of the four tests.

The Summarizing Procedure

Due to certain technical limitations of the project, the graphologist reduced the three Wittlich (1971) criteria to two combined categories, namely:

a) Disturbances of Rhythm
b) Disturbances of Form and Space Arrangement

a) Disturbances of Rhythm

This category includes the quality of the pen stroke (tension, grippressure), mainly along the lines of Pophal's (1966) researches on writing movement, showing that cerebral processes influence muscle function in handwriting. Pophal defines **handwriting as brain writing,** and established a typological system, classifying types of motoric behavior as reflected in the handwriting patterns, showing the functional dominance of different parts of the brain. His method has been further developed by additional research over more than three decades, and constitutes one of the cornerstones of Wittlich's classification technique. By the use of these methods, it is now possible to diagnose from the measure and quality of pressure and tension, functional capability, the influence of fear and anxiety, the impact of traumatic events and the socio-communicative attitudes of the writer.

The movement structure (or individual rhythm) represents mainly basic direct and unconscious urges and impulses, transmitted to the muscles performing the writing. Disturbances in the flow of the individual writing rhythm generally indicate obstacles and impediments affecting the flow of energies or, in other words, the flow of libidinous potential.

b) Disturbances of Form and Arrangement

The form represents, first and foremost, the cognitive functions, such as the conscious relationship of the writer to his or her self-image and to the world about him. Secondly, the form structure reflects the writer's functional adaptability to environmental and existential conditions and demands. It also reflects signs of integrative faculties and interpersonal skills; it shows the writer's will and/or ability to communicate with others and to express himself clearly and openly, to make himself comprehensible — to be "readable." Disturbances of form and space arrangement in the handwriting consist of numerous signs of structure detrioration, deformations of letter and word shapes, exaggerations or other signs of negligence, omissions, disharmonious and defective configurations.

18 Signs of Disturbance

Eighteen signs of disturbance were selected, nine of them relating to disturbances of rhythm and nine relating to disturbances of form and arrangement. Some of these signs are specific and can be observed and measured by simple means: height and width, slant, broken and tremulous strokes, etc. Others are syndromes, or groups of single signs, which have an inherent mobility, such as exaggerated forms, extremely irregular arrangement, extreme rigidity or flaccidity of the stroke, etc.

(i) Signs Indicating Disturbances of Rhythm

1. Disproportion (disharmonious relations between movement structures in different parts of the writing).
2. Non-rhythmic alterations of writing angle (inclination).
3. Non-rhythmic alterations in stroke direction (against standard).
4. Alterations in degree of connection.
5. Uneven changes in size (height, width) of letters.
6. Obsessive, cramped tracing.
7. Tremulous strokes.
8. Broken strokes, "solderings."
9. Sudden changes in stroke pressure.

(ii) Signs Indicating Disturbances of Form and Arrangement

1. Strange, unusual form structure.
2. Exaggerated shapes.
3. Different shapes of same model.
4. Excessive additions.
5. Excessive entanglements.
6. Excessive adornments.
7. Disorders of arrangements.
8. Unevenness of distances.
9. Disorders in punctuation and diacritical marks.

The Results of the Graphological Test

Table I displays the most significant differences between the two main sample groups, the Psychiatric and Holocaust groups—namely, disturbances of form and arrangement (ii), which came out 1:4 (10% vs. 40%), and disturbances of rhythm (i), where the ratio was 1:2 (38% vs. 70%). Amongst the four groups, the "Holocaust" handwriting samples exhibited the highest frequency of deterioration and disorders, both in movement and form-arrangement.

The statistical summary of the graphological analysis provides conclusive evidence on the central topics of the research project:

a. The Holocaust group displays the highest incidence of disturbances in rhythm, as well as form-arrangement.
b. An interesting item is the low frequency of form disturbances among the Psychiatric group. This indicates adaptability of interpersonal behavior.

c. The difference between the Psychiatric and the Holocaust groups in the frequency of **all** writing disturbances is statistically significant: (P < .01). It indicates different modes of behavior which are generally "calm" for the Psychiatric and "restless" for the Holocaust subjects.

d. An interesting and perhaps surprising factor is the statistically significant differences between the Psychiatric group and the other control group, the Nazi-persecuted group (who left **before** World War II), concerning the number of Form-Arrangement disturbances (P < .05). This indicates higher cognitive social competence and adaptability for Group 1 (Psychiatric) than for Group 2 (Nazi-persecuted). This may be partly related to the low reliability of graphology in detecting valid signs of latent psychosis. It may also be the outcome of the Nazi-persecuted subjects' experiences with the pre-war Nazi regime.

e. As to movement/rhythm disturbances, mainly indicating enhanced stress, severe anxiety and communication disorders, the differences btween Group 3 (Holocaust) and Group 2 (Nazi-persecuted) are obvious (P < .01). This is fairly conclusive evidence as to the disastrous impact of the Holocaust experience on its surviving victims.

f. Another interesting finding is the fact that in the handwriting of the Holocaust group (without O. B. D.), the number of rhythm disturbances is twice that of arrangement disturbances.

TABLE I

Statistical Data on the Handwriting Analyses

The table gives the sizes of samples, mean values, standard deviations and significance of differences between the pairs of groups for number disturbances of rhythm and form arrangement.

Disturbance	Group	N	Mean	Standard Deviation	1-2	2-3	1-3	3-4	1-4
Movement Rhythm Disturbances	1. Psychiatric	17	3.294	1.572	N.S.	P<.01	P<.01	P<.05	P<.01
	2. Nazi-Persecuted	24	2.792	1.215					
	3. Holocaust	119	6.773	1.710					
	4. Holocaust with O.B.D.	24 / 184	7.792	1.285					
Form and Arrangement Disturbances	1. Psychiatric	17	0.529	0.624	P<.01	P<.05	P<.01	P<.01	P<.01
	2. Nazi-Persecuted	24	2.600	1.224					
	3. Holocaust	119	3.537	1.645					
	4. Holocaust with O.B.D.	24 / 184	5.208	1.933					

Some Qualitative Observations

In the Holocaust group, we found a great number of oversized scripts, and also many inflated, exaggerated and complicated structures, which point to enhanced tension, problems of self-confidence and problems with inter-personal relationships (Figs. 1-2). Very often, the tracing is hampered by a non-rhythmic interplay of flow and interruption, exhibiting broken strokes, tremors, etc. Such tracing is typical of acute and continuous conflict and emotional instability (Fig. 3). More than 70% of the handwriting samples taken from the Holocaust group exhibited a high degree of compulsive motion. All this hints at anxiety, feelings of hostility and aggressiveness towards others, towards society and towards the self. These traits go naturally with a low level of ability to adjust to, and cope with, social demands.

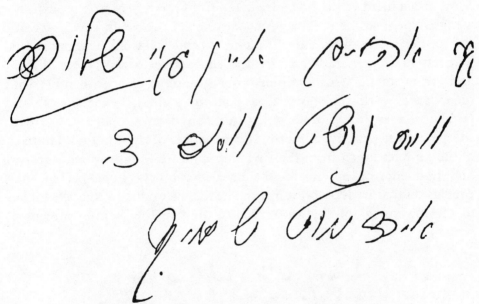

Figure 1. ♂ 49 (Holocaust) Oversized inflated structure.

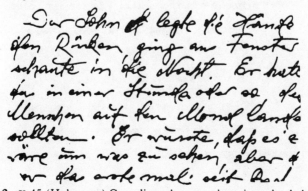

Figure 2. ♂ 45 (Holocaust) Complicated cramped tracing — hurled strokes.

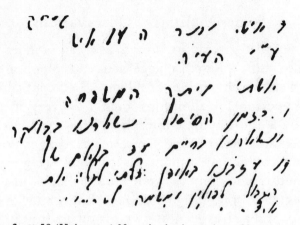

Figure 3. ♂ 58 (Holocaust) Non-rhythmic tracing — Uneven pressure.

Most of the handwriting samples taken from the Psychiatric group have a more fluent and easier rhythm pattern than those of the Holocaust group, but the stroke quality is often extremely flaccid, without tonus. The letters are generally smaller and show fewer disturbances of form and arrangement. This signifies fewer situations of open conflict with the external world. However, these signs of "stability" — the smooth and regular shapes, the simple structures and even proportions — are in sharp contrast with the numerous disturbances of rhythm found in most of the samples taken from the Psychiatric group — signs which signify a high frequency of repressed and concealed conflicts (Fig. 4). Hence the conclusion that with both groups the incidence of disturbances is higher in the movement of rhythm structure than in the form-arrangement structure.

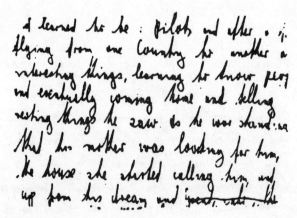

Figure 4. ♂ 63 (Psychiatric) Regular simple narrow structures — non-even pressure, slow compulsive tracing.

It appears, therefore, that most writers in the Holocaust group, as well as in the Psychiatric group, are not devoid of functional and communicative abilities. However, with the Holocaust population, these abilities are often hampered by a state of severe tension and stress (Figs. 5-6).

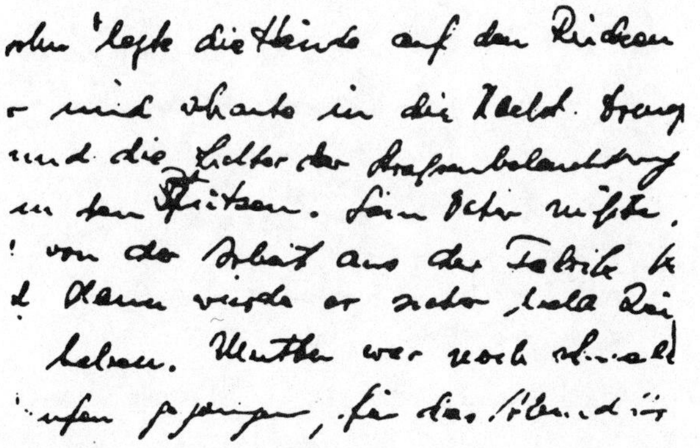

Figure 5. ♀ 52 (Holocaust II) Form structure appropriate—movement structure disturbed.

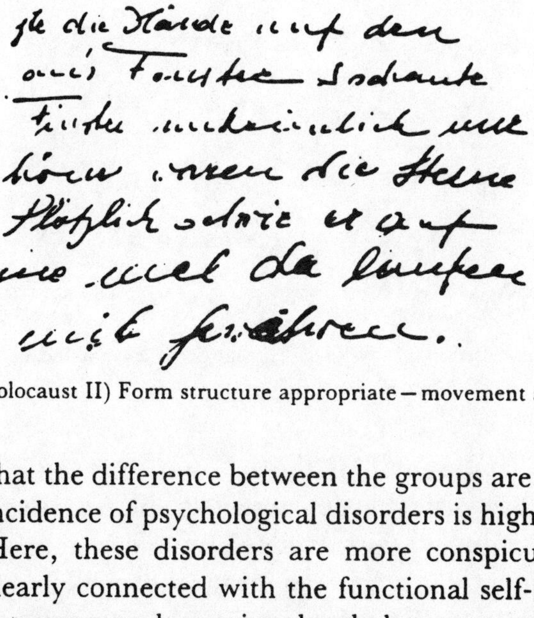

Figure 6. ♀ 53 (Holocaust II) Form structure appropriate—movement structure disturbed.

Table I shows that the difference between the groups are statistically significant. The incidence of psychological disorders is highest in the Holocaust group. Here, these disorders are more conspicuous, externally manifest and clearly connected with the functional self-image. Signs of aggressiveness, trauma and emotional unbalance are more frequent in the Holocaust handwriting samples than in those of all the other groups.

The final summary of the results revealed that distortions, deviations, disproportions, etc., are most frequent in the handwriting of the 24 Holocaust with O. B. D. subjects—as expected (Fig. 7). As to the Psychiatric group, their more evenly flowing, more regular scripts often bear signs of deep introversion (Fig. 8). This leads us to the conclusion that there might be some cases of latent psychosis among these writers, a condition which cannot be reliably diagnosed by graphological examination.

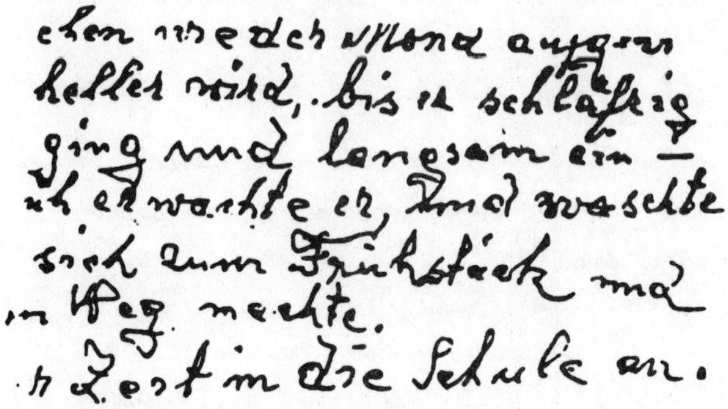

Figure 7. ♂ 68 (Holocaust + O. B. D.). Local stroke distortion tremor.

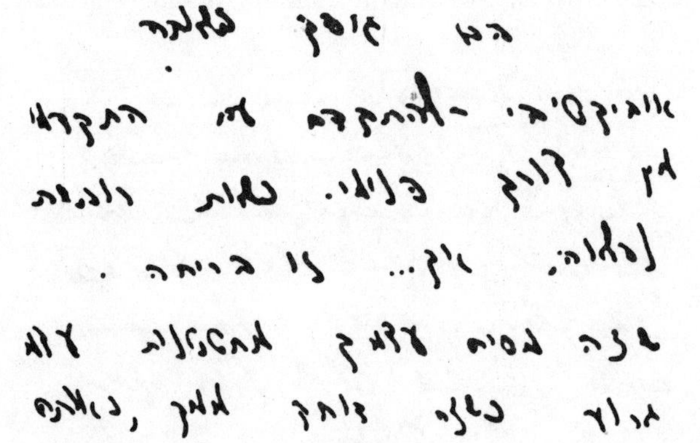

Figure 8. ♀ 27 (Holocaust + O. B. D.). Simple proportional forms, slow tracing, even strokes.

A qualitative assessment of the handwriting samples reveals that form and structure disturbances, such as dilated, swollen and over-adorned shapes, mingled with compulsive movement patterns, which are a dominant "contrast-syndrome" of most of the Holocaust handwriting samples, reflect the existence of a personality structure, in which psychological disorders are concealed inside a compulsive, harnessed "persona," which continues to function according to standard norms, despite severe neurotic impediments (Figs. 5-6). This inference calls for further investigation, all the more so, since the other tests involved in the project produced similar results.

THE OTHER TESTS OF THE BATTERY

Some concise information will now be given about the other tests involved in the project, although the author of this chapter took no active part in their performance.

The items are transmitted according to the report of the project edited and published by the Research Staff.

A. The Bender-Gestalt Test

This test, dealing with visuo-motoric graphical performance, bears a notable affinity to the psycho-graphological test; therefore the high correlation rate between the two tests is of special interest.

The material of the Bender-Gestalt Test was assessed by the psychologists, A. Shafir, S. Shepps and M. Hirsch (1975), according to the Pascal-Suttel FN (formniveau) method, which produces a quantitative measurement index for the comparison of the groups. The results of their assessment showed that statistically, the Holocaust groups (with and without organic brain damage) are more severely damaged than the other surviving group (the Nazi-persecuted).

B. The Draw-a-Person Test

This test was devised by Dr. B. Shalit and carried out on 1,000 drawings of human figures made by the research subjects. The drawings were examined according to two different methods: the Fisher method and the Witkin method. The results of the two tests show a higher capacity for self-protection with the Holocaust group than with the two other groups, the groups falling into the sequence of 3-4-1-2 (Holocaust, Holocaust with O. B. D., Psychiatric, Nazi-persecuted). This means that the Holocaust group displays the highest capacity for coping with immediate environmental threats (pain, acute danger, etc.). According to the Fisher conception, this does not enable us to predict general, constant adaptation ability.

The results of the Witkin test bring us back to the 1-2-3-4 sequence. This test dealt with the capacity of the subject to define himself as a separate identity and to evaluate his environment with a certain degree of self-confidence. Here again, the Psychiatric group scored highest and the Holocaust group lowest.

C. The Rorschach Test

Despite its limited reliability for statistical assessment, the Rorschach Test was included in the battery as an additional device for comparison. The method employed was that of Bohm. Summing up the results of this complicated test, it may be said that, in general, the items obtained show that the sequence of the four groups is almost always 1-2-3-4.

CONCLUSION: THE SIGNIFICANCE OF THE GRAPHOLOGICAL TEST AS PART OF A BATTERY OF TESTS PERFORMED IN A COMPREHENSIVE RESEARCH PROJECT.

The material from each test in the battery was analysed according to the specific field associated with that test: Bender-Gestalt, for the investigation of perception and recall abilities; Draw-a-Person, for measuring the quality of body image; Rorschach, for the interpretation of personality structure; and graphology, for the analysis of psychological dynamics and pathology.

The two control groups chosen consisted of people who had applied to the Mental Health Clinic for psychiatric treatment, with various different motives and complaints. The Psychiatric group consisted of patients with various psychological disorders, who had requested psychiatric help. The Nazi-persecuted group was composed of people seeking compensation for psychological damage caused by the Nazi regime. The experiences which they reported were less traumatic than those recalled by the Holocaust survivors, whose reason for applying to the Mental Health Clinic was the same. The Nazi-persecuted group was also chosen partly in order to check the validity of the allegation that many of the Nazi-persecuted and Holocaust survivors had advanced false claims. This allegation had to be ultimately rejected, because, had it been justified, the test results of the two groups would have displayed a much greater degree of similarity.

Despite the fact that the psycho-graphological examination covered only a part of these symptoms, because it was limited to a predefined range of characteristics, it nevertheless produced conclusive evidence as to the exclusivity of the damage caused by the Holocaust, and its irreversibility. Moreover, the high level of correspondence between the results of the different tests confirmed the validity of this research scheme.

Graphology is rarely used for research as one of the tests in a battery, and in Israel it has hardly ever been done before. That it **was** done this time is due to the initiative of the late A. Shafir.

It may be stated that in this project, the reliability and the validity of the psycho-graphological test stands out clearly amongst the other psychological tests, producing the same, if not more significant, statistical results — a fact which was verified and confirmed by the research staff. In view of the success of this approach, it is to be expected that it will be followed up in the future.

REFERENCES

Heiss, R. (1964). *Die Deutung der Handschrift*. Hamburg: P. U. F.

Pophal, R. (1968). *Graphologie in Vorlesungen. Band 2: Eidetische Graphologie*. Frankfurt: Fischer.

Pophal, R. (1968). *Graphologie in Vorlesungen. Band 3: Kinetische Graphologie*. Frankfurt: Fischer.

Shafir, A., Hirsch, M. & Shepps, S. (1975). *The delayed mental influence of the Holocaust experience as projected in psychodiagnostic battery*. Mental Health Clinic, Kupat Holim and Tel Aviv University Medical School.

Wittlich, B., Fiebrand, H. & Wessely, E. (1968). *Neurosenstrukturen in der Handschrift*. Frankfurt: Dipa.

Wittlich, B. (1971). *Konfliktzeichen in der Handschrift*. Munchen: Reinhardt.

NOTES

1. The author of this chapter owes a debt of gratitude to the late A. Shafir for his confidence and cooperation, as well as to the late Prof. F. Bruehl and his assistants, the psychologists, S. Shepps and H. Hirsch, for their open-minded and unbiased approach to a topic which often has to face over-emotional and misinformed criticism, instead of factual and objective inquiry.

8

CAN GRAPHOLOGISTS IDENTIFY INDIVIDUALS UNDER STRESS?

GIORA KEINAN

Summary

THIS STUDY investigated graphologists' ability to identify, through graphoanalysis, individuals who had been subjected to intense psychological stress. Three graphologists, three graphic artists, and three lay persons analyzed biographies and attitude statements written by 56 cadets in a parachuting course. The scripts were written under stress (before the first night jump) and in a relaxed situation (at the end of the course). The three groups of raters were asked to identify which script was written under stress and which in a relaxed state. Although the night jump elicited considerable stress, the three groups of raters failed to classify the scripts beyond chance. Moreover, no significant differences among the success rates of the three groups were found. The success rate of only one rater, a graphologist, exceeded chance. Possible explanations for the findings and suggestions for future research are discussed.

Introduction

Graphologists' ability to diagnose relatively stable personality traits or characteristics has been assessed in a number of studies. For example, the diagnostic power of graphoanalysis was tested with regard to self-confidence (Kimmel & Wertheimer, 1966; Lemke & Kirchner, 1971), introversion-extroversion (Lester, McLaughlin & Nosal, 1977; Williams et al., 1977) and neuroticism (Lester & McLaughlin, 1976; Eysenck, 1948). In contrast, little attention has been paid by researchers to graphologists' ability to diagnose temporary or transient emotional states. The evaluation of such ability was undertaken in the present study. More specifically, I evaluated graphologists' ability to identify a state of psychological stress, resulting from threats to individuals' self-esteem and physical integrity.

What Constitutes Psychological Stress?

Although the concept of stress is frequently used by both scientists and lay persons, attempts to define stress have resulted, to date, in numerous varied and partially contradictory definitions. McGrath (1970, 1976), pointed out several elements that any definition of stress ought to take into consideration.

(a) Stress results from an imbalance between external demands and individual capabilities.

(b) The imbalance can result from excessive demands (over stimulation) as well as from the absence of demands (stimulus deprivation).

(c) Stress results from imbalance between **perceived** demands and the individual's **perceived** ability.

(d) The individual will experience stress only when it is truly important for him not to fail in his fulfillment of the demands.

The terminology employed in the following is one that is becoming quite widely accepted in stress research: **stressor** is defined as a stimulus that produces **stress**. The latter is a state with the organism. **A stress reaction** is any behavioral or verbal response elicited by the stress experienced by the individual.

In the present study, night parachuting was chosen as a prototype of a stressful situation. Let us now examine the characteristics of this stressor.

Parachuting as a stressor. A number of researchers have employed parachuting as a prototype of stressors. Basowitz, Persky, Korchin & Grinker (1955) argued that the emotional state engendered by parachute jumps is similar in its intensity to anxiety states, encountered in the clinical context. Fenz (1975) emphasizes that parachuting is an ideal situation for stress research due to the intensive involvement of the individual. Parachute jumps, particularly night jumps, constitute significant and powerful stressors. First, they pose a significant physical threat. Second, failure to cope adequately with the task, or salient manifestations of fear, can hurt the individual's self-image and self-esteem. Third, parachuting and especially night jumps are fraught with uncertainty.

The Effect of Stress on Handwriting: Theoretical Explanations.

Assumptions as to the effect of stress on handwriting can be justified on several grounds.

Physiological processes. Exposure to stressors induces various physiological responses, such as increased hormonal activity, sweating, and heightened muscle tones. These responses might conceivably affect the fine motor activity required in writing (see Vroom, 1964).

Focus of attention. Stressed individuals tend to focus more on danger cues than on the task they are asked to perform (Kern, 1966; Keinan, 1979). They might thus pay less attention to, and invest less effort in, the precision of their handwriting.

Psychoanalytic explanation. Handwriting reflects the ego's power in balancing the impulses and effects of the id and superego (Bar-El, 1984). It may be assumed that impulsive effects are enhanced under stress, resulting in an imbalance. Such imbalance is presumably revealed by handwriting.

These explanations are not mutually conclusive.

The Effect of Stress on Handwriting: Empirical Evidence.

Stress was found to affect a variety of motor skills that are involved or required in handwriting, such as hand-eye coordination (Willis, 1967), manual dexterity (Berkun, Bialek, Kern & Yagi, 1962), hand coordination (Kiener & Hugow, 1973), tracking (Bergstrom & Arenberg, 1971) and visual scanning (Friedland & Keinan, 1982).

Direct evidence of the effect of stress on handwriting can be found in empirical research and in the writings of graphologists. Squire (1967) asked students to copy sentences twice, at a two-week interval—the second time being closer to the end-of-term examinations. He examined nine indices that are common in graphoanalysis, and found a high test-retest reliability in all but one.

The exception was the handwriting slant, which supposedly reflects the writer's emotional state.

Baddeley, Defigueredo, Hawkswell and Curtis & Williams (1968) reported that numbers copied by divers in deep water were larger than those copied while diving in shallow water. The same effect was found when the numbers were copied in a dry pressure chamber. The authors concluded, therefore, that the effect could not be attributed to nitrogen narcosis but rather to the stress induced by the diver's environment.

Frederick (1968) examined suicide notes. He asked graphologists, detectives and secretaries to identify the suicide notes out of groups of four notes. Each group contained the original note and three notes which were written later. All four notes were equal in content, precluding the reliance on content for the identification of the original note.

Graphologists were significantly more successful than detectives and secretaries in identifying the suicide notes beyond chance. Frederick concluded that "there might be something operating within the individual at the time he is preparing to commit suicide which would reveal itself in a motor-expressive act such as handwriting" (p. 266).

Wing & Baddeley (1978) presented data showing that alcohol consumption had an effect on the size of cursive handwriting, on increase in the average size of ticks and on variability of tick size. These authors concluded that they had found in handwriting an index for the intensity of stress experienced by individuals. Odem (1981) presented in his book **Handwriting and Reality,** the handwriting of individuals who had experienced hardship or excitement. On the basis of these handwriting specimens he concluded that excitement leads to over activity which results, among other things, in the enlargement of the middle area, more leftward movement, widening of strokes, and more connections in the handwriting.

The above examples do not invariably show the direct effect of psychological stress on handwriting. One could argue, for instance, that alcohol content in the blood rather than psychological stress is accountable for the results of the Wing & Baddeley (1978) study. Nevertheless, these examples contain sufficient data to suggest that stress affects handwriting. It remains to be ascertained whether graphologists are capable of detecting stress-induced changes in handwriting. This question was addressed in the present study.

METHOD

Subjects

56 Israeli soldiers participated in the study. They were 19-20 years old. At the time of the study they were undergoing parachute training.

Instruments

The State-Trait Anxiety Inventory (STAI)

This inventory was originally developed by Spielberger, Gorsuch & Lushene (1970) to assess individuals' chronic and state anxiety. In the present study, only the items designed to assess state anxiety were employed. The questionnaire was adapted and translated into Hebrew by

Teichman & Melnick of Tel-Aviv University. It contains 20 items that reflect the anxiety experienced by the respondent while answering the questions. The respondent is asked to indicate on a 4-point scale the frequency with which (s)he experiences the anxiety symptoms ("almost never" to "almost always"). Borus (1978) reports that the STAI is the most frequently used instrument in psychological research for the measurement of anxiety.

Handwriting Specimens

Each of the 56 soldiers was asked to write two essays on the following topics: "Censorship of movies and shows: For or against" and "Death penalty for terrorists: For or against." Each essay was written on a separate, unlined page. In addition, each participant was asked to write on separate pages part of his biography; first, from birth until age 15, second, from age 15 until present. The participants used sharpened pencils.

Raters

The handwriting specimens were analyzed by three groups of raters: three graphologists, three graphic designers and three lay persons. The last two groups served as controls for the first.

The three graphologists chosen to participate in the study, had an accumulated experience of at least five years in graphoanalysis and made their living by it. The graphic designers were chosen as representatives of a profession which, although unrelated to graphology, requires attention to line and pattern and aesthetic judgment. The group of lay persons consisted of a housewife, an industrial plant manager and a student. Members of this group lacked any formal training either in graphology or in graphic arts. They provided a comparative basis for the other two groups.

Procedure

The 56 soldiers were assembled twice, under stressful and relaxed conditions.

Writing Under Stress

The soldiers were invited into a large hall, one hour and a half before performing, for the first time in their life, a night parachute jump. They were told that they were to participate in a psychology experiment, sponsored by the Tel-Aviv University designed to test relationships between life events, personality traits and attitudes toward various issues. Following this introduction, the participants were asked to fill out the STAI and then write on separate pages an attitudinal essay and biographical passage.

Writing Under Relaxed Conditions

The soldiers were gathered after the completion of the course, before going on leave. They were informed that they were to take part in the second part of the Tel-Aviv University experiment. Once again, they filled out the STAI, wrote an additional attitudinal essay and the remaining biographical passage.

The topics for the attitudinal essays and the biographical passages which the participants were asked to write, were counterbalanced between the stressful and relaxed conditions. Following the completion of the second part the true purpose of the study was revealed.

Each of the raters received the handwritings of all the soldiers. The raters' task was to identify which of the handwritten material was written under stress and which in a relaxed state. Each rater was asked, in addition, to indicate in a 7-point scale (1 = not at all stressed, 7 = very stressed) the intensity of stress experienced by the writer of each essay or biographical passage (henceforth, "stress score").

RESULTS

In order to ascertain that the night jump was in fact a stressful experience, the average STAI score measured before the night jump was compared to that obtained at the end of the course. State anxiety was found to be significantly higher before the night jump ($t(55) = 6.09$, $p < .001$).

Table I depicts the average number of correct identifications of material written under stressful and relaxed conditions. The differences between graphologists, graphic designers and lay persons were not found to be significant. ($X^2 (2) = 1.212$, NS).

Moreover, the average performance of the three groups did not exceed the 50% chance level.

Table I :   Average correct classifications in the three rater groups.[1]

	Graphologists	Graphic artists	Laypersons	Total
Correct classifications	32 (57.14%)	24 (42.86%)	26.6 (47.5%)	82.6
Incorrect classifications	24 (42.86%)	32 (57.14%)	29.4 (52.5%)	85.4

[1] Percentage of correct classifications out of 56 possible classifications presented in the parentheses.

Table II depicts individual success rates of the 9 raters. It can be seen that only one rater (graphologist No. 1) significantly exceeded the chance level by correctly classifying 67.85% of the cases ($z=1.67$, $p<.05$).

Table II: Average correct classifications by individual raters.[1]

Rater No.	Graphologists	Graphic Artists	Laypersons
1	38 (67.85%)	23 (41.07%)	26 (46.42%)
2	29 (51,78%)	26 (46,42%)	32 (57.14%)
3	29 (51.78%)	23 (41.07%)	22 (39.28%)

[1] Percentage of correct classifications out of 56 possible classifications presented in the parentheses.

The raters' success in identifying scripts written before the night jump and those written at the end of the course could conceivably be related to the difference between the degrees of stress experienced in the two situations. To evaluate this possibility, the difference between the STAI score each subject received before the jump and his score at the end of the course was calculated. The sample was then divided at the median to a "high difference" group and to a "low difference" one.[1]

Table III shows the number of correct identifications in each of the two categories.

Table III: Average correct classifications above and below median. [2]

	Graphologists	Graphic Artists	Laypersons	Total
Above median	16 (64%)	13.3 (53.3%)	15.3 (61.3%)	44.66
Below median	14 (56%)	8 (32%)	7.66 (30.6%)	29.66

[2] Percentage of correct classifications out of 50 possible classifications presented in the parentheses.

On the average, more correct identifications were achieved in the "high difference" than in the "low difference" category ($z = 2.287$, $< .05$). Yet, no difference was found among the success rates of the three groups of raters, for the "high difference" case ($X^2 (2) = 0.642$, NS) and for the "low difference" case ($X^2 (2) = 4.255$, NS).

Table IV: Correlations between STAI and Stress Scores in the Stressful and Relaxed Conditions.

	Stressful Condition	Relaxed Condition
Graphologists	.08	.18
Graphic Artists	.19	.03
Laypersons	.17	.14

Table IV depicts correlations between stress scores assigned by the raters (on 7-point scales) and the STAI scores. None of the correlations was found to be statistically significant.

DISCUSSION

The present results indicate that the soldiers in the sample experienced more stress before the night parachute jump than after it. However the different stress levels experienced by the soldiers, before and after the night jump, were not detected by the graphologists beyond chance. In fact, the average rate of correct classifications, by graphologists, did not differ from that obtained by graphic designers or lay persons (X^2 (2) = 1.212, NS).

The various raters' failure to classify the scripts could be attributed to the absence of an effect of stress on the soldiers' handwriting. This interpretation is inconsistent, however, with the previously presented evidence of the effects of stress on fine motor activity, handwriting in particular. A more plausible explanation derives from the possibility that stress affects differently the handwriting of individuals who differ in personality attributes. This may have hindered the graphologists' ability to detect unidirectional graphological signs, characteristic of the whole sample, leading to their failure, as a group, to classify the scripts correctly. Support for this explanation derives from findings that stress has different physiological and motor effects on individuals with different personality characterisics (e.g., McGrath, 1970).

The results show that the various raters' success in classifying the scripts was higher when the difference between the stress experienced before and after the jump was high than when it was low (z = 2.887, p < .05). It appears then that there exists a relationship between individuals' stress and changes in their handwriting. It should be noted, however, that even when the scripts of the more stressed individuals were examined, the raters' success rate was only 59%. This rate does not differ significantly from chance.

Interestingly, the success rate of one of the graphologists (67%) exceeded chance. This finding is consistent with previous results which indicate that graphologists differ in their ability to predict behavior or to classify individuals according to various characteristics (Borenstein, 1985; Fredrick, 1968; Keinan, Barak & Ramati, 1984). Future research may attempt to identify the characteristics of successful graphologists and to assess the extent to which they can pass on their expertise.

To sum up, the present study did not show that graphologists, as a group, are capable of identifying, through graphoanalysis, individuals subject to psychological stress. Future research designed to collect systematic information on changes in handwriting, due to exposure to different stressors, might provide graphologists with a basis for more valid and precise judgements.

REFERENCES

Baddeley, A. D., Figueredo, J. W., Hawkswell Curtis, J. W., & Williams, A. N. (1968). Nitrogen narcosis and performance under water. *Ergonomics, 11,* 157-164.

Bar-El, N. (1984). *Interrelations among graphological judgements, psychological assessments and self-ratings of personality trends.* M.A. Thesis, Tel-Aviv University, Israel.

Basowitz, H., Persky, H., Korchin, S. J., & Grinker, R. R. (1955). *Anxiety and Stress.* New York: McGraw-Hill.

Bergstrom, B., & Arenberg, P. (1971). Heart rate and performance in manual missile guidance. *Perceptual and Motor Skills, 33,* 352-354.

Berkun, N. M., Bialek, H. M., Kern, R. P., & Yagi, K. (1962). Experimental studies of psychological stress in man. *Psychological Monographs, 76,* 1-39.

Borenstein, Y. (1985). *The Utility of Graphological Assessment as a Tool in Selection Process in the Israeli Defense Forces.* M.A. Thesis, University of Haifa, Israel.

Buros, O. K. (1978). *The Eighth Mental Measurement Yearbook.* New Jersey: Gryphon.

Eysenck, H. J. (1948). Neuroticism and handwriting. *Journal of Abnormal and Social Psychology, 43,* 94-96

Fredrick, C. J. (1968). An investigation of handwriting of suicide persons through suicide notes. *Journal of Abnormal Psychology, 73,* 263-267

Friedland, N., & Keinan, G. (1982). Patterns of fidelity between training and criterion situation as determinants of performance in stressful situations. *Journal of Human Stress, 8,* 41-46.

Keinan, G. (1979). *The effects of personality and training variables on the experienced stress and quality of performance in situations where physical integrity is threatened.* Ph.D. Dissertation. Tel-Aviv University, Israel.

Keinan, G., Barak, A., & Ramati, T. (1984). Reliability and validity of graphological assessment in the selection process of military officers. *Perceptual and Motor Skills, 58,* 811-821.

Kern, R. P. (1966). A conceptual model of behavior under stress with implications for combat training. *HumRRO Technical Report,* 66-12.

Kiener, F., & Hugow, K. (1973). Influence of stress on the fine motor movements in students. *Zietschrift für Entwicklungspsychologie und Pädagogische Psychologie, 5,* 293-302.

Kimmel, D., & Wertheimer, M. (1966). Personality rating based on handwriting analysis and clinical judgment: A correlational study. *Journal of Projective Techniques, 30,* 177-178.

Lemke, L. A., & Kirchner, J. H. (1971). A multivariate study of handwriting intelligence, and personality correlates. *Journal of Personality Assessment, 35,* 584-592.

Lester, D., & McLaughlin, S. (1976). Sex deviant handwriting and neuroticism. *Perceptual and Motor Skills, 43,* 770.

Lester, D., McLaughlin, S., & Nosal, G. (1977). Graphological signs for extraversion. *Perceptual and Motor Skills, 44,* 137-138.

McGrath, J. E. (1970). *Social and Psychological Factors in Stress.* New York: Holt.

McGrath, J. E. (1976). Stress and behavior in organizations. In: M. D. Dunnette (Ed.), *Handbook of Industrial and Organizational Psychology* (pp. 1351-1396). Chicago: Rand McNally College Publishing Company.

Odem, I. (1981). Handwriting and Reality. Tel-Aviv: Dvir.

Spielberger, C. D., Gorsuch, R. L., & Lushene, R. E. (1970). *Test Manual for the State-Trait Anxiety Inventory.* Palo Alto, California: Consulting Psychologists Press.

Squire, H. W. (1967). *Graphology as a method of selecting employees.* M.A. Thesis, The Ohio State University, Ohio.

Vroom, V. H. (1964). *Work and Motivation.* New York: Wiley.

Williams, M., Berg Croso, G., & Berg Croso, L. (1977). Handwriting characteristics and their relationship to Eysenck's extraversion-introversion and Kagan's impulsivity-reflectivity dimensions. *Journal of Personality Assessment, 41,* 291-298.

Willis, M. P. (1967). Stress effects on skills. *Journal of Experimental Psychology, 74,* 460-465.

Wing, A. M., & Baddeley, A. D. (1978). A simple measure of handwriting as an index of stress. *Bulletin of the Psychonomic Society, 11,* 245-246.

NOTES

1. This analysis was carried out on 50 cases. Four soldiers were excluded as their post-jump STAI scores were higher than their pre-jump scores. A fifth soldier did not fill out the STAI. One additional soldier was excluded in order to obtain an even number of cases.

9

TEMPORARY CHANGES IN HANDWRITING REVEALING MENTAL ATTITUDES AND THEIR FORENSIC SIGNIFICANCE[1]

ARIE L. NAFTALI

Summary

WHEN THE EXAMINER of a Questioned Document (QD) tries to identify a person by his handwriting he must also consider behavioral factors that influence a writer's movement on paper. Experts rarely venture into interpretation of peculiarities of handwriting that is not directly related to identification, except when forced to explain differences between two otherwise similar samples of writing. There are, however, some well established areas of physiological symptoms and/or temporary changes in handwriting which may contain evidence beyond the mere matter of identifying a writer: namely "identifying" his state of mind or body at a time relevant to other facts under investigation or to be decided on by the court. Here are some examples:

1) Clearing up conflicting evidence in cases of contested wills: Eyewitness against eyewitness, and medical or other expert evidence.
2) Adding some physiological proof to, or disproving the claim of "irresistible impulse" or temporary insanity which is mostly based on the time element and the psychiatrist and without taking into account the body/hormone type of a person.
3) Eliminating and narrowing down suspects in police investigations to the most likely personality in cases of theft, fraud, manslaughter, murder and sex offenses in group screening, classification and tentative identification.

Methods of Identification

"Identification" in the legal sense may be considered as the definite recognition of an object, person or activity on the basis of prior knowledge. Generally speaking, there are two distinct kinds of identification. One is the "objective" method of comparing, measuring or analysing physical characteristics by identification and chemical analysis. The other is the direct, non-analytical method of identifying faces, familiar objects, voices, tunes and other "Gestalt" patterns by the process of quick comparison with earlier impressions retained as memory traces. These complex memory traces provide a subjective certainty of definite knowledge, usually called familiarity.

The Logic Behind Identification

The objective method of identification relies on two factors: on the unchangeable character of classifiable physical properties observed, and on reasoning concerning the probabilities of the type, combination, and pattern of identical signs occurring by chance in two different objects. In this method the prior knowledge required in any identification procedure is provided by standard procedures accessible to all and the evidence of identity may be demonstrated to any intelligent observer by quantitative examination or by direct inspection. This is not so in the subjective, non-analytical method of identification where prior knowledge cannot be communicated to others because it is based on memory, for instance in an identification parade where the process of identification takes place in the central nervous system of the identifier. A combination of objective and subjective methods is also used in medical diagnosis where laboratory techniques and clinical signs or impressions lead to the identification of a disease.

Forensic Identification and Handwriting

Likewise the entire legal procedure consists of a chain of identifying processes in establishing facts, defining a point of law or determining the motive of an offender by inference from his overt behavior. Even the credibility of a witness is "identified" **inter alia** from his behavior in the witness box.

It is the purpose of this paper to suggest that the forensic examiner of questioned documents should branch out into that area of behavioral science which today uses handwriting analysis as a psycho-diagnostic tool for the purpose of classifying and identifying human behavior patterns related to court proceedings. With the definite localization of brain centers connected with writing and with the identification of neuro-hormones that influence human behavior, the analysis of handwriting has entered the area of the natural sciences. It is therefore a fallacy to relate handwriting analysis exclusively to psychological theory. This same fallacy still confuses the issue in some schools of psychiatry where exhaustion is misdiagnosed as "depression" and where temporary changes in the hormone level are diagnosed as "psychosis," ending in ruinous chemotherapy and years of mental acrobatics called "psychotherapy." This misguided, dualistic division of human behavior into body and mind has confused court proceedings, causing conflicting statements by opposing psychiatrists.

Body Types and Behavior

Previous biological studies of behavior have pointed out the importance of genetic "constitutional types" as a predicate for certain behavioral patterns — legal or otherwise (Kretschmer, 1977; Pavlov, 1956; Sheldon, 1940, 1949). Others made early conditioning the center of their theories. Glueck & Glueck (1950) and Eysenk (1964) laid stress on extrovert and introvert types with the addition of early conditioning as a decisive factor. Grassberger, in defining motivation in criminal behavior stated that they WANT more, they want to BE more or they need more LOVE. The neurologists J. H. Schutz & W. Luthe (1959), proposed, instead of the dualistic body/mind approach to behavior studies, a diagnosis and relaxation therapy on the basis of four functional systems. These systems are, in fact, the anatomical and physiological parallel of earlier typologies. The four systems each work on the principle of closing and opening in a semi-independent circle but they are interwoven and influence each other. The first — and most external — is the moving system consisting of skeletal muscles, joints and bones. The second is the inner transportation system consisting of heart, blood vessels and the lymph channels. The third is the metabolic system consisting of the digestive tract and the blood chemistry. These three systems are under the guidance of the fourth, most sophisticated system which is the neuro-hormone system, consisting of the hypothalamus with the glands of the inner secretion and the vegetative, or "autonomous" nervous system. This fourth system is our adaptation and defence apparatus, which works through chemical messengers, inside, as it were, the former three systems. This neuro-physiological system is frequently confused with mind and soul and accordingly causes misguided psychotherapy.

Tension, Neurosis and Crime in Handwriting

Schultz & Luthe (1959)—like Darwin, and much later, Wilhelm Reich—observed that people under stress tense up their skeletal muscles and contract their bodies like animals against attack. In sleep, feeding and lovemaking these muscles relax. Biological rhythm of contraction and release, of closing and opening frigidity and elasticity, was likewise used by **Pophal** (1949), the Hamburg psychiatrist, in establishing five grades of muscular tension—permanent or temporary—as shown in handwriting. He became the physiologist of graphology by identifying the causes of extreme rigidity or slackness of handwriting in the brain, be they expressed in movement, spacing or form of the letters. **Rhoda Wieser** (1952) in her classification of criminal types by their handwriting and manifest behavior used a combination, similar to **Pavlov's** (1956), of strong/elastic, strong/rigid, weak/elastic and weak/rigid. She found that the strong/rigid is more vulnerable in the area of "passive" (sometimes clever) offences.

A Working Model of Success and Failure in Life

On the basis of these earlier studies, and on observation of medical and criminal borderline cases, the attached socio-physiological model for the study of human adjustment was developed. At first, changes in handwriting tension after psychotherapy were observed during a study of 170 patients at the psychosomatic clinic of Hamburg. Physical examination and interviews with these patients revealed that improvement of neurotic symptoms produced a better coordinated, smoothly flowing handwriting as an expression of rhythmic elasticity of physical/mental functions. This biological balance—not too tense and not too slack—was claimed by **Pophal** (1949, 1938) to be the ideal of moderate tension combining alertness with relaxation.

Applying this principle to road accidents and crime, the Hamburg study explained why failure to cope with adjustment problems may be caused by high tension or slackness, when alertness and relaxation deteriorate into their caricatures of over-reaction and fatigue: active crime or passivity causing indolence, negligence, self-indulgence and drug-dependence.

Fig. 1 is self-explanatory in that it shows the gradual accumulation of activating and restraining elements in a human being on the left side, and their interplay with the values behind each immediate goal on the right.

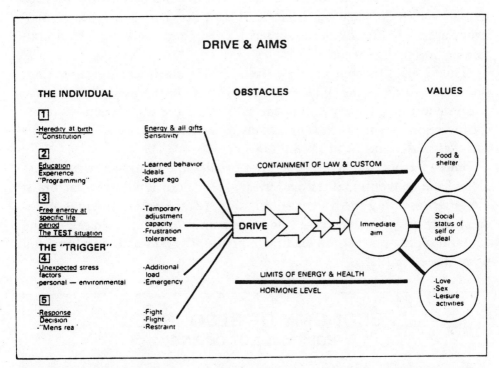

Figure 1. The Accident-Prone, the Neurotic and the Potential Criminal. Patterns of Adjustment as Shown in Handwriting.

The inborn constitutional factor at No. 1 indicates not an absolute degree of urge or aggressiveness, but the relation of energy (hormone/sugar/oxygen) to sensitivity. **Pavlov** (1956) proposed four types of temperaments: the strong/stable, the strong/excitable, the weak/stable and the weak/excitable as his classification of stress resistence and relative vulnerability. If we add human qualities to Pavlov's (1956) formula, and multiply the basic relationship of energy/sensitivity by intelligence and other attributes, we get, as a mathematical formula, the complex raw material, the "type" pointing to the kind of defense mechanism a person will choose in later life.

The Test Situation — Predicting the Breaking Point

No. 3 represents the state of balance between individual needs and their present gratification. "Free energy" means the capacity to respond appropriately to additional stimulation — neither too hearty, nor too indolent. The Hamburg study shows that handwriting will reveal the life-elasticity at a specific time, and also the relative importance of the three human values depicted on the right side of the model, i.e., the dependency or lack of interest of the subject according to his type, to his conditioning and actual needs.

This is also the common test situation for all psychological testing, but handwriting is the only single test revealing the available physical and intellectual capacity and at the same time the motivation — namely the direction in which a person is likely to use his capacity at work, in his social attitudes and/or in self-indulgence.

Three factors in this model are not predictable from handwriting, let alone from conventional test batteries: (1) the additional stress factors at No. 4 representing the trigger stimulation; (2) the environmental obstacles before an immediate goal (the "opportunity" in criminology); (3) the actual response or decision leading to action, containment or a breaking point. (See Fig. 2.)

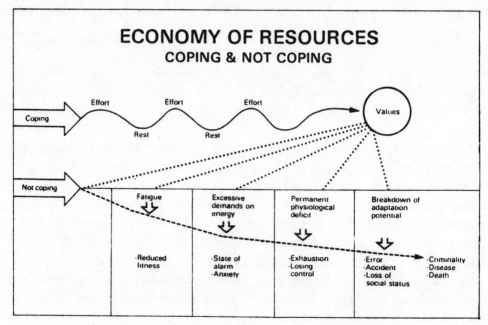

Figure 2. Economy of Resources. Coping and not Coping.

Breaking Out — Breaking Down

The application of the model to accidents and criminality has shown that human failure is sometimes, and with certain body hormone types, related to overstimulation—permanent or temporary—leading ultimately to exhaustion (Selye, 1956) of energy sources, and sometimes to slow reaction time and apathy. In criminal behavior we find, at one end of the spectrum, compulsion, irresistible impulse and aggression, and, at the other end, criminal negligence and all forms of "passive" crime. The "straw that breaks the camel's back" in a trigger situation is a mere random factor added to the accumulated activating and restraining elements shown in the model. But longitudinal samples of handwriting applied to this model will help to estimate how near to his breaking point a person has come and how the conflict with reality might be resolved: by breaking out, breaking down or prolonged containment, resignation and depression.

Clinical Use of the Model

For the last five years, hospitals in West Germany have been using handwriting to establish the biochemistry responsible for adjustment problems, testing 100 neurotics daily in one hospital alone, to identify their neuroleptic threshold. The physiological and psychological evidence thus accumulated serves as a basis for decision as to treatment by medication, exercise or otherwise (Haase, Bitter & Dreher, 1982). There is no reason why adequate samples of handwriting as used in medical diagnosis should not furnish information for forensic purposes in the areas suggested earlier—of course with all due reservations.

Possible Forensic Applications

Applying the Hamburg model to contested wills, it was on several occasions possible, after establishing the biological type of the writer, to identify a chain of gradual deteriorations or fluctuations with the help of dated samples of handwriting. In comparing this chain with medical diagnosis (and the intake of medicine) one can often answer the court's question: whether at a specific time the testator was capable of producing a well defined signature as claimed by eyewitnesses, i.e., did he do so of his own free will, considering his state of mind and health. Of course, QD examiners agree that on handwriting evidence alone, most of these questions cannot be answered, but very often it can be shown that one version as to how a signature was obtained is definitely untrue. Various problems of heart action and respiration exclude certain well defined forms and line qualities. Therefore, it is not always "the mind" but often certain physiological limitations that may help to identify or date a signature.

Furthermore, in the early stage of police investigation into a particular offense it was often possible to establish from handwriting the physical (body) type, the intelligence and dominant needs of suspects at a specific time in their lives. This helped to eliminate the most unlikely suspects and to narrow down suspects to the most likely personalities, thereby adding another dimension to the **modus operandi** (four samples). In the same way it is sometimes possible to supplement physiological evidence from handwriting or to disprove the claim of irresistible impulse or temporary insanity which is mostly based on the time element, on continuity of events and on the psychiatrists. There are certain body types identifiable by their handwriting whose compulsion to execute an envisaged scenario — of murder, for instance — is so strong, that it will be active in the brain for a long time through various "distracting" events until an appropriate trigger situation will simply put it into motion.

Conclusion: Look at the Evidence

Let me conclude with the remarks of Klara Roman (1980) on the clinical and forensic uses of graphology:

> The intense research of the past few decades has equipped the well trained and clinically oriented graphologist with shortcuts to the recognition of key syndromes. In group screening the normal can be separated from the potentially delinquent. Further, through indications of particular behavior-disorders in the handwriting [. . .] one is able to classify groups and also pick out, as in a police line up, those whose specific personality type fits a specific crime. I may add from my own experience with handwritings of criminals and sick people for the last 40 years, that it is time to discard the prejudice against graphology and start looking at the evidence.

REFERENCES

Eysenck, H. J. (1964). *Crime and Personality*. London: Routledge and Kegan Paul Ltd.

Glueck, S. and Glueck, E. T. (1950). *Unravelling Juvenile Delinquency*. New York: The Commonwealth Fund, Harvard University Press.

Haase, H. J., Bitter, I., and Dreher, A. (1982), Der elektronische neuroleptische schwellenindikator. *Therapiewoche, 32,* 3396.

Kretschmer, E. (1977). *Korperbau und Charakter.* Springer Verlag.

Naftali, A. (1965). Behavior factors in handwriting identification. *The Journal of Criminal Law, Criminology and Police Science, 56,* 4.

Pavlov, I. P. (1956). *Selected Works.* Moscow: Foreign Languages Publishing House.

Pophal, R. (1949). *Zür Psychophysiologie der Spannungsercscheinungen in der Handschrift.* Rudolstadt: Greifenverlag.

Pophal, R. (1938). *Grundlegung der Bewegungsphysiologischen Graphologie.* Leipzig; J. A. Barth.

Pophal, R. (1949). *Die Handschrift als Gehirnschrift.* Rudolstadt: Greifenverlag.

Roman, K. G. (1980). *Encyclopedia of the Written Word.* New York: Fredrick Ungar Publishing Co.

Schultz, J. H., and Luthe, W. (1959). *Autogenic Training.* New York and London: Grune and Stratton.

Selye, H. (1950). *The Physiology and Pathology of Exposure to Stress.* Montreal: Acta Inc.

Selye, H. (1956). *The Stress of Life.* New York, Toronto, London: Hill Book Co.

Sheldon, W. H. (1940). *The Varieties of Human Physique.*

Sheldon, W. H., Hart, E. M. & McDermott. (1949). *Varieties of Delinquent Youth.* New York: Harper.

Wieser, Rhoda. (1952). *Der Verbrecher und seine Handschrift: 649 Shriften Krimineller und 200 Schriften Nichtkrimineller.* Stuttgart: Alstdorfer Verlag.

NOTES

1. This chapter is based in part on earlier publications by the author:
   (1) (1965) Behavior factors in handwriting identification. *Journal of Criminal Law, Criminology & Police Sciences. 56,* 528-539.
   (2) *Temporary changes in handwriting revealing mental attitudes and their forensic significance.* Paper presented at the 10th International Meeting on Forensic Sciences, Oxford 1984.

PART III
VALIDITY STUDIES

10

GRAPHOLOGY AND JOB PERFORMANCE: A VALIDATION STUDY

AMOS DRORY

Summary

HANDWRITING SCRIPTS of sixty employees in an industrial organization were analyzed by a graphologist and rated on 13 job related items. Supervisory assessments of on the job behavior were obtained using the same items. The correlations between the graphological ratings and the subjective assessment of performance were highly significant for 10 of the items. A multiple regression of the graphological predictions on the criterion accounted for 60 percent of the variance. The results are discussed in terms of the potential application of graphology in the personnel selection context.

Introduction

In spite of the fact that graphology has been widely applied for personnel selection purposes in Europe (Levy, 1979) and that some 3000 American firms currently incorporate this technique into their selection systems, it has rarely been considered by psychologists as a legitimate subject for research — many psychologists tending to regard it as a dubious practice, on a level with astrology and palmistry. Consequently, little research is available on the psychometric properties and the predictive validity of handwriting analysis.

Graphoanalysis is a quick, technically simple and relatively inexpensive procedure. The active cooperation of the applicant is not required and faking is very unlikely. These features make it an attractive selection tool if its validity can be demonstrated. The importance of investigating the validity issue is particularly important in view of the fact that graphology is already widely practiced as a selection tool. The results of a systematic effort to examine its validity should lead either to defining more clearly the specific purposes for which it may be useful or, if validity cannot be demonstrated, for deterring practitioners from indiscriminant application. The research available so far suggests that the reliability of graphological measures is acceptably high in terms of the consistency in handwriting attributes (Birge, 1954; Wallner, 1975). The interrater reliability of handwriting analysis was also found to be satisfactory (Galbraith & Wilson, 1964; Prystav, 1971; Rafaeli & Klimoski, 1983). Evidence pertaining to the validity of the graphoanalysis technique is far less conclusive. Conflicting findings exist regarding the relationships between handwriting and mental health, personality attributes and intelligence (Klimoski & Rafaeli, 1983). It should be noted however that the number of studies addressing this issue is very limited and their lack of standardization in terms of criterion measures and analysts' expertise makes the comparison among them rather problematic. Little is known about the relationship between graphology and work criteria. The few studies which examined the question yielded conflicting results (Sonneman & Kernan, 1962; Zdep & Weaver, 1967; Jansen, 1973; Rafaeli and Klimoski, 1983).

The limited number of studies using job related criteria make it impossible to draw even tentative conclusions. Further research is needed in order to establish a clearer picture with regard to the utility of graphology as a selection tool. The present study was designed to examine the validity of the handwriting analysis in a sample of industrial and clerical employees utilizing a predictive validity design. It was generally hypothesized that graphological predictions will be correlated with superiors' judgements of on the job behavior.

METHOD

Subjects

Sixty employees in a medium size soft drinks plant were included in the sample. Subjects were employed in technical jobs such as machine operators and maintenance men or in clerical jobs. The sample comprised 45 males and 15 females; their mean age was 32.

Measures

A 13-item scale was constructed for the purpose of this study. Items pertaining to relevant job behavior domain were generated through discussions with management personnel of the firm and related to the following areas: 1) Understanding instructions; 2) Perseverance; 3) Thoroughness; 4) Verbal expression; 5) Independence; 6) Discipline; 7) Interpersonal relations; 8) Responsibility; 9) Honesty; 10) Leadership; 11) Initiative; 12) Motivation; 13) Productivity. The items were rated on a 5-point scale with explanatory comments attached to each point. For example:

Understanding Instructions

1. Understands new instructions quickly after short explanation.
2. Understands instruction after a detailed explanation.
3. Sometimes needs additional explanations.
4. Almost always requires additional explanations in order to understand instructions.
5. Has difficulties in understanding instructions even after repeated explanations.

The scale was used for the purpose of graphological ratings and for supervisory ratings of job behavior. Subject supervisors also rated their subordinates on a single global item assessing overall performance on a five point scale ranging from "Excellent" to "Very Poor."

Procedure

All subjects were assessed by a female graphologist when they originally applied for the job (betweeen a year and two years prior to the time of the study). The graphologist, who had years of experience in this practice, provided the service on a commercial basis using an essay type assessment. Hiring decisions were made on the basis of a number of predictors including a personal interview conducted by the firm representative and depending on the selection ratio in each particular case. Selection decisions were made in a clinical fashion and the weight given to the graphological assessment was generally low. It was therefore quite common for a person assessed unfavorably by the graphologist to be hired or vice versa; thus no serious restriction of range existed in the sample. The graphologist never met any of the subjects and the only source of information besides the handwritten script was the subject's sex and the job applied for. The script itself consisted of a short half page autobiographic note handwritten in pencil. Subjects were not instructed to cover any particular details and there was little consistency in terms of the script content across subjects. At the time of the study the graphologist requested to go back to the original script and the essay type report, which was written before the hiring decision was made, and this time provide a structured response by rating each item on the scale. The graphologist was unaware of the present status or the actual job behavior of the subjects and had no access to the employees or their superiors. At the same time all immediate superiors of the subjects were introduced to the same rating scale. After explaining and discussing the various items they were asked to rate their employees, taking into consideration the last six months on the job. In addition they were asked to assess their subordinates on a global 5-point item rating overall performance from "very poor" to "excellent." The raters were told that their assessments would remain confidential. Since the original interpretations of the scripts were made prior to the hiring decision, the design of this study may be considered predictive rather than concurrent.

RESULTS

The graphological and supervisory ratings were subjected to correlational and regression analysis. Table I presents the Pearson correlations between the graphological and supervisory ratings for the separate scale items. It may be observed that for 10 out of the 13 items significant correlations were yielded, most of them of a fairly high magnitude relative to validity coefficients commonly found for selection tests. In order to assess the combined effect of the graphological predictors, two stepwise multiple regressions were conducted with the graphological rating items as predictors. The intercorrelations among the graphologist's item ratings ranged from .02-.52 with a median of .39. In the first analysis the additive combination of the supervisory rating items was used as the criterion. In the second analysis the graphological predictors were regressed against the global assessment item rated by superiors. Tables II and III present the summary of the regression analyses. Approximately 60 percent of the criterion variance was accounted for in each analysis with individual item correlations with the criterion ranging from .17-.62.

TABLE I

Pearson Correlations Between Graphological and Supervisory Ratings of

Scale Items.

Item	r
1. Understanding	.32**
2. Perseverence	.43**
3. Thoroughness	.44**
4. Verbal Expression	.26*
5. Independence	.17
6. Discipline	.20
7. Interpersonal Relations	.27*
8. Responsibility	.55***
9. Honesty	.41**
10. Leadership	.42**
11. Initiative	.13
12. Motivation	.51***
13. Productivity	.51***

* p<.05   ** p<.01   *** p<.001

TABLE II

Multiple Regression of Graphological Ratings on Composite Performance Assessment Criterion

	Predictor	Multiple R	R^2	r	Significance of Predictor	Overall Significance
1.	Interpersonal Relations	.57	.32	.57	.001	.000
2.	Responsibility	.68	.46	.56	.01	.000
3.	Understanding	.70	.50	.52	N.S.	.000
4.	Thoroughness	.73	.53	.49	N.S.	.000
5.	Productivity	.74	.55	.43	N.S.	.000
6.	Verbal Expression	.75	.56	.50	N.S.	.01
7.	Independence	.76	.58	.17	N.S.	.01
8.	Leadership	.77	.60	.34	N.S.	.01
9.	Motivation	.78	.60	.54	N.S.	.01
10.	Initiative	.78	.61	.34	N.S.	.05
11.	Honesty	.78	.61	.43	N.S.	.05

TABLE III

Multiple Regression of Graphological Ratings on Global Performance Assessment Criterion

	Predictor	Multiple R	R^2	r	Significance of Predictor	Overall Significance
1.	Interpersonal Relations	.62	.38	.62	.000	.000
2.	Responsibility	.68	.46	.44	.05	.000
3.	Motivation	.71	.51	.52	N.S.	.000
4.	Initiative	.74	.55	.24	N.S.	.000
5.	Verbal Expression	.75	.56	.42	N.S.	.000
6.	Understanding	.76	.57	.47	N.S.	.000
7.	Honesty	.76	.58	.38	N.S.	.010
8.	Productivity	.76	.58	.35	N.S.	.010
9.	Independence	.77	.59	.18	N.S.	.050
10.	Thoroughness	.77	.59	.36	N.S.	.050

DISCUSSION

The results of the present study lend support to the graphologists' claim that job performance can be predicted on the basis of handwriting analysis. The magnitude of the relationship between graphological ratings and supervisory assessment of job performance was fairly high in comparison to most if not all traditional selection tools commonly in use. Obviously the merit of a new selection device cannot be established on the basis of a single sample particularly when previous investigations are not always supportive. However, the present results should serve as an indication of the potential promise of graphoanalysis and as an encouragement for further research on the issue. Most of the very few studies which previously addressed the validity issue in organizational settings, with the exception of Sonneman and Kernan (1962), did not yield such promising results. Rafaeli and Klimoski's (1983) study which somewhat resembles the methodology of the present study, did not find any significant relationships between graphoanalysis and objective performance appraisal. Such inconsistencies are not easily interpretable and may hypothetically be attributed to any discrepancy between studies' conditions and samples.

The magnitude of the present results may simply reflect a random sampling error. It is not impossible that in a sample of the present size such fluctuation may occur by chance alone and the results simply do not represent the true relationships in the population.

Greater efforts should be made in the future to increase the sample size of single studies and to attempt to apply meta-analysis techniques to enable greater confidence in the interpretation of the results.

Another possible interpretation is that the particular graphologist who provided the predictions in this study is exceptionally skillful. Although the present design does not allow for the testing of this hypothesis, the effect of individual differences among graphologists should be examined in the future. Research in this direction may lead to the identification of effective practices and methods employed by the more successful graphologists. Such findings may in turn be used for training purposes in an attempt to improve the effectiveness of other practitioners in this area.

Yet another variable which could have affected the present results may be the nature of the relationship between the graphologist and the organization. The graphologist in the present study had rendered her services to the organization for a number of years. Her familiarity with the organizational practices, and possibly with the organizational culture and expectations, may have contributed to her understanding of the kind of individual qualities leading to job success in this given setting. Considering the lack of direct and controlled experimental comparison, this argument remains rather speculative. However, the effect of experience and familiarity with the organization on the validity of graphological prediction deserves some direct research attention in the future.

To sum up, the results of the present study leave the author with an unusual task of speculating about the causes for the exceptionally highly positive results. Limitations of the study should be noted. One is due to the fact that the scripts consisted of autobiographical notes. It may be argued that the content of the script had a conscious or unconscious influence on the graphologist's ratings. Two points can be made in defense of the present data. First, Rafaeli and Klimoski (1983) compared the validity of autobiographical notes to that of neutral scripts and found no difference between the two. Secondly, although biographical information may serve as a basis for very useful selection tools (Owens, 1976) the validity of such information depends to a large extent on a high level of standardization and systematization in data gathering and scaling and on a careful empirical development of the tool. The information available to the graphologist in this case was rather sketchy and highly unstandardized. It is hard to believe that validity coefficients of the magnitude found in this study could be obtained on the basis of a few lines of unsystematic information intuitively interpreted by a person lacking basic training in industrial psychology. In conclusion, the present results suggest that the potential importance of graphology in the selection context should not be dismissed and that this potential should be further explored in order to enrich the presently existing capacity of predicting job performance.

REFERENCES

Birge, W. R. (1954). An experimental inquiry into the measurable handwriting correlates of five personality traits. *Journal of Personality, 23,* 215-223.

Jansen, A. (1973). *Validation of Graphological Measures.* Paris: Mouton.

Klimoski, R. J., and Rafaeli, A. (1983). Inferring personal qualities through handwriting analysis. *Journal of Occupational Psychology, 56,* 191-202.

Levy, L. (1979). Handwriting and hiring. *Dun's Review, 113,* 72-79.

Owens, W. A. (1976). Background data. In M. Dunette (ed.), *Handbook of Industrial/ Organizational Psychology.* Chicago: Rand McNally.

Rafaeli, A., and Klimoski, R. J. (1983). Predicting sales success through handwriting analysis: An evaluation of the effects of training and handwriting sample content. *Journal of Applied Psychology, 68*, 212-217.

Schmidt, F. L., and Hunter, J. E. (1980). The future of criterion related validity. *Personnel Psychology, 33*, 41-59.

Sonneman, U., and Kernan, J. P. (1962). Handwriting analysis — A valid selection tool? *Personnel, 39*, 8-14.

Wallner, T., Hypotheses of handwriting psychology and their verification. *Professional Psychology, 6*, 8-16.

Zdep, S. M., and Weaver, H. B. (1967). The graphoanalytic approach to selecting life insurance salesmen. *Journal of Applied Psychology, 51*, 295-299.

11

A VALIDATION STUDY OF GRAPHOLOGICAL EVALUATION IN PERSONNEL SELECTION

GERSHON BEN-SHAKHAR, MAYA BAR-HILLEL & ANAT FLUG

Summary

THREE GRAPHOLOGISTS independently rated eighty bank employees on several traits relevant to their jobs. The ratings were based on handwritten autobiographies. In order to establish a control for the biographical information, the scripts were also rated on the same traits by a psychodiagnostician with no knowledge of graphology. The criterion employed was the ratings, on the same traits and rendered in the same format, of the employees' supervisors, all of whom had had on-the-job acquaintance with their workers for at least one year. The reliability coefficients of the graphologists on the different traits were around 0.4, and their correlations with the criterion were typically between 0.2 and 0.3. The same (or even slightly higher) correlations were achieved by the psychodiagnostician, suggesting that such validities as graphologists achieve from handwritten autobiographies might be attributable to the non-graphological information they contain. A systematic attempt was then made to extract such information (e.g., level of education, army record, quality of verbal expression, aesthetics of the script, etc.), and combine it into a simple, a priori defined, linear formula. The score achieved turned out to be more valid than the ratings of the four judges. Even the score on the single variable "quality of essay" was as valid as that of the graphologists.

Introduction

The measurement and prediction of personality traits presents a major obstacle for personnel selection. Traits such as honesty, responsibil-

175

ity, independence, sociability, etc., seem desirable and even necessary
for many occupations, yet traditional psychological testing devices typically fail to predict them with anything approaching satisfactory vigor.
The increasing demand for better personnel selection, combined with
the weakness of standard personality tests, has led many firms to turn to
alternative prediction methods — most notably, graphology. Levy (1979)
reported that graphology is routinely used in the hiring of personnel by
85% of firms in Europe. Rafaeli & Klimoski (1983) estimated that 3000
American firms use this tool, and the number appears to be growing. In
Israel, graphology is more widespread than any other single personality
test, and in certain areas (e.g., banking) **all** firms use it as a screening
device.

   In view of this trend, it is surprising to note the paucity of serious research efforts to assess the validity of graphology in predicting job performance. Such research as is available typically suffers from one or
more of the following methodological problems.

a. Non-Standardized Assessments

   The typical graphological output is a free-style overall qualitative
personality description, which is hard to correlate with any independent
criterion. There are two ways to deal with the problem — by standardiz-
ing the assessments, or by choosing an evaluation methodology that can
handle the non-standard assessments. With respect to the first, the
graphologists may be requested to dispense with the overall description,
and merely to rate the writers on several predefined traits. However,
most graphologists find it unnatural to work this way, for reasons that
are at least partially valid (see Bem & Allen, 1974). With respect to the
second, Crumbaugh & Stockholm (1977) developed what they called a
holistic technique, which is based on requesting judges who are acquainted with all the writers in a sample to match the graphologists' free-
style descriptions, from which direct references to the writers have been
deleted, against the names of the writers. If the correct matches exceed
chance expectation, this is taken as evidence that the descriptions carry
at least some valid information about the writers.

b. Flawed Criteria

   When graphologists attribute to writers' traits such as honesty, responsibility, etc., satisfactory validation criteria are hard to come by, as
these traits are not directly observable, and can seldom be indepen-

dently ascertained with sufficient certitude. The most commonly used criteria are the predictions of other, more standard, personality tests, or the subjective evaluations of people who are well acquainted with the writers. The problem with these criteria is that personality tests have notoriously low validities themselves, and subjective evaluations are often unreliable. This makes it hard to conclude which prediction is at fault if a mismatch is found between the graphologists' predictions and the criteria. Other possibilities are to ask for the predication of traits that are so extreme as to be readily verifiable (e.g., "psychotic"), or to use a behavior for criterion, rather than a disposition (e.g., embezzlement, rather than dishonesty). However, even were graphologists to perform successfully in such tasks, this does not mean that they can successfully predict the more mundane attributes which interest most clients, but which are neither as extreme as the first possibility, nor as situationally specific as the second.

c. Contaminated Texts

This factor refers to the confounding of graphological information with other sources of information. Contamination is most apparent when the handwritten text is a brief autobiography of the writer, as it typically is in personnel screening contexts. Clearly, such texts contain a great deal of information about the writer that is relevant for predicting job performance criteria, such as education, previous work record, etc. Moreover spontaneous text is also contaminated by information of non-biographical nature, most notably the writer's verbal abilities, such as vocabulary, articulateness, clarity of expression, etc. These are correlated with intelligence, which, in turn, is correlated with successful performance in many jobs. Since graphological validity refers to the form, rather than content, of written material, the confounding of the two makes it difficult to assign the appropriate weight to the one versus the other.

This difficulty is almost inherent, because many graphologists will analyze only spontaneously produced text, claiming that standard or cited text changes the graphological characteristics of the written material. To be sure, the graphologists also claim that they attend only to the graphological features of the text, ignoring its contents. However, besides the a priori implausibility of this claim, studies typically find that non-graphologists achieve the same (low) validities with spontaneous text as do graphologists (e.g., Jansen, 1973; Rafaeli & Klimoski, 1983), or even outperform them (e.g., Frederick, 1965). Although this does not logically rule out the possibility that non-graphologists attend to content, while graphologists attend to form, such results clearly shift the burden of proof (that their validities are not due to content) to the graphologists.

It should therefore come as no surprise that validation studies of graphology have shown a mixed bag of results. In general, the tighter a study's methodology, the less impressive the graphologists' performance. At the same time, the tighter the methodology, the less the graphologists are working in their natural mode with their preferred material. For what it is worth, however, we offer a brief review of some validation studies of graphology.

Studies by Jansen (1973) and by Vestewig, Santee and Moss (1976) failed to find any systematic relationship between the graphological predictions and the criterion. Since, however, the criterion was psychological test results, this failure can hardly be held against the graphologists. Studies that used independent assessments by people who knew the writers were performed by Jansen (1973), Rafaeli & Klimoski (1983), Sonneman & Kernan (1962), and Zdep & Weaver (1967). Most of these studies found low or no correlations between the predictions and the criteria. In the few instances where correlations (which were always low) were significant, contaminated text, such as autobiographies, was employed. When the same texts were assessed by non-graphologists, they performed at the same level as the graphologists.

Crumbaugh and Stockholm's (1977) study, using the holistic matching technique, found the graphologists able to do significantly better than chance. The effect, however, was very small — an average of 1.72 matches out of five against a chance expectation of 1 out of 5. In a study carried out by Frederick (1965), graphologists could distinguish psychotic patients from students at better than chance level only when the handwritten sample was a spontaneous, rather than a standard, text. Even then, they did no better than non-graphologists presented with the same material. Only when required to distinguish between real suicide notes — written just prior to the suicide — and fake ones (Frederick, 1968), did graphologists perform at a level significantly better than chance. It is likely, however, that the handwritten suicide notes reflected the situational stress under which they were produced, rather than any enduring personality characteristics.

The present study represents another attempt to validate graphology in a personnel selection set-up. This study used as criterion the evaluations of people acquainted with the writers, but in a context where it can be argued that it is more or less these evaluations that the graphologists were attempting to predict in the first place, since success on the job is so closely linked with satisfactory supervisor ratings. The scripts were handwritten autobiographical sketches, but measures were taken to allow for text contamination.

In addition, we attempted to extract from the script some objective quantifiable information and derive a simple linear model for predicting the criterion from this information. The intention was to check whether such information can account for such validity as graphologists have, and whether — by integrating it formally rather than leaving the integration to be done intuitively by the human judges — the graphologists' validity can even be surpassed (see, e.g., Dawes, 1979; Dawes & Corrigan, 1974; Meehl, 1954). This aspect of the present study represents a novel contribution to the validation of graphology.

METHOD

Subjects and Material

The handwritten material was taken from the files of employees of two large Israeli banks. These files had been compiled by a reputable professional Israeli firm for preemployment screening and personnel evaluation. We shall refer to the firm as PT. The handwritten samples had been submitted, by request, upon application for the job, one to three years prior to our study. Almost all of them were brief (up to one page) autobiographical sketches. The search for material was halted when 80 scripts were found belonging to people still in the banks' employ. No selection was exercised.

The scripts were assessed four times. The assessors were three professional graphologists employed by PT, and an experienced psychodiagnostician with no knowledge of graphology. Additionally, each writer was assessed by a battery of psychological tests developed by the firm. The criterion was provided by the assessments of the employees by their direct supervisors (these underwent a standardization procedure developed by PT, to control for individual differences among different supervisors in using the rating scales). The assessors were told the purpose of the study, and the nature of the criterion, and were asked to make their predictions on a simplified form derived from that used in the firms by the employees' supervisors for the purpose of evaluation and promotion. Thus, the supervisors made a routine evalution on familiar forms, in their natural mode, while the assessors adjusted their judgments to a standardized format.

The evaluation form consisted of 3-6 items in each of three job-related areas:

    a. Level of performance and ability (e.g., "ability to learn from mistakes and make appropriate adjustments").

    b. Interpersonal relations (e.g., "willingness to help fellow workers").

    c. Loyalty to the job and compliance with job requirements (e.g., "shows up on time to work").

There was also a single summary item called "overall evaluation". All items were scaled from 1 (poorest) to 6 (best).

Besides the scripts, the files contained the predictions, on similar scales, that had been made at the preemployment screening by the firm's psychologists on the basis of an entire battery of aptitude and personality tests and other observations, such as small-group interactions, interviews, etc. We extended some of our analyses to these evaluations as well, merely for the purpose of comparison of what validities can be achieved using any data one cares to gather.

The attempt to build a linear model of information contained in the scripts was guided initially by informal and intuitive considerations. Nine variables were chosen, and their values defined. These are sumarized in Table I. The selection of variables was made a priori, guided only by considerations of general knowledge and by the casual introspection of the clinical psychologist as to what variables she felt had influenced her judgments when reading the scripts. The values were also assigned a priori, based on our intuitions only. Each script was scored on each variable separately and independently by two graduate students who worked as research assistants in this study.

RESULTS

Data Reproduction

For purposes of data reduction, we elected to reduce the set of scores given each writer to five scores. For each judge, the specific scales within each of the three areas (level of performance, interpersonal relations and job compliance) were averaged to arrive at a single score for that area.

Table I

Nine items of non-graphological information contained in the scripts,

and their a priori assigned values.

V1 - Education. University graduate.   V1= 4.
               College studies without degree.   V1= 3.
               High School graduate with matriculation. V1= 2.
               12 years of school without matriculation.V1= 0.
               Less than 12 years of school.   V1=-2.

V2 - Army rank. Officer.   V2= 5.
               Enlisted man in commanding position.   V2= 0.
               No army service, or enlisted man.   V2=-1.

V3 - Arrival in Israel.
               Prior 1967 and Israeli born.   V3= 0.
               Eetween 1967 and 1971.   V3=-1.
               Later than 1971.   V3=-2.

V4 - Marital Status.
               Married.   V4= 1.
               Single.   V4= 0.

V5 - Vocational interests.
               Theoretical, commercial.   V5= 2.
               Other or none.   V5= 0.

V6 - Overall quality of written essay.
               Very good.   V6= 3.
               Good.   V6= 1.
               Fair.   V6= 0.
               Poor.   V6=-1.
               Very poor.   V6=-2.

V7 - Aesthetic evaluation of script
               Beautiful or nice.   V7 = 1.
               Fair or poor.   V7 = 0.

V8 - Grammatical or spelling errors.
               None.   V8 = 1.
               Almost none.   V8 = 0.

V9 - Overall impression of writer.
               Good.   V9 = 2.
               Fair.   V9 = 0.
               Poor.   V9 =-1

In addition, a simple average of the three area scores was computed to arrive at a grand average. Along with the original scale of "general evaluation," this yields 5 scores per writer, three specific and two general.

Validities

Each of the five judgments (three graphologists + one clinical psychologist + the firm test battery) was correlated, with respect to each of the above five scores, with the corresponding five supervisor ratings. The Pearson coefficients are presented on the left hand side of Table II.

Where the table reports a number of cases smaller than 80, this is due to a failure on the part of the corresponding judge to rate the script. The graphologists were reluctant, for example, to judge scripts which were not written by native speakers of Hebrew. To facilitate meaningful comparisons of the correlations, these were recommended for those 58 scripts which were evaluated by all the judges, and the new correlations presented in Table II are positive, indicating some predictive ability, almost none exceed .4, and only about half are significant (at these sample sizes, significance at the .05 level occurs at about .25).

The right hand side of Table II shows that the psychodiagnostician outperformed all three graphologists on the global criteria, and compared favorably even with the firm's test battery. With respect to the specific areas, her performance was about on par with the graphologists,' better than some, worse than others.

A regression analysis for each of the five judges was conducted on the criterion of "general evaluation." The first test battery accounted for 11.2% of the criterion variance; none of the other judges contributed significantly to the percentage of explained variance. The total multiple correlation was .45 which is significantly greater than 0 (at the .05 level).

The Linear Model

To arrive at a single score for each writer on each of the nine variables, the average of the two independent assessors was taken. Their interjudge reliabilities on the extraction and rating of the nine variables were measured by computing the Pearson correlation between their ratings, and are displayed in the first column of Table III. Note that some of the variables are strictly objective (e.g., V1, V2, V3, V4), whereas others involve some subjective judgment (e.g., V6, V7, V9). Not sur-

Table II

Correlations between the predictions of five judges and supervisor ratings

Supervisor Ratings

	Based on all available information					Based on the common core, n = 58				
	general evaluation	level of job performance	job compliance	human relations	average	general evaluation	level of job performance	job compliance	human relations	average
Grapho-logist A (n=66)	0.24	0.31*	0.17	0.11	0.22	0.21	0.34*	0.18	0.07	0.21
Grapho-logist B (n=72)	0.21	0.37*	0.26*	0.11	0.27*	0.21	0.42*	0.25	0.10	0.29*
Grapho-logist C (n=64)	0.25*	0.07	0.33*	0.11	0.29*	0.21	0.05	0.39*	0.06	0.25*
Clinical psycholo-gist(n=75)	0.21	0.33*	-0.13	0.27*	0.24*	0.28*	0.34*	-0.08	0.42*	0.34*
Firm test battery (n=79)	0.33*	0.28*	0.12	0.12	0.37*	0.33*	0.32*	0.13	0.07	0.34*

* significant at the .05 level, two-tailed test.

prisingly, the reliabilities were higher for the more objective variables, and lower where subjective judgment was exercised. The correlations between the assessors' average rating and the two general criteria (the supervisors' general evaluations, and the computed average of the three area scores) are displayed, for each of the nine variables, based on a sub-sample of 52 of the original 80 scripts, for which **all** nine variables could be defined, since some texts failed to include information on some of the variables.

Table III

Interjudge reliabilities and predictive validities for nine variables

extracted from 52 scripts.

	Interjudge reliability	Predictive validity for "general evaluation"	Predictive validity for average
Education V1	0.95	0.20	0.21
Army rank V2	1.00	0.17	0.12
Arrival in Israel V3	1.00	0.17	0.12
Marital status V4	0.95	−0.11	−0.15
Vocational interests V5	0.77	−0.07	−0.03
Quality of essay V6	0.50	0.27	0.28
Aesthetics of script V7	0.53	0.24	0.28
Language errors V8	0.53	0.24	0.27
Overall Impression V9	0.20	0.22	0.25

On the whole, and in spite of their lower reliabilities, the more sub-jective variables (V6-V9) produced larger validity coefficients than the more objective biographical data (V1-V3).

We clearly failed in our a priori guess at the manner in which marital status and vocational interests (V4 and V5, respectively) should be scored. Nonetheless, in accordance with the a priori rationale, we went ahead to combine all nine variables into a single predictor, by computing a simple sum of the nine variables. This predictor, correlated .28 and .30 with the two general criteria, respectively. By eliminating V4 and V5 ad hoc, these correlations were raised to .35 and .35, respectively. To see how these validities compare with the validities of the five judges, we computed the latter on the same subsample of 52.

Table IV

Correlations between various predictors and two general criteria for

subsample of 52 writers.

	Criterion	
	supervisor's general evaluation	average supervisor rating
graphologist A	0.16	0.21
graphologist B	0.21	0.29
graphologist C	0.19	0.08
clinical psychologist	0.22	0.34
firm test battery	0.31	0.34
sum of V1-V9	0.28	0.30
sum of V1-V3 with V6-V9	0.35	0.35
bootstrap of graphologist A	0.14	0.13
bootstrap of graphologist B	0.26	0.29
bootstrap of graphologist C	0.04	0.08
bootstrap of psychologist	0.27	0.28
bootstrap of test battery	0.32	0.34

The results are presented in the top half of Table IV. Note that the subjective variables V6 — V9 predicted the two criteria better than any of the three graphologists (the exception is graphologist B's correlation with the average score, .29. Indeed, the single variable of "script aesthetics," V7, had a higher validity coefficient than any of the three graphologists and the psychodiagnostician), and the corrected formula outperformed the firm test battery as well. We did not attempt to find the optimal weights for combining the nine variables, since with a sample of 52, the results would not have been robust enough to justify the effort.

Table V

Regression weights of the nine variables with respect to "general evaluation" for five judges.

	grapho-logist A	grapho-logist B	grapho-logist C	clinical psychologist	firm test battery
V1	0.06	−0.09	0.06	0.12	0.32[*]
V2	0.12	−0.27	−0.39	0.03	0.31[*]
V3	−0.16	0.03	0.04	−0.18	0.00
V4	0.06	−0.09	0.06	0.12	−0.32[*]
V5	−0.41	−0.24	−0.17	−0.12	−0.10
V6	0.16	0.40	0.33	0.37	−0.03
V7	0.22	0.11	0.13	0.26	−0.07
V8	0.39[*]	0.22	0.00	0.28[*]	0.00
V9	−0.04	0.15	0.24	−0.08	0.24
R	0.57	0.62	0.65	0.68	0.58
R^2	0.32	0.38	0.42	0.46	0.34
adjusted R^2	0.17	0.25	0.30	0.34	0.24

Bootstrapping the Judges

The final analysis was a bootstrap of the five judges. A regression analysis was performed on the nine variables to construct the linear combination which best fits each of the five judges. The regression weights and the multiple correlations for the five analyses are presented in Table V. These weights should be taken with a pinch of salt, because of the large number of variables relative to the sample size. In any event, the negative weights indicate that the judge in question weighted the variable in question in the opposite direction that we did. For V5, this reflects our error; for V2 it reflects the graphologists' error.

For all five judges, the percentage of explained variance is rather small. The adjusted R^2, which corrects for shrinkage, giving an estimate of what value might be expected in a new sample, is, of course, even smaller. The weights of the nine variables differ for the different judges, making it difficult to generalize much from the present results. The overall quality of the written essay (V6) and the grammatical and spelling errors contained therein (V8) seem to be the only factors with any consistent influence on the judgments of the three graphologists and the psychodiagnostician.

A "best" linear combination of the nine variables was computed for each judge using the weights of Table V. These five bootstrapped scores were correlated with the two general criteria, and are displayed in the bottom half of Table IV. The bootstrapping did not consistently affect the validities. It improved the validity of graphologist B, reduced those of graphologists A and C, and hardly affected those of the firm test battery or of the psychodiagnostician.

DISCUSSION

The present study consists of two parts. The first applied standard validation methods to test the predictions made by three graphologists against certain job performance criteria, with results which largely replicate results of previous validity studies and lead to the same conclusion, namely, that when graphologists base their judgments on spontaneously produced text, such as autobiographical sketches, they can achieve positive, if low (i.e., between .2 and .3), validities against a criterion such as supervisor ratings; however when non-graphologists analyze the same texts, they achieve similar, if not higher, validities.

The second part of the study attempted to extract from the scripts items of information that are also available to non-graphologists which could account for the positive correlations that the four judges managed to achieve. The results of this section demonstrated how even a naive and clearly non-optimal first attempt to extract such information proved as successful as the professional efforts of experienced graphologists.

In light of some recent literature which recommends the use of biographical information in personnel selection (e.g., Cascio, 1978), it is of some interest that such information, at least when extracted from freehand autobiographical sketches, had validities that were inferior to the "softer" properties of the written text. As shown in Table III, nonbiographical properties of the writers, such as the quality of their writing in terms of grammar, aesthetics or articulateness, produce validity coefficients comparable to those achieved by professional graphologists. A possible reason for the advantage of "script variables" over biographical variables is that the former are more directly related to ability and intelligence than the latter. This does not account, however for the superiority of the "script aesthetics" variable, which—unlike writing quality and linguistic errors—does not seem related to ability or intelligence. Since the aesthetic features of one's handwriting are, at least to some extent, under one's voluntary control, perhaps this variable is a good predictor of supervisor satisfaction since it might reflect some willingness to please, to "do well," to match up to some standard. Further research might be needed to clarify this point.

These results imply that even in studies that use standard scripts (i.e., studies where not only biographical information is excluded, but also information about the quality of language use by the writer), it is still worthwhile to utilize a control group of non-graphologists. The aesthetic features of a handwritten script may be a graphological variable, but our results suggest that it is the kind of variable that is intuitively accessible to non-graphologists as well. The burden of proof that graphologists can extract graphological information that transcends this holistic judgment of a script's appearance rests with the graphologists. It is also important not to generalize from the validity of a script's aesthetics to predicting success on the job; personality characteristics such as honesty, leadership, sense of humor, etc., may bear no relationship to this variable.

The linear models of the judges extracted by the bootstrap technique failed, in general, to do better than the judges themselves (see Table IV). This suggests that some of our judges, especially graphologists A and C, may have relied on other items of information inferrable from the texts in addition to the ones we chose to focus on. Note, however, that overall these two judges were the least valid of all five judges, so there are no grounds to believe their choice of variables was better than our own.

Although the bootstrapping was disappointing, a simple linear combination of seven variables extracted from the scripts was the best predictor in this entire study. To be sure, this formula was not totally determined on an a priori basis, having been derived from the a priori formula by omitting the two variables, V4 and V5, that on our scoring were negatively correlated with the criteria. However, to quote Dawes & Corrigan (1974, p. 105): "the whole trick is to know what variables to look for and then to know how to add."

An additional aspect of this study relates to the validity of the test battery employed by the firm PT for personnel selection. Although this validity was higher than that achieved by the other four judges (though not than that of even the a priori linear model), the differences are small and insignificant. This is rather dismaying, considering that the test battery included a great deal of information elicited at considerable effort from aptitude, situational, and personality tests, as well as from interviews. What might account for this poor performance?

Several possibilities come to mind. First, the information gathered in the test battery was evaluated and integrated by the firm's psychologists in an intuitive manner, rather than in the formal manner that typically leads to better results (see, e.g., Dawes, 1979; Meehl, 1954; Sawyer, 1966). Second, a variable such as "success on the job" may have a natural limitation in terms of its predictability, since it clearly involves situational factors as well as the dispositional ones towards which psychological tests are geared.

It is tempting to close with some clearcut recommendation for or against the use of graphology for personnel selection. On purist or academic grounds, we would wish to recommend against such usage, since there is little if any evidence that graphology per se is a valid predictor of job success, or that it adds anything to what can be achieved by standard psychological tests. On the other hand, pragmatic considerations speak for its use, since graphologists who are allowed to work with their natural — and contaminated — material seem to do better than chance, and almost as well as a whole battery of more conventional psychological tests, at what seems to be a far lesser cost. Note, however, in a similar vein, that placebos can cure many headaches as effectively as aspirin.

We should also recall that our analysis showed that the low levels of validity achieved by graphologists are easily replicated by non-graphologists as well, and can be surpassed by extracting a few simple characteristics from the script and combining them crudely. This means that even if one were to use handwritten scripts for personnel selection, there is no particular reason to have them analyzed by professional graphologists. Indeed, one ought to be wary of "professional graphologists," since graphology is not a profession in the standard sense of the word. In most countries there are no official credited schools where it is taught, training programs which meet preset criteria, accreditation procedures, etc. The practice is not regulated by law, or bound by a code of ethics. Hence, if anything that graphologists can achieve can also be achieved by simple rules of script evaluation, we would probably all be better off formalizing the latter than relying on the former.

REFERENCES

Bem, D. J. & Allen A. (1974). On predicting some of the people some of the time: The search for cross situational consistencies in behavior. *Psychological Review, 81,* 506-520.

Cascio, W. F. (1978). *Applied Psychology in Personnel Management,* Englewood Cliffs: Prentice Hall.

Crumbaugh, J. C. & Stockholm, E. (1977). Validation of graphoanalysis by "global" or "Holistic" method. *Perceptual and Motor Skills, 44,* 403-410.

Dawes, R. M. (1979). The robust beauty of improper linear models in decision making. *American Psychologist, 34,* 571-582.

Dawes, R. M. & Corrigan, B. (1974). Linear models in decision making. *Psychological Bulletin, 81,* 95-106.

Frederick, C. J. (1965). Some phenomena affecting handwriting analysis. *Perceptual and Motor Skills, 20,* 211-218.

Frederick, C. J. (1968). An investigation of handwriting and suicide persons through suicide notes. *Journal of Abnormal Psychology, 73,* 263-267.

Jansen, A. (1973). *Validation of graphoanalysis judgements: An Experimental Study.* The Hague: Mouton.

Levy, L. (1979). Handwriting and hiring. *Dun's Review, 113,* 72-79.

Meehl, P. E. (1954). *Clinical versus statistical prediction: A theoretical analysis and a review of the literature.* Minnesota: University of Minnesota Press.

Rafaeli, A. & Klimoski, R. J. (1983). Predicting sales success through handwriting analysis: An evaluation of the effects of training and handwriting sample context. *Journal of Applied Psychology, 68,* 212-217.

Sawyer, J. (1966). Measurement and prediction, clinical and statistical. *Psychological Bulletin, 66,* 178-200.

Sonneman, U. & Kernan, J. P. (1962). Handwriting analysis—A valid selection tool? *Personnel, 39,* 8-14.

Vestewig, R. E., Santee, A. M. & Moss, M. K. (1976). Validity and student acceptance of a graphoanalytic approach to personality. *Journal of Personality Assessment, 40,* 592-598.

Zdep, S. M. & Weaver, H. B. (1967). The graphoanalytic approach to selecting life insurance salesmen. *Journal of Applied Psychology, 51,* 295-299.

NOTES

We wish to thank Hagit Benziman for giving us her valuable time and the benefit of her expertise as a psychodiagnostician. Thanks are also due to Micha Weiss and Vered Kozachok who assisted in the data gathering stages of the study. Micha also assisted in the data analysis.

12

GRAPHOANALYSIS FOR MILITARY PERSONNEL SELECTION

GIORA KEINAN

Summary

THIS CHAPTER describes two studies designed to assess the usefulness of graphoanalysis for the selection of military personnel. In the first study 6 graphoanalysts, 6 psychologists and 6 lay persons examined the handwritten biographies of 65 candidates for the Israel Defense Force Officer School. Twelve scales were used by the 18 raters to describe the candidates' personalities and to predict their success in the officers' course. The second study differed from the first in that the likelihood of the candidates' success in the course was rated on the basis of biographical scripts and neutral scripts. Success ratings were made by 3 graphologists, 3 psychologists and 3 lay persons who examined 214 scripts. In both studies, reliability coefficients among the graphologists were significant though moderate in size. Their validity coefficients were significant yet low, particularly when graphological evaluation was carried out on neutral scripts ($r = .12$). No reliable difference was found between the success predictions made by graphologists and by psychologists on the basis of either biographical or neutral scripts. These findings suggest that the employment of graphoanalysis as the sole basis for military personnel selection is premature.

Introduction

Graphology is frequently applied, nowadays, to decisions concerning personnel selection and placement. In Europe, 85% of the companies are estimated to use it (Levy, 1979; Sharman & Vardling, 1975). In the United States, despite some opposition to graphological analysis, more than 3000 firms routinely employ graphologists in the process of personnel selection and screening.

Graphology offers several advantages as a screening device. The evaluation process is fast and inexpensive, in comparison with evaluations based on batteries of psychological tests. It minimizes the imposition on the applicant and does not require his/her involvement. In fact, the applicant is often unaware of the evaluation. Lastly, the risk of faking is significantly reduced.

Research on the effectiveness of graphology in the process of personnel selection dates back to the early sixties. Its reliability and validity were evaluated with respect to a variety of occupations (see, for example Sonneman & Kernan, 1962; Zdep & Weaver, 1967; Jansen, 1973; Flug, 1981; Rafaeli & Klimoski, 1983). Interestingly, there is little published evidence to suggest that the military, which often leads in the development and application of selection procedures, has evaluated the usefulness of graphology.

The present chapter is addressed to the reliability and validity of graphoanalysis for the selection of military personnel. One of the earliest studies in this field (Gaussin, 1963) tested the validity of graphology in predicting the success of flight cadets in the French army. The author's conclusion — that an individual's success as a pilot can be predicted on the basis of graphoanalysis — was supported neither by quantitative data nor by statistical analyses. The two studies described below are therefore unique in their rigorous application of sound methodology to the evaluation of graphoanalysis as a predictor of military performances.

STUDY 1

A study, designed to assess the reliability and validity of graphoanalysis as a predictor of success in the officers' training course of the Israel Defense Forces (IDF), was conducted by Keinan, Barak, & Ramati (1984). Sixty-five cadets were selected at random from the list of course participants. Sampling was carried out after the completion of the course. Thus, each subject's performance in the course was known. Moreover, the random selection assured that the various degrees of success and failure in the course were proportionally represented in the sample.

Handwriting specimens consisted of brief autobiographies which the cadets had written in the process of being screened several months before the commencement of the course, since the graphologists who took part in the study claimed that valid handwriting analysis requires that the writer be involved in the written subject matter.

The 65 specimens were analyzed by three groups: 6 practicing graphologists, 6 psychologists who were employed by the IDF's officers' selection unit and who were unfamiliar with graphoanalysis, and 6 lay persons with no training either in graphology or in psychology. The second and third groups served as controls. Analyses by psychologists were deemed necessary in order to account for the possibility that the graphologists would rely more heavily on the content of the cadets' personal histories than on their handwriting. The lay group provided a comparative basis for the evaluation of both graphologists' and psychologists' predictive ability.

In contrast to other studies, a special effort was made to familiarize the raters thoroughly with the criterion. Course instructors and psychologists provided the graphologists with substantial information on the course contents, cadet evaluation procedures, typical causes of drop-out and characteristics of successful cadets. In addition, the graphologists were given 50 handwriting specimens; half written by cadets who had successfully graduated from the course and the other half by cadets who had failed it. The lay group was exposed to the same information about the officers' course and the evaluation system as the graphologists. All members of the lay group had completed full military service and some were officers. They were thus familiar with an officer's role in the IDF. Lastly the 6 psychologists, by nature of their occupation in the officers' selection unit, were thoroughly familar with the course.

Each of the 65 handwriting specimens was analyzed by each of the 18 raters, on 12 scales. These were developed, in consultation with the graphologists, to allow the rating of characteristics such as intelligence, sociability, and mental maturity. In addition, each rater was asked to indicate on a general evaluation scale, the cadet's likelihood of success in the course.

The criterion to which the raters' assessments were compared was the cadets' actual success or failure in the course. An 8-point success-failure scale was defined.

Reliability coefficients for the 13 scales ranged from .21 to .37 among the graphologists, .17 to .36 for the psychologists, and .09 to .20 for the lay group. For the general evaluation scale, the graphologists' reliability coefficient was practically identical to that of the psychologists (.37 and .36, respectively), but higher than the lay persons' (.16). It was also found that the extent of agreement between graphologists and psychologists was lower than the agreement within each of the two groups. By contrast, the agreement among the lay persons was lower than their agreement with either the graphologists or the psychologists.

Regarding predictive validity, the median coefficients obtained in the graphologists' group ranged from .11 to .26, in the psychologists' group from .07 to .23, and in the lay group from − .5 to .17. The median validities of the general evaluation scale were .26, .20 and .11, for the graphologists, psychologists, and lay persons, respectively. Among these, only the difference between the validity of the graphologists' and lay persons' ratings turned out to be significant. A consideration of the correlations between the general evaluation scale and success in the course, computed for individual raters, revealed that 4 were significant among the graphologists; 3 among the psychologists; and none among the lay persons.

STUDY 2

A continuation and extension of the Keinan et al. (1984) study was recently completed by Borenstein (1985), who attempted to address an argument which has been raised by some authors (e.g., Frederick, 1965). Graphologists, so it is argued, predicate their personality diagnoses on the content of handwritten autobiographies rather than on morphological cues of the handwriting. Accordingly, Borenstein's raters were asked to analyze brief, handwritten autobiographies as well as handwriting specimens which contained no information about the writers. It was assumed that this procedure would provide grounds for the assessment of the productive validity of "pure graphoanalysis."

Handwriting specimens were taken from a sample of 214 cadets in the IDF officers' course. During the screening process of the course each candidate was asked to write a brief autobiography. In addition, each was asked to copy a passage describing a battle, answer several questions about that battle, and sign the written pages.[1] The handwriting specimens were given to three practicing graphologists (two of whom had participated in the first study), three psychologists from the staff of the officers' selection unit who were unfamiliar with graphoanalysis, and three lay persons who had no training in either graphology or psychology. The raters were familiarized with the officers' course in the same way as their counterparts in the previous study.

Each rater analyzed, first, handwriting specimens of one kind (either autobiographical or neutral) and then the other. Ratings were given in a dichotomous "passed/failed" fashion as well as on a 9-point scale which expressed likelihood of success in the course. The criterion for the validity of the ratings was the cadets' final grades. Those who had failed the course were assigned the score of 50 as a final grade.

Reliability coefficients among the graphologists ranged from .13 to .39 for autobiographical scripts and from .33 to .58 for neutral scripts. Among psychologists, reliability ranged from .43 to .60 and from .43 to .48 for autobiographical and neutral scripts respectively. In the lay group, the range of reliability coefficients was from .31 to .49 for the autobiographies and from .16 to .28 for the neutral scripts. All reliability coefficients were statistically significant as were intergroup reliability coefficients. Biographical scripts yielded a correlation of .65 between psychologists and lay person, .55 between psychologists and graphologists, and .49 between graphologists and lay persons. In the case of neutral scripts, the correlations were somewhat lower: .49 between psychologists and graphologists, .35 between psychologists and lay persons, and .28 between graphologists and lay persons.

The analyses of biographical specimens yielded significant but low predictive validity coefficients: .20 in the lay group, .16 in the psychologists' group, and .14 in the graphologists' group. In the case of neutral specimens, the validity coefficients were very low, although in the graphologists' group the coefficient was significant ($r = .12$, $p < .05$). For the remaining two groups, the validity coefficients were non-significant (.11 for the psychologists and .02 for lay persons). Of the 9 raters, only one graphologist and one psychologist achieved significant validity coefficients (.15 and .12 respectively). The differences among the validity coefficients obtained in the three groups, in the case of both biographical and neutral scripts, were non-significant.

DISCUSSION

Inter-Rater Reliability

In both studies, reliability coefficients among graphologists, although statistically significant, were only low to moderate. Similar reliability levels were found in previous studies which had adopted a holistic approach to handwriting analysis (Cantril & Rand, 1934; Crider, 1941; McNeil & Blum, 1952; Birge, 1954; Rafaeli & Klimoski, 1983). This is not to suggest that graphology is unreliable. Nevertheless it is clear that low reliabilities set a low level to the potential validity of graphoanalysis.

Borenstein's study (1985) revealed that intercorrelations among graphologists' ratings were higher when neutral scripts were analyzed than when autobiographical scripts were analyzed. The opposite pattern was found in the case of psychologists and lay persons. It appears that individuals' life histories help psychologists and lay persons achieve a higher degree of agreement than morphological handwriting signs. Graphologists, on the other hand, achieve greater uniformity of judgement on the basis of morphological signs.

Predictive Validity

The two studies point to the conclusion that the predictive validity of graphoanalysis is low or even extremely low. This conclusion is consistent with the results of previous studies (e.g., Jansen, 1973; Rafaeli & Klimoski, 1983).

The results of the two studies fail to offer unambiguous support to the contention that graphologists rely more heavily on the content of handwriting specimens than on the shape of handwriting. Some support for this contention derives from the finding that in both studies, graphologists' analysis of autobiographical specimens did not significantly differ in validity from the psychologists' analysis. Yet in Borenstein's study, the graphologists' analyses of biographical and neutral specimens yielded validity coefficients which did not significantly differ from each other. It appears then, that additional research is needed in order to clarify this ambiguity.

Individual Differences in Predictive Ability

The results of the two studies reveal significant differences among individual graphologists' predictive ability. This is understandable in view of the fact that in graphoanalysis, a person is the measurement instrument. Thus, different graphologists might achieve different levels of predictive ability due to differences in personal attributes or training. It may be added, that similar degrees of variability were found in studies that evaluated the diagnostic ability of clinical and occupational psychologists (cf. Wiggins, 1973).

The considerable variability in graphologists' predictive ability gives rise to an important question: to what extent are graphologists who achieve high predictive validity capable of training their less proficient colleagues? Empirical research is obviously needed in order to answer this question. It stands to reason, however, that graphologists who employ a holistic approach to handwriting analysis would be less successful in passing on their expertise than those who rely on an atomistic method.

Differences Between the Results of the Two Studies

Validity coefficients obtained in the analysis of biographical scripts, were somewhat higher in the first than in the second study. Two explanations for this difference may be offered:

(a) Two different groups of graphologists participated in the two studies. Only two of the graphologists who had taken part in the first study participated in the second. Moreover, one graphologist, who had shown a particularly high predictive ability in the first study, did not take part in the second.

(b) The course from which the study 1. cadets were sampled was twice as long as the course from which the study 2. sample was taken. Hence, instructors in the former course may have had a better opportunity to become acquainted with the cadets. Criterion scores, in other words, might have been more valid in the first study than in the second study.

In the absence of additional supporting data it is clearly impossible to ascertain which of two possible explanations accounts for the difference between the two studies. It might be that both have to be taken into consideration.

Were the Graphologists Given a Fair Chance to Prove Themselves?

The graphologists who participated in the two studies were given a fair opportunity to prove their ability. In contrast to previous studies, which examined the usefulness of graphology for personnel selection, a special effort was made in the two studies described herein to allow the graphologists' familiarization with the criterion. Moreover, the graphologists were given an opportunity to examine the handwriting of successful and unsuccessful cadets, in order to identify the unique writing patterns of each of the two groups.

Previous studies (e.g., Jansen, 1973; Flug, 1981) have tested the predictive power of graphoanalysis against criteria of unproven validity or criteria which consisted of psychological evaluations. By contrast, the studies described above employed a tested, unambiguous criterion, which does not derive from psychologists' evaluations. Data collected by the army over many years attest to the relatively high reliability and validity of this criterion. In addition, the rating scales employed in the first study were designed in consultation with the graphologists.

The opportunity to achieve high levels of predictive validity notwithstanding, the graphologists' ability, as revealed in the two studies, leaves a lot to be desired. One redeeming circumstance should nevertheless be mentioned. This is the fact that the criterion range did not include applicants to the course who were rejected in the screening stage. Such a restriction of range may have somewhat lowered the validity coefficients.

The Applicability of Graphoanalysis to Military Personnel Selection

The results of the two studies cast doubt on the usefulness of graphoanalysis for military selection. This conclusion is underscored by the poor validity coefficients which were obtained by "pure" graphoanalysis; that is, the analysis of neutral as opposed to autobiographical handwriting specimens.

To sum up, present results, along with those obtained in previous systematic and controlled studies carried out in civilian contexts (Jansen, 1973; Rafaeli & Klimoski, 1983), appear to suggest that the widespread use of graphology as the sole device for personnel selection is premature.

REFERENCES

Birge, W. R. (1954). An experimental enquiry into the measurable handwriting correlates of five personality traits. *Journal of Personality, 23,* 215-223.

Borenstein, Y. (1985). *The utility of graphological assessment as a tool in selection process in the Israeli Defense Forces.* M.A. Thesis, University of Haifa, Israel.

Cantril, H. & Rand, H. A. (1934). An additional study of the determination of personal interests by psychological and graphological methods. *Character and Personality, 3,* 72-78.

Crider, B. (1941). The reliability and validity of two graphologists. *Journal of Applied Psychology, 25,* 323-325.

Flug, A. (1981). *Reliability and Validity of Graphological Evaluations in Personnel Selection.* M.A. Thesis, Hebrew University, Jerusalem, Israel.

Frederick, C. J. (1965). Some phenomena affecting handwriting analysis, *Perceptual and Motor Skills, 20,* 211-218.

Gaussin, B. (1963). Une nouveaute: La graphologie au service de l'armee. *La Graphologie, 90,* 5-14.

Jansen, A. (1973). *Validation of Graphological Judgments.* Paris: Mouton.

Keinan, G., Barak, A. & Ramati, T. (1984). Reliability and validity of graphological assessment in the selection process of military officers. *Perceptual and Motor Skills, 58,* 811-821.

Levy, L. (1979). Handwriting and hiring. *Dun's Review,* March, 72-79.

McNeil, E. B., & Blum, G. S. (1952). Handwriting and psychosexual dimensions of personality. *Journal of Projective Techniques, 16,* 476-484.

Rafaeli, A. & Klimoski, R. (1983). Predicting sales success through handwriting analysis: An evaluation of the effects of training and handwriting sample content. *Journal of Applied Psychology, 68,* 212-217

Roman, K. G. (1952). *Handwriting: A key to personality.* New York: Pantheon.

Sharman, J. M. & Vardling, H. (1975). Graphology — what handwriting can tell you about an applicant. *Personnel, 52,* 57-63.

Sonneman, U. & Kernan, J. P. (1962). Handwriting analysis — A valid selection tool? *Personnel, 39,* 8-14.

Wiggins, J. S. (1973). *Personality and Prediction: Principles of Personality Assessment.* Massachusetts: Addison — Wesley.

Zdep, S. M. & Weaver, H. B. (1967). The graphoanalytic approach to selecting life insurance salesman. *Journal of Applied Psychology, 51,* 295-299.

NOTES

1. The choice of a battle description was designed to elicit emotional involvement. Graphologists, as mentioned, maintain that without such involvement, a handwriting specimen does not constitute a "soul's mirror" (Roman, 1952).

13

BASIC RHYTHMS AND CRIMINAL DISPOSITION IN HANDWRITING, by H. HÖNEL: CRITICAL REVIEW AND REANALYSIS

BARUCH NEVO

Summary

IN 1977, Dr. H. Hönel reported on a study which sought an empirical relationship between graphological assessments and the external criterion of criminality. In two consecutive experiments, an impressive list of correlations between predictors and criterion was reported.

In this article, an attempt is made to:

a. Provide a short description of Hönel's study.
b. Point out the weak spots in methodology and statistical analysis of the study.
c. Re-analyse some of the data.

The results of the re-analysis show that when irrelevant variables are controlled and statistical techniques improved, the correlations—as reported in the original paper—between graphological ratings and actual criminality, decrease. On the other hand, Hönel's data gives some support to the idea that handwriting does contain interesting clues as to the writer's personality.

Introduction

In 1977, Dr. Herbert Hönel, the editor of "Zeitschrift für Menschenkunde" published in that journal a paper called: "Grundrythmus und Kriminelle Disposition in der Handschrift," reporting on a study which sought an empirical relationship between graphological assessments and the external criterion of criminality. The importance of the Hönel study cannot be overstated. First, it focuses on the one trait which is considered by the business world as the "Forte" of graphology. Unlike personnel psychologists who are modest about their ability to evaluate peoples' criminal tendencies, graphologists provide that kind of service with much less reservation. Second, this particular research project is of a high standard: the sample size is satisfactory, cross validation is exercised and the criminality criterion is objective.

Unfortunately, the article was ignored by English-speaking scientists, mainly because it was never translated. In this chapter, I would like to bring that study to those who were unable to acquaint themselves with it and also to add some input of my own. The chapter will be divided into three sections, in which I will attempt to:

a. provide a short description of Hönel's study;
b. point to the weak spots in the methodology and statistical analysis of the study;
c. re-analyze some of the data and discuss the new findings.

A. SHORT DESCRIPTION OF HÖNEL'S STUDY

Hönel's 1977 project consisted of two not dissimilar studies or experiments, in which the second improved on the first.

Experiment I

Subjects

Experimental Group: 41 male prison inmates including larcenists, embezzlers, sex offenders and murderers.

Control Group: 48 men who were reported to be honest, loyal, responsible, and without criminal record. They had all been employed at the same enterprise for at least five years, and the judges of their non-criminality were the personnel directors of their places of employment.

Different levels of education and various types of professions were represented in both samples. No special effort however, was made to match the samples on socio-economic, educational, or professional variables (see an elaboration on this point in section C).

Handwriting Materials

Scripts were taken from the subjects' files, either from the prison archives or from the enterprise archives. All samples were spontaneous, natural writings, several months or several years old, written by the subjects with ink or ballpoint pen, on normal size paper, and signed by the writer. An attempt was made to exclude handwritings which could provide any external clue as to the affiliation of the writer.

Raters

Four graphologists (A, B, C, D) and one psychologist (P) participated, without pay.

Graphological Evaluation of the Handwritings

The raters were asked to assess each of the 89 scripts twice. First, they rated the samples on a unidimensional five-point "basic rhythm" ("grundrhythmus") scale, developed by the graphologist, Rhoda Wieser. Psycho-diagnostically, the "basic rhythm" of the handwriting reflects "general qualities of the writer's personality," his "personality depth," "genuineness of life," and "sociability." ("Basic rhythm" seems to be to personality what "g" is to intelligence.) After an interval of several months during which the raters had no access to the writing samples, they were asked to classify the scripts into three categories according to the perceived criminal disposition of the writer: criminal, intermediate, non-criminal. Raters were allowed to omit any handwriting which they felt completely unable to classify. The ratings were performed independently — both intra-rater and inter-rater.

Supervision

The project was carried out by Dr. Hönel and supervised by the Psychological Institute of the Vienna University. The Institute personnel approved the methodology, constructed and operated safeguards to prevent various artifacts which could affect the results, and provided advice on the statistical analysis of the results. According to Dr. Hönel, the basic attitude of the Institute was skeptical, and he felt as if in a "lion's cage."

Findings

Technical reasons preclude reproduction of Hönel's tables and the reader is referred to the original article. Hönel's Tabelle I (p.23) details the raw data of Equipment I. In the table, Hönel detailed the ratings of the "basic rhythm," (1, . . ., 5), and the "criminality disposition" ("+" for criminal classification; "−" for non-criminal; "∿" for cases in which the graphologist was not certain), as rated by each graphologist and by the psychologist.

Statistical Analysis

Three validity measures of the basic rhythm and the criminality disposition were calculated for each rating: contingency coefficient, Spearman rank-order correlation and percentage of "hits" ("∿" was taken as "+"). The third measure was calculated for "criminality disposition" only. Table I details the three indices as reported by Hönel (p.34).

TABLE I: Validity Measures (Experiment I)

(Spontaneous Handwriting)

Rater	A	B	C	D	P
N	89	89	89	89	89
Contingency Coefficient	.84	.35	.31	.68	-
Rank-order Correlation	.67	.22	.07	.48	-
Contingency Coefficient	.91	-	-	.77	.27
Rank-order Correlation	.81	-	-	.64	.27
Percentage of "Hits"	91	-	-	76	63

Experiment II

The second experiment was carried out in order to correct a major methodological weakness detected in Experiment I—the fact that the scripts were spontaneous and personal and could therefore have led the graphologists to correct ratings based on the **content** of the scripts rather than on their graphic characteristics. The design of the second experiment is very similar to the first with the exception that the handwriting content samples collected were standardized.

Subjects

113 male and female volunteers, 53 criminals and 60 non-criminals. 18 and 26 members of each group respectively were women. The definitions of criminality and non-criminality were similar to those in Experiment I.

Handwriting Materials

Subjects were asked to write down a standard dictated paragraph of about 120 words, with neutral content. A standard white sheet of paper was provided by the experimenter.

Raters

Five graphologists (one of whom participated in Experiment I) and a psychologist performed the ratings.

Graphological Evaluation of the Handwritings

As in Experiment I, raters were asked to score each handwriting sample as to its "basic rhythm" (1 to 5) and as to the perceived "criminal disposition" ($+$, $\sim$, $-$).

Supervision

As in Experiment I, supervision was provided by the University of Vienna.

Findings

The results of Experiment II are presented in Hönel's Tabelle II (p.32). Numbers and symbols here used there should be interpreted as in Tabelle I. For unknown reasons, Hönel did not provide any values for the contingency coefficient and the rank-order correlations for the psychologist's ratings, other than the fact that they were not significant. The conclusions drawn in this chapter are based by and large on the aforementioned Tabelle II, except that superfluous information provided by Hönel regarding the severity of crimes was not taken into account.

Statistical Analysis

The same three indices of validity used in Experiment I were applied here. Results are summarized and presented in Table II.

TABLE II: Validity Measures (Experiment II)

(Standard Handwriting)

	Rater	A	E	F	G	H	P
Basic Rhythm	N	111	113	112	113 (112)	113 (105)	113
	Contingency Coeficient	.60	.50	.73	.24	.47	-
	Rank-order Correlation	.43	.35	.48	.09	.30	-
Criminality Disposition	Contingency Coefficient	.57	.38	.71	.13	.45	NS
	Rank-order Correlation	-	.28	.54	.10	.32	NS
	Percentage of "Hits"	71	63	78	53	67	55

Reliability Measures

Normally, a researcher would study the reliability of the predictors **before** embarking on an investigation of the relations between predictors and criteria. This tactic stems from a well-known psychometric fact — the square root of the reliability coefficient creates an upper limit for the validity. In other words, if reliability is low, validity cannot be very high. There is then no point in continuing the research until an improvement of the predictors' measurement is reached (i.e., by means of extra training for the raters). Thus, Dr. Hönel took a great risk by postponing the reliability analysis to the last stage of his research.

The two major types of reliability were studied: inter-rater reliability and test-retest reliability.

Inter-Rater Reliability

Calculations of the inter-rater reliability were based on the data (ratings) collected in Experiment II (standard text). Intercorrelations between pairs of raters were calculated separately for the basic rhythm and the criminal disposition ratings. Five graphologists were involved in Part II and the rank-order correlations among them are presented in Table III. In each cell the higher figure represents the inter-rater correlation of the basic rhythm and the lower figure relates to criminality disposition.

TABLE III: <u>Rank-Order Inter-Correlation Among Five Graphologists</u>

	H	G	F	E
A	.57	.41	.66	.82
	.42	.37	.59	.41
E	.37	.44	.52	
	.40	.47	.34	
F	.42	.29		
	.42	.21		
G	.28			
	.31			

The general level of inter-rater reliability is low and in retrospect, it is regrettable that greater efforts were not made to study and improve inter-rater agreement. One may assume that the **validities** of Graphologists G and F, for instance, may have been improved with proper rater training.

Test-Retest Reliability

Graphologist A rated the same sample scripts twice (N = 111) at an interval of 10 months. His rank-order correlations for basic rhythm and criminal disposition were .82 and .81 correspondingly. These figures are based on one rater only and therefore should not be relied upon. However, if they are representative in any way, then the poor inter-rater agreement cannot be related to the instability of each individual graphologist, but rather to disagreements among them. This strengthens the argument that extra training for the raters would have helped.

B. CRITICAL COMMENTS

Statistical Indices of Association Between Predictors and Criterion

Hönel makes thorough use of the contingency coefficient, whose figures are most impressive. The problem with this coefficient is that it measures strength of association between two variables regardless of the direction of that relation. The contingency coefficient would be sufficient if, for example, the researcher, wishes to know whether there is any connection at all between basic rhythm rating and criminality. But if there is a specific hypothesis regarding the character of this connection (e.g., the higher the basic rhythm rating, the greater is the possibility of being a criminal), then the contingency coefficient would become an inflated, biased statistic. This is the case in this study. The directionality is essential and cannot be ignored.

The second index of association which was employed by Hönel was the rank-order correlation (Spearman correlation). When choosing the appropriate correlational technique, the researcher must base his choice on the properties of the distributions of the two variables. The qualities of the distributions for the **three** variables involved (criminality, criminal disposition, and basic rhythm) are certainly not typical of situations calling for rank-order correlation: all three of them, and especially the first two, consist of huge clusters of **ties**. In such a situation, the application of rank-order correlation is not highly recommended (Hays, 1973) although not illegitimate. This author believes that when dealing with the relation between factual criminality and criminal predisposition, as measured in the Hönel study, phi (ϕ) correlation should be employed. This coefficient was designed to measure the relationship between two dichotomous variables, certainly the case here. Each of the subjects in the study was either a criminal or a non-criminal. The gap between the two groups was **intentionally** made as wide as possible. The task of the raters was originally **defined** for them in a trichotomous fashion ($+$, $-$, $\sim$), but the intermediate category was employed very rarely (except in the case of graphologist G) so it could be cancelled, the few cases belonging in this category being deleted from the analysis or being added to the ($+$) category. Its cancellation also sharpens the picture. The original 3 x 2 categorization would thus be reduced to a 2 x 2 table and a phi (ϕ) correlation could be employed. (Guilford, 1973, p. 306-310.)

When dealing with the relation between factual criminality and the basic rhythm rating, we have a case of two variables, one of which is a true dichotomous variable, while the other (basic rhythm) is continuous in its nature. The index which is generally recommended for that situation is the Rp.bi — Point-biserial correlation (Guilford, 1973, p. 297-300). In the following section these two coefficients — ϕ and Rp.bi — will be employed in the re-analysis.

Methodological Problems

Spontaneous vs. Standard Writing

In Experiment II, which was designed solely for the purpose of neutralizing script content, scripts were collected via dictation and the content was standard. It is possible that in changing from spontaneous to standard handwriting some of the projective value of the writing was lost. However, the graphologists who participated in Experiment II agreed to this condition, believing that they could effectively rate standard scripts. We too, shall focus on standard writing, and re-analysis will be performed only on Experiment II data.

Sampling Biases

In order to prove that experts can differentiate between handwritings of criminals and non-criminals, an attempt must be made to control for irrelevant variables so that no external cues will be given to the experts. Extending the study to include standard handwritings (Experiment II) was, in fact, a control of this type. But what about the educational and socio-economic status of the subjects? For the sake of argument, let us assume that all criminals are people whose level of education is very low (e.g., 3-4 years of primary school), and all the non-criminals are university graduates. Would this situation not help the graphologists to identify the criminals? We have no way of knowing whether or not the graphologists in Hönel's study utilized external cues (e.g., spelling errors). However, it is the researcher's duty to minimize such possibilities.

The involvement of female writers in Experiment II creates another sampling problem and that is the representation of the sexes. Fortunately, Dr. Hönel provided details regarding the sex, age and profession of each Experiment II subject. An inspection of this information reveals that the sample is unbalanced from at least two aspects:

a) Women are slightly over-represented in the non-criminal subsample;
b) The proportion of people from white collar and technological professions is much higher among the non-criminals.

To correct these biases, a new sample was created by an independent research assistant, in which the criminal and non-criminal subsamples were matched for sex, age group, and profession. Naturally, the new sample is smaller than the original (44 subjects vs. 113 subjects) but the statistical analyses are much more meaningful and "clean." No parallel data regarding Experiment I subjects' professions was provided by Hönel, a fact that strengthens our decision to omit Experiment I data from our analysis.

C. RE-ANALYSIS OF THE DATA AND CONCLUSIONS

Following the line of thought presented above, we have limited our re-analysis to criminal disposition ratings and to basic rhythm ratings of graphologists A, E, F, G, and H in Experiment II.

First, for each graphologist, a 2 x 2 table was prepared with the graphologist's rating (criminal vs. non-criminal disposition) and the actual criminality (criminal vs. non-criminal disposition) as the two dimensions. This procedure was repeated twice;

a) with the indecisive ratings ($\backsim$) considered as ($+$) (as was suggested by Hönel himself);

b) with the indecisive ratings ($\backsim$) deleted — together with their matches — from the calculations. Table IV details the resulting validity co-efficients.

TABLE IV: Validity Co-efficients (ϕ Correlations)

for Four[*] Graphologists

Graphologist	A	E	F	H
a) ($\backsim$) ratings considered as ($+$).	.19 (44)	.14 (44)	.32 (44)	.23 (44)
b) ($\backsim$) ratings deleted.	.11 (38)	.29 (28)	.25 (40)	.23 (36)

[*] Graphologist G was excluded because 38 of his 44 ratings were indecisive ($\backsim$).

Most of the correlations, except F(a), are not significantly higher than chance level.

Second, the number of "hits" for each graphologist was counted — a "hit" being defined as a correspondence between the graphologist's rating and reality. This was done twice:

a) with the indecisive ratings ($\backsim$) considered as (+);
b) with the indecisive ratings ($\backsim$) deleted. Again, Graphologist G was not included.

TABLE V: Percentage of Hits for Four

Graphologists (Chance Level = 50%)

Graphologist	A	E	F	H
a)	59.1%	56.8%	65.9%	61.4
	(44)	(44)	(44)	(44)
b)	55.3%	64.3%	62.5%	61.1%
	(38)	(28)	(40)	(36)

Table V is based on the same data employed in Table IV. The only difference lies in the way the results are presented (percentages rather than correlations).

Third, the point-biserial correlation was calculated for each graphologist, between the basic rhythm ratings and actual criminality. The results are shown in Table VI.

TABLE VI: Validity Coefficient for the

Basic Rhythm Ratings (NS 44)

Graphologist	Point-Biserial Correlations
A	.15
E	.25
F	.20
G	-.04
H	.10

Finally, an attempt was made to combine the input of the criminal disposition ratings of the four graphologists A, E, F, and H into one index, and to check the validity of this index. The assumption made here is that the "joint effort" or "common wisdom" of all raters together is stronger than that of each individual rater, because their individual mistakes cancel each other out. As an index, the total sum of the criminal disposition ratings was employed, where (+) was weighted 1 and ($\sim$) was weighted 0.5. If the total sum was 1.5 or higher, the writer was classified as a "predicted criminal." If the total sum was 1.0 or less, the writer was classified as a "predicted non-criminal." The ϕ correlation between the combined index and actual criminality was .33 ($N = 44$) and the significance level is $p < .05$. Similar attempts with regard to the basic rhythm ratings failed.

Conclusion

The results of our re-analysis show that the validity of graphological ratings is lower than Hönel's article implies. When irrelevant variables were controlled and statistical techniques improved, the correlations between predictors and criterion decreased dramatically. Only a combined index, based on four graphologists together, discriminated in a statistically significant way between criminals and non-criminals. One may perhaps conclude by saying that there is **some** information in a person's handwriting regarding their criminal tendencies (or lack of them), but the accuracy of criminality predisposition ratings is much lower than the claims put forward by some practitioners who try hard to market their skills as know-all graphologists.

Another issue which deserves some attention is the fact that handwriting apparently reflects the socio-economic status of the writer. In our re-analysis, this variable (socio-economic status) was treated as an "irrelevant" factor which should be "partialled out." But in a different context, one might adopt a different view and make the relationship between handwriting and socio-economic status the **focus** of one's research. In fact, Dr. Hönel proved the great value of Rhoda Wieser's basic rhythm — and he should be praised for that — by showing that this variable is indeed related to that factor to which it is related in theory. This relationship is by no means a trivial one, and certainly deserves further study.

REFERENCES

Guilford, J. P. & Fruchter, B. (1973). *Fundamental Statistics in Psychology and Education* (5th ed.), New York: McGraw-Hill.

Hays, L. W. (1973). *Statistics for Social Sciences* (2nd ed.), New York: Holt, Rinehart & Winston.

Hönel, W. (1977). "Grundrhythmus und Kriminelle disposition in der Handschrift." *Zeitschrift für Menschenkunde, 41*, 1-55.

14

INTELLECTUAL ABILITIES AND HANDWRITING

LOTHAR MICHEL

Summary

THIS CHAPTER summarizes a body of research on the questions of reliability and validity of graphological assessment with regard to intelligence. The author differentiates between the investigation of particular (graphometric) signs and the study of their interpretation, both in relation to intelligence measures. Specific signs, especially those which are based on form structure, show a positive, if weak, association with the writer's intellectual level. Employing graphological analysis and interpretation, a rough classification of the intelligence level is possible. It will be emphasized that the qualitative aspects of graphological diagnosis of talent (beyond mere intellectual capacity) have not yet been fully researched.

Introduction

Over the last eight years, approximately thirty studies have been published on the possible use of handwriting analysis in the diagnosis of intelligence. Looking at them en masse, it is not easy to arrive at a general conclusion. The reasons are various. New studies inevitably refer to earlier concepts, which often fail to conform to the demands of modern planning. The method, extent and type of writing required by the researchers vary considerably. Furthermore, various external criteria are employed, and a common definition of "intelligence" has not been agreed on.

Several studies were carried out on the **sign level.** These investigated the relations between graphical signs (or sign syndromes) and intellectual abilities. Other studies dealt with **interpretation:** graphological diagnoses of intelligence were checked to see whether they agree with each other and with the external criteria.

1. RESEARCHES ON THE LEVEL OF SIGNS

Gesell (1906) was probably the first to study the relationship between graphical signs and intellectual abilities. Taking public school pupils as his subject (N = 1,260), he noted a correlation (perceived by a layman) between "accuracy" of the handwriting and school performance on the one hand, and independently estimated "general intelligence" on the other hand.

Oinonen (1961), quoted by Wallner (1965), reports comparable results with pupils in the first two grades at public school, aged 7-9 (N = 122). He ascertained a correlation of .38 between intelligence as measured by a test of school readiness and quality of handwriting. However, both Gesell and Oinonen carried out a comparison of extreme contrast groups. Lockowandt (1980), whose sample covered a more complete range of intelligence of second to fourth grade public school pupils, found no indication "that the judgement of children's handwriting by the teacher has any significance" (p.429). Furthermore, there is some question as to the validity for adult handwriting of the correlations found by Gesell and Oinonen. In a study of 130 students, Omwake (1925) could find no association between writing characteristics (such as cleanliness, beauty and readability) and Army Alpha scores. Similarly, Forster's (1927) graphological scale of intelligence could not be confirmed. Although he obtained positive results, his study was carried out on ten subjects only, he did not make use of external criteria and his methodology was questionable, so his results have little significance. The value of Birge's (1954) validity study is also doubtful, because of the methodological basis and the choice of variables. In a comparison of contrast groups where subjects were rated by their peers on five personality traits, and their handwriting was later re-examined to see if its components were related to the peer-rating, very few significant correlations were found between the 22 writing signs measured and the five personality traits. Even Paul-Mengelberg (1971) is not fully satisfied with her results in grading intelligence according to the handwriting.

Wallner (1966) studied the relationship between writing variables and general intelligence, as well as special talents and knowledge. In the framework of a diagnostic aptitude study of 112 transfer pupils, data was collected through a relatively extensive test battery, aptitude judgements of a vocational counsellor and several graphoimpressionistic variables (e.g., regularity measure, fullness, maturity of writing style, expansiveness and the number of words in the curriculum vitae). Only a few correlations were found to be significant and it was the non-graphological variable "Number of words per curriculum vitae" which exhibited the closest connection to the aptitude criteria, such as intelligence.

Of three other words dealing with analytical cognitive factors (Adolph, 1963; Fahrenberg, 1965; Timm, 1967), only Timm discovered signs and sign syndromes which could be referred to as intelligence indicators. Timm's research on the reliability and validity of 84 graphometric and graphoimpressionistic signs was based upon writing samples of eighty persons of both sexes aged from 20 to 40, with a medium to high level of education. Three criteria of intelligence were employed: the Intelligence Structure Test (I.S.T.), the Figure Reasoning Test and the "General Intelligence" scale of the 16-PF test. The results of all three were then combined to give a criterion "total intelligence." Of the 84 writing variables, twelve showed significant correlations ranging between .24 and .37 with the external criterion. It is noteworthy that the signs of intelligence mentioned in the graphological literature — such as simplification, formrichness, originality and speed — showed significant correlations with the criterion in this study too. However, higher correlations were found for these variables with the criterion of "education." The multiple correlation between predictors and the criterion of "total intelligence" was R = .50. When the variables "sex" and "education" were included in the regression equation, a remarkably high R was attained (R = .70). Timm notes: "This result is obviously of little importance, as schooling in any case correlates with intelligence at a rate of between .63 and .66 . . . but if the level of formal education is not known, then the set of graphological signs represents the criteria which may be predicted with the highest accuracy from the handwriting" (p.350). Even if the result of multiple regression which has not been tested in a replication study is not fully satisfying, it may still show "that statistically significant correspondence exists between handwriting signs and different intellectual and affective variables" (p.350).

2. RESEARCHES ON THE LEVEL OF INTERPRETATION

2.1. Reliability of Graphological Diagnosis of Intelligence

The subject of reliabiliy of graphological diagnosis of intelligence concerns two aspects, namely, inter-rater agreement and intra-rater consistency in the interpretation and assessment of handwriting in regard to intellectual abilities. The issue of how a rater, interpreting different handwriting samples of the same person, will reach the same diagnosis each time, concerns the general question of internal consistency and stability of graphic signs, which is the topic of this discussion.

So far, only Crider (1941) has reported on research into the intra-rater consistency of graphological assessments of intelligence. A graphologist who had already rated eighteen scripts for twelve personality traits (including intelligence), was confronted one month later with the same samples. According to Crider, the graphologist rated the scripts in essentially the same manner on both occasions.

There are additional studies on the question of inter-rater agreement of judgements of intelligence. But some earlier works are methodologically defective and therefore have relatively little significance. For instance, Schorn (1927) noted agreement in a comparison of five graphological assessments of a single script regarding the intelligence of the writer. However, the statements of the five graphologists are so general and vague that the term "agreement" has little meaning here. In the aforementioned research by Crider (1941), two graphologists ranked eighteen handwriting samples amongst other samples with regard to intelligence. This gave the results rho = .39 (which is not significant) but apparently, the qualifications of the graphologists were inadequate. In contrast, the studies presented independently by Mields (1964) and Michel (1969) are methodologically satisfying. Both have, in the framework of general research, considered the diagnostic possibilities of various procedures in rating intelligence, including the analysis of the handwriting. Mields used writing samples of 24 females in the 15-40 age group. The distribution of the IQs of these writers, measured by the Wechsler Adult Intelligence Scale (WAIS), may be seen as widely representative, but is slightly inclined to the right (M = 108.4). Between the eighteen raters, Mields ascertained a concordance rate of rho = .63.

Michel (1969) studied three random samples of six, seven and seven students at the average ages of 18 and a half, 18 and a half, and 23 and a half years. The scripts were judged independently by seven certified psychologists with a thorough education in graphology, and ranked for intelligence. As a measure of agreement, the Kendall concordance coefficient was calculated. The values for the three studies are as follows: I: .36; II: .65; III: .69. All three figures are significantly higher than zero. The studies carried out by Mields and Michel showed significantly high agreement between the ratings of the judges, but these values are clearly inferior still to reported reliability coefficients of many psychological tests. Furthermore, the written materials employed in the two studies were not standardized; they carried some content significance.

Schneevoigt (1968) subjected a random sample of 151 men (students and soldiers) to two intelligence tests (I.S.T. and L.P.S.) and obtained a standard dictated handwriting sample from each. On the basis of their performance in the intelligence tests, three samples of six writers each were created:

I. widely scattered IQs between 53 and 130;
II. slight scattering in the upper IQ area: 91-127;
III. slight scattering in the lower IQ area: 70-101.

Only certified psychologists with several years of experience served as raters. Thirteen of the raters had received a thorough training in graphology ("graphologists"). The others had not had any serious education in the subject ("psychologists"). In the following table, the concordance indices of the ratings are presented.

Rater	Writing Samples		
	I	II	III
"Graphologists" (N = 13)	.88**	.73**	.63**
"Psychologists" (N = 12)	.72**	.54**	.31*

*P < .05   **P < .01

This shows a greater degree of agreement amongst the psychologists who had studied graphology. As expected, the highest concordance appears in the widely scattered random writing samples. Furthermore, it seems that persons with a higher IQ can be more reliably rated through their writing than those with a lower IQ.

2.2. Validity of Graphological Diagnosis of Intelligence

Historically, the first study of validity was carried out by Binet (1906). Studying the ratings of three graphologists, he noted an accuracy of their ratings of intelligence which was above chance level. Later works (e.g., Seeseman, 1929; Jacoby, 1936; Gross, 1955) reach a more or less positive result regarding the possible diagnosis of intelligence or talent by graphological analysis. But various methodological deficiencies greatly reduce their value as evidence. A further series of works (published between the 1920s and the 1950s) are relatively better shaped, although they are still far from being even close to perfect (Hartge & Marum, 1933; Hartge, 1938; Super, 1941; Crider, 1941; Hönel, 1950). By careful examination of data given by the authors, one may conclude that global graphological ratings of intellectual abilities seem to be possible with regard to different types of borderline groups, but they normally show a limited general validity. Omwake (1925), Broom & Basinger (1932), Middleton (1941) and Eysenck (1945) reported negative results, but the external criteria they used for the validation were weak.

The first study of the validity of graphological ratings of intelligence to be relatively satisfying from a methodological point of view, was presented by Schonfeld and Simon (1935). They examined 100 primary school pupils by means of twelve intelligence tests, and had their handwritten curriculum vitae rated by graphologists. Not only the question of the general "level of intelligence" was put to the graphologists, but also questions of some qualitative aspects of intelligence and thinking. Intelligence was rated on a five-point scale. The authors found an average correlation of r = .34 between the graphological ratings and psychometric scores. The qualitative statements unfortunately could not be quantitatively evaluated. However, in a very general way, in 65% of the cases, the graphological statements agreed with the psychometric profile, when indicating a more practical versus a more theoretical way of thought. The authors conclude: "The graphological method is undoubtedly useful for a first rough selection" (p.120). It should be added, that the authors express reservations as to the legitimacy of making psychometric scores the criteria of validation of graphology (p.121). However, they explicitly leave open the question as to whether the more developed writing of an adult would perhaps enable a more accurate diagnosis of intelligence.

Rasch (1957) studied the correspondence rate between graphological ratings and assessments made by the subjects' superiors at work. A random sample of 114 persons was examined, mostly employees aged between 23 and 40. Structured scales were filled by psychologists with graphological training on the one hand and by the subjects' superiors in the firm on the other. As to intellectual ability, there was a correlation of r = .29 (P < .05). After excluding 39 cases which could not be definitely rated by the firm, the correlation rose to r = .35. With the evaluation of this coefficient, it is obvious that the limited value of the external criteria has to be considered. Wallner (1965) provided further data on the validity of the graphological diagnosis of ability. The first examination was carried out with 118 persons, who underwent intelligence tests prior to embarking upon vocational schooling. For each examinee, an average stanine was calculated. These values were correlated with a 9-point graphological evaluation of general intelligence. The result was r = .20 (P < .05). For a second examination, 88 applicants for the task of foreman were chosen and their handwritten curricula vitae were rated by a graphologist for general intellectual level. This evaluation of intelligence correlates to r = .20 (P < .10; N.S.) with a "corresponding talent for studies" which was ascertained by means of tests. For 24 examinees, teachers' ratings were also available; these correlated significantly with the graphological rating of intelligence on the level of 1% in the following aspects: quality of verbal expression, quality of written expression, independence of thinking and interest in learning. In a third, similarly constructed study with 91 applicants for the job of foreman, the correlation coefficient between graphological ratings and psychometric scores was r = .23 (P < .05). In the already mentioned studies by Mields (1962, 1964), the correlation coefficient between the graphological ratings of intelligence and the Wechsler — IQ Test (WAIS) varied in the range of .17 to .46, with a median of .33. However, Mields did not find significant differences between a trained, practicing graphologist, a psychologist less schooled in graphology, and a layman, as to their ability to rate intelligence.

Michel (1969) gave the following average correlation coefficients with five external criteria:

	I.S.T.	WAIS	Raven Matrices	Teacher's Rating	School Records
Study I	.16	.27	*	.27	.27
Study II	.37	.16	.66	.46	.40
Study III	− .35	− .09	− .18	− .08	− .19

* Was not yet used in Study I.

Reasons for the wide scatterings of results cannot be specified. Random errors are not at all unusual with respect to the relatively small writing samples (N = 6 or 7). In comparison with other studies, those of Michel and Mields showed graphology in the poorest light. Higher correlations with external criteria resulted through evaluation of intelligence by facial expressions and the Rorschach test (Mields), through the sound of voice (Wartegg), by means of a drawing test, by peer-rating and by the Four Picture Test (Michel). Michel could find no connection between the subjective optimism of the graphologists' experience and the objective correctness of their rating of intelligence.

Those studies so far reported show far-ranging differences as to the validity of graphological ratings of intelligence. For the most part, they also show above chance-level relations with external criteria of intellectual ability. At the same time, they show that these correlations are rather low. Yet Castelnuovo-Tedesco (1948) reports manifestly **higher** correlation coefficients. His examination is, accordingly, on the one hand often quoted as evidence for the possibility of diagnosing intelligence by means of graphology and on the other hand, considered an exception "which is very difficult to explain" by critics of graphology such as Guilford (1959, p.278). Castelnuovo-Tedesco used a very heterogenous group consisting of students, prison inmates and retarded persons aged 18 to 24. The IQs of the examinees were established by several tests combined into an IQ measure. Group 1 included 100 examinees with IQs between 68 and 132; they had to copy out a newspaper text as a writing sample. Group 2 was composed of examinees with IQs between 82 and 132; these had, in addition, to recount the story of the copied text in writing. Five laymen with partial knowledge of graphology were asked to classify the handwriting samples into five categories (Group 1) and four categories (Group 2) of intelligence level, with intervals ranging from 12 to 14 IQ units. For a second rating, graphological criteria according to Klages were assigned to them by a trained graphologist: speed, simplification, original and independent letter forms, as well as aesthetic distribution of area. The contingent coefficients (C) for the worst and best raters are, according to Castelnuovo-Tedesco:

Group 1 (copy)		Group 2 (copy and recount)	
Laymen's Judgement	Graphologists' Judgement	Laymen's Judgement	Graphologists' Judgement
.59/.59	.59/.63	.45/.47	.49/.56

The knowledge of graphological indicators of intelligence had only a small influence on the quality of ratings.

All in all, the contigency coefficients are remarkably high and correspond to the Pearson r-values between .52 and .70. In evaluation of these coefficients, one should take into account—and this should be a decisive factor—that the levels of correlation coefficients are stochastically dependent on the homogeneity of the samples. The samples employed by Castelnuovo-Tedesco show a high degree of heterogeneity, especially in Group 1, which encompasses both retardation and high intelligence. How far the raters in Group 2 considered contents, orthographic, grammatical and other non-graphic signs, must remain a separate subject.

The work of Schneevoigt (1968) clearly demonstrates the dependence of the level of correlation on the variance of samples used. For three handwriting samples, he presented the following correlations with criteria:

Rater	Writing Samples		
	I	II	III
Graphologists (N = 13)	.88**	.43**	−.24
Psychologists (N = 12)	.78**	.31*	.11

*P < .05   **P < .01

Comparably high coefficients of validity were obtained only with the extremely heterogenous sample I, while sample III (small scattering in the lower IQ area) resulted in a negative correlation with the graphologists and a zero-order correlation with psychologists. Furthermore, it seems remarkable that there was no systematic difference in the ratings of certified psychologists with and without graphological education.

3. SUMMARY, DISCUSSION AND PROSPECTS

1. Significant correlations between various handwriting signs and the intellectual level of the writer certainly exist. Signs of form and formation are especially significant. However, single signs do not show sufficiently close and consistent relations as to enable diagnosis of intelligence of a given individual.

2. Indeed, graphological assessment of intelligence is never based on single signs, but on sign complexes (syndromes), which are grasped in a more or less intuitive way. The result of this process, the graphological estimation of the intelligence level, has been the object of a series of reliability and validity studies. The resulting correlations may reach satisfactory levels, but only with writing samples which originate from intellectually heterogenous writers. A rough classification of the level of intelligence seems to be possible, but no fine grading, which should be left — so it seems — to psychometric tests.

3. There is fragmental evidence that certain groups are less susceptible than others to graphological analysis (Michel & Iseler, 1968). In particular, it may be surmised that the writings of children or others not used to writing are unsuitable for the diagnosis of intelligence.

4. Laymen have, in some cases, reached the same validities as graphologists when rating intelligence by handwriting. This requires further explanation.

5. Graphologists have objected to pure examinations of intelligence, as the concept "intelligence" has not been plainly defined and agreed upon. (See, for example, Mueller & Enskat, 1965, p.771.) On the one hand, one may agree with Kretschmer (1950) that this concept may be useful as a "word accepted in practice." On the other hand, basing ourselves on Mields and on Timm, it seems that this index is primarily a measure of the writer's educational level. Timm actually mentioned the supposition that a "graphological intelligence" syndrome reflects merely the fact of being accustomed to writing.

In the last three decades, the rating process has indeed been made the target of many studies of psychological diagnostics (Summary in Jäger, 1982.) In graphology, this subject was dealt with by Lockowandt (1973). In our context, there is so far hardly any useful information available. The multiple regression equations extracted by Timm can be seen as a simulation of the graphological ratings process. Furthermore, it should be stated that in addition to additive linear models, there are other statistical models suitable for an optimal syndrome formation, as suggested by Michel and Iseler (1968).

6. In reported evaluation studies, the qualitative aspects of the diagnosis of talent in a wider sense (beyond mere intellectual capacity) have so far been neglected.

Graphology was measured in much too one-sided a manner in comparison with intelligence tests. With regard to possible exactitude in the measuring of general intelligence, intelligence tests are certainly superior to graphology. Graphology, in the sense used by Cronbach & Gleser (1965), represents a subjective process, in which lie both its strength and its weakness. This weakness, as well as graphology's possibilities vis-a-vis traditional psychometric intelligence testing, has been by and large explained. Its strength, and its limitations within the framework of talent diagnostics in a wide sense, remain largely unresearched.

REFERENCES

Adolph, K. (1963). *Faktorenanlytische Untersuchung der gerbräuchlichsten Handschriftvariablen.* Doctoral dissertation, Freiburg University.

Binet, A. (1906). *Les révélations de l'écriture d'après un contrôle scientifique.* Paris.

Birge, W. R. (1954). An experimental enquiry into the measurable handwriting correlates of five personality traits. *Journal of Personality, 23,* 215.

Broom, B. & Basinger, M. (1932). On the determination of the intelligence of adults from samples of their penmanship. *Journal of Applied Psychology, 16,* 515.

Castelnuovo-Tedesco, P. A. (1948). A study of the relationship between handwriting and personality variables. *Genetic Psychology Monograph, 37,* 167.

Crider, B. (1941). The reliability and validity of two graphologists. *Journal of Applied Psychology, 25,* 323.

Cronbach, L. J. & Gleser, G. C. (1965). *Psychological Tests and Personal Decisions* (2nd Ed.). Urbana: University of Illinois Press.

Eysenck, H. J. (1945). Graphological analysis and psychiatry: an experimental study. *British Journal of Psychology, 35,* 70.

Fahrenberg, J. & Conrad, W. (1965). Eine explorative Faktorenanalayse graphometrischer und psychometrischer Daten. *Z. exp. angewand. Psychol., 12,* 223.

Förster, J. (1927). Verfahren und Möglichkeiten der Schriftbeurteilung. *Industr. Psychotech., 4,* 129.

Gessell, A. (1906). Accuracy in handwriting as related to school intelligence and sex. *American Journal of Psychology, 17,* 129.

Groel, E. (1963). *Untersuchungen zür Handschriftdeutung mit kurzzeitiger und langzeitiger Schriftdarbietung.* Doctoral dissertation, University of Mainz.

Gross, A. (1955). Zür Graphologie der Gelehrtenhandschrift. *Zeitung für Menschenkunde, 19,* 41.

Guilford, J. P. (1959). *Personality.* New York: McGraw-Hill.

Hartge, M. (1938). Graphologie in der Pädagogik und Berufsberatung. *Z. angew. Psychol., 54,* 92.

Hartge, M. & Marum. O. (1933). Die Sicherheit graphologischer Intelligenzbeurteilung. *Z. angew. Psychol., 44,* 321.

Hönel, H. (1950). *Untersuchungen zum Problem der Bewahrheitung graphologischer Gutachten.* Doctoral dissertation, Vienna University.

Jäger, A. O. (1960). Zum prognostischen Wert psychologischer Eignungsuntersuchungen. *Psychol. Rdsch., 11,* 160.

Jäger, R. S. (1982). Diagnostische Urteilsbildung. In: Groffmann, K. J. & Michel, L. (Eds.) *Psychologische Diagnostik*, Vol. 1, Gottingen, Verlag für Psychologie.

Jacoby, M. (1936). Die Bedeutung der Graphologie für die Berufsberatung. *Die Schrift, 2*, 155.

Kretschmer, E. (1950). Medizinische Psychologie. Stuttgart.

Kristof, W. (1957). Zür Frage der statistischen Sicherung von Profildifferenzen. *Z. exp. angew Psychol., 4*, 692.

Lockowandt, O. (1973). Der Prozess der Urteilsbildung in der Schriftpsychologie. *Zeitung für Menschenskunde, 37*, 135.

Lockowandt, O. (1980). Schreiben und Schulerfolg. *Zeitung für Menschenskunde, 44*, 423.

Michel, L. (1969). Empirische Untersuchungen zür Frage der Obereinstimmung und Gültigkeit von Beurteilungen des intellektuellen Niveaus aus der Handschrift. *Arch. ges. Psychol., 121*, 31.

Michel, L. & Iseler, A. (1968). Beziehungen zwischen klinischen und psychometrischen Methoden der diagnostischen Urteilsbildung. In: Groffmann, K. J. & Wewetzer, K. H. (Eds.) *Person als Prozess*. Bern.

Middleton, W. C. (1941). The ability of untrained subjects to judge intelligence and age from handwriting samples. *Journal of Applied Psychology, 25*, 331.

Mields, J. (1962). *Untersuchungen der Möglichkeit der Intelligenzbeurteilung*. Doctoral dissertation, Heidelberg University.

Mields, J. (1964). Möglichkeiten der Intelligenz-Diagnose bei Team-Work. *Diagnostica, 10*, 15.

Mueller, W. H. & Enskat, A. (1965). Grundzüge der Graphologie. In: Kirchhoff, R. (Eds.) *Ausdruckspsychologie (Handbuch der Psychologie*, Vol. 5). Göttingen: Verlag für Psychologie.

Oinonen, P. (1965). Huono käsiala psykologisena ongelmana. *Acta Academiae Paedagogicae Jyväskyläensis, 21* (quoted in: Wallner, T., 1965).

Omwake, K. T. (1925). The value of photographs and handwriting in estimating intelligence. *Publ. Pers. Stud., 3*, 2.

Paul-Mengelberg. M. (1971). Die Einstufung der Intelligenz nach der Handschrift. *Zeitung für Menschenkunde, 35*, 18.

Rasch, W. D. (1957). Hat sich die Graphologie bewahrt? Bern: Huber.

Schleussner, C. A. (1955). Der Aussagewert graphologischer Prüfungen. *Umschau in Wissenschaft und Technik, 5*, 150.

Schneevoigt, I. (1968). *Die graphologische Intelligenzdiagnose*. Doctoral dissertation. Mannheim University.

Schonfeld, W. & Simon, W. (1935). *Die graphologische Intelligenzbeurteilung*. Prague.

Schorn, M. (1927). Untersuchungen zur Kritik der graphologischen Gutachten. *Indust. Psychotech., 4*.

Schwager, J. (1955). Entgegnung zu Schleussner. *Ausdruckskunde, 2*, 186.

Seesemann, K. (1929). Bewährungsprobe graphologische Gutachten. *Indust. Psychotech., 6*.

Super, D. E. (1941). A comparison of the diagnoses of a graphologist with results of psychological tests. *Journal of Consulting Psychology, 5*, 127.

Timm, U. (1967). Graphometrie als psychologischer Test? *Psychol. Forsch., 30*, 307.

Wallner, T. (1965). Graphologie als Objekt statistischer Untersuchungen. *Psychol. Rdsch.*, *16*, 282.

Wallner, T. (1966). Zusammenhänge zwischen Prognosedaten, Handschriftenvariablen und Ausbildungsergebnissen. *Psychol. Beitr.*, *9*, 449.

15

VALIDATION OF GRAPHOANALYSIS BY "GLOBAL" OR "HOLISTIC" METHOD[1]

JAMES C. CRUMBAUGH and EMILIE STOCKHOLM

Summary

GRAPHOANALYSIS is a projective expressive movement which is neither better nor more poorly validated than most projective techniques as a means of personality assessment. This is inadequate validation because the subjectivity of the latter makes statistical study difficult. With all projective techniques, "sign" or "trait" validation has been minimal, and the best validation has come from "global" or "holistic" methods. The present chapter presents a paradigm for the latter type of approach to handwriting analysis, using a matching technique with probabilities of 1/5, wherein five subjects were matched by people who knew them to one of five blind Graphoanalyses of the subjects' writing. This design is herein replicated five times, with total data significantly different from chance expectation ($p < .001$), supporting the hypothesis that it is possible to evaluate personality through analysis of handwriting.

Introduction

Handwriting is an expressive movement which, like drawings, has an excellent rationale for the assumption that personality is projected into the activity. Projective techniques assume this true of all forms of behavioral expression as well as of stimulus interpretation or perception. Textbooks of psychology have usually agreed that there ought to be "something to" handwriting analysis, though some have contended that it has never been pinned down.

A survey of the literature has led the first author to believe that graphology (the generic term for all handwriting study) has been neither

231

better nor worse validated than a majority of the projective techniques currently in use (Crumbaugh, 1970; IGAS Research Department, 1970). In the opinion of the present writers the approach called Graphoanalysis has been more systematically developed, presented in greater detail, more effectively taught, and better researched than any other method of handwriting analysis. For this reason we have used it as the basis of validation research.

We set out along the lines of trait or "sign" validation, but soon found that — as in the case of other projective techniques, like the Rorschach — results here are minimal. We did obtain significant correlations between ratings of several traits by Graphoanalysts from handwriting samples and ratings of the same traits done by people who knew the subjects; but in general the source of error variance (such as raters' unreliability, and un-reliability of the interpretations of definitions of traits) made effective study difficult. As Weinberg, Fluckiger & Tripp (1962), graphologists from a different background of study, had succeeded in validation by the global or holistic approach, we next turned our attention in this direction.

METHOD

In a pilot study five subjects well known to each other as well as to five other people (two Graphoanalysts and three non-Graphoanalysts) were selected. Each subject gave a standard handwriting sample consist-ing of a page of copied book material. Each of these five samples was sent to a competent Graphoanalyst with instructions to write a single-page summary of the salient features of personality of the subject. Only age and sex were specified to the participating Graphoanalyst, who did not know the subjects personally. Several Graphoanalysts were used; all five samples were not done by the same analyst.

Upon receipt of the five personality summaries they were coded and given successively to 10 people who knew well all five subjects: three non-Graphoanalysts, two Graphoanalysts (who were different from, and had no contact with, the analysts who wrote the personality descrip-tions), and the five subjects themselves.

Instructions were to "match these five personality descriptions to the following five people whom you know. (The five names were specified.) The descriptions are coded A through E. On each description write the name of the person among these five who in your opinion is best described by it."

The reason for choosing five subjects, with resultant chance probabilities of 1/5, was that preliminary exploratory work had indicated that 10 subjects were more than most matchers could hold in mind (and it was also hard to get 10 subjects well known to any matcher), and fewer than five subjects would increase the chance factor to such an extent that an extremely high level of success in matching would be required to "beat chance." It was found that most matchers could hold in mind about five single-page personality descriptions at once as they made their comparisons but that their capability in this respect decreased rapidly upon the addition of more subjects.

The results of this pilot study were, as we shall see in the next section, encouraging: the general approach was therefore replicated five times under the following paradigm:

A cooperating researcher (usually a Graphoanalyst) was asked to select five subjects who were all well known to three people, to obtain a standard handwriting sample from each of these subjects and to submit these samples to the second writer. The second writer then sent the five samples to independent expert Graphoanalysts, who had no knowledge of the subjects. These Graphoanalysts were instructed to write concise single-page summaries of the salient features of personality which appeared in each handwriting sample, being told only the age and sex of the writer. The five personality summaries were then coded and returned to the research cooperator, who independently submitted them to each of the three persons who knew all five subjects with the following instructions: "These five personality sketches are of five people you know (The five people were then named.) On each sketch write the name of the one of these individuals it most resembles." The three matchers functioned independently of each other with no knowledge of matchings other than their own. All data were then returned to the second writer and analyzed by the first writer.

RESULTS

The results of the pilot study are shown in Table I; the results of the replications including the pilot study are presented in Table II. The portion of the pilot study included is Set A in Table II, which corresponds to the non-Graphoanalyst matchers of Table I. This is the only portion of the pilot study which is actually replicated by Sets B through F of Table II.

TABLE I

PILOT STUDY RESULTS: ABILITY OF MATCHERS TO SELECT CORRECT GRAPHOANALYTIC

PERSONALITY DESCRIPTION BASED ON A GIVEN SUBJECT WELL-KNOWN TO THEM

Set Matchers	Ss 1	2	3	4	5	Matchers' scores	Chance expectation	= chance	M matching score	n (no. trials)
A Non-Graphoanalysts										
a		x		x	x	3	1			5
b	x			x		2	1			5
c			x	x	x	3	1			5
Totals	1	1	1	3	2	8	3	5	2.66	15
B Graphoanalysts										
I	x		x	x		3	1			5
II	x	x	x	x	x	5	1			5
Totals	2	1	2	2	1	8	2	6	4.00	10
C Subjects themselves as matchers										
1	x		x	x		3	1			5
2	x	x	x	x	x	5	1			5
3	x		x	x		3	1			5
4	x	x	x	x	x	5	1			5
5		x			x	2	1			5
Totals	4	3	4	4	3	18	5	13	3.60	25
Total, sets	7	5	7	9	6	34			3.40	50
Chance	2	2	2	2	2		10			
= chance	5	3	5	7	4			24		

Note – SE of chance expectation: $\sqrt{NPQ}$ = 2.82; corrected for "dependent events" =2.88;
t ratio = 24/2.88 = 8.3, p<.001.

TABLE II

COMBINED RESULTS OF SET A OF PILOT STUDY PLUS
FIVE REPLICATIONS OF THIS SET

Set	Matchers	Ss 1	2	3	4	5	Matchers' scores	Chance expectation	+/− chance	M matching score	n (no. trials)
A	a		x		x	x	3	1			5
	b	x			x		2	1			5
	c			x	x	x	3	1			5
	Tot.	1	1	1	3	2	8	3	5	2.66	15
B	a	x					1	1			5
	b	x					1	1			5
	c						0	1			5
	Tot.	2	0	0	0	0	2	3	−1	0.67	15
C	a	x	x		x		3	1			5
	b	x	x	x	x	x	5	1			5
	c				x	x	2	1			5
	Tot.	2	2	1	3	2	10	3	7	3.33	15
D	a						0	1			5
	b	x	x	x	x	x	5	1			5
	c						0	1			5
	Tot.	1	1	1	1	1	5	3	2	1.67	15
E	a	x					1	1			5
	b						0	1			5
	c						0	1			5
	Tot.	1	0	0	0	0	1	3	−2	0.33	15
F	a				x	x	2	1			5
	b		x	x			2	1			5
	c	x					1	1			5
	Tot.	1	1	1	1	1	5	3	2	1.67	15
	Total, sets	7	6	3	9	6	31	18	13		90
	Chance	3.6	3.6	3.6	3.6	3.6					
	+/− chance	3.4	2.4	−0.6	5.4	2.4					

Note − SE of chance expectation: $= \sqrt{NPQ} = \sqrt{90\ (1/5 \times 4/5)} = 3.79)$;
t ratio = 13/3.79 = 3.43, p<.001.

It will be seen in Table I that the total results of the 10 matchers exceed chance expectation at a significant level and that three of the 10 matched all five personality descriptions perfectly to the subject upon whose handwriting Graphoanalysts had based these descriptions. In all 10 cases the chance expectation of one "hit" was exceeded.

It will also be noted that Subject No. 4 was correctly hit by nine of the 10 matchers, suggesting that there may have been unique features of personality which made this individual easier to assess both from handwriting and from personal recognition. All five subjects were, however, correctly matched considerably more frequently than chance.

For practical reasons only Set A was replicated. The results of the replication (Table II) are seen to be less above chance than those of Set A with the one exception of Set C (though there is no statistically significant difference between sets because of the small samples).

There is no rationale for expecting matching to be better among Graphoanalysts than among either non-Graphoanalysts or the subjects themselves, as occurred in the pilot study (Table I). One might presume that, since the subjects included their own cases in their matching and might know themselves best, they would do better. Actually they were in the middle between Graphoanalysts and non-Graphoanalysts. They may in reality have matched their own descriptions more poorly because of the possible tendency to pick an overly favorable description if they had strong egos or a tendency to pick the opposite if self-esteem were low. Since there was no good reason to believe that these three classes of matchers would vary from each other much if they knew the subjects pretty well, non-Graphoanalysts as in Set A seemed the most feasible choice for the replications.

Table II shows that these replications, while generally yielding results less above chance expectation than Set A, in total combination still show significant consistency. One rater in Set C and one in Set D matched all five descriptions perfectly. It should be noted that the subjects were different from set to set in these replications, so that the number of hits for a given subject can vary only from 0 to 3. One subject in Set A and one in Set C was identified by all three matchers, which suggests that these individuals may have had unique features of personality which showed both in handwriting and in their behavior as observed by the matchers. But the number of matchings per subject is too small here for any conclusion.

DISCUSSION

It is clear that the data of Tables I and II summarize significant results. The writers submit that no feasible interpretation of these results exists other than the assumption that at least some Graphoanalysts have written personality sketches of some subjects, based upon their handwriting alone, which have been correctly recognized by at least some matchers who know the subjects. The important conclusion from these data is that it can be done and therefore that evidence has thus been presented by the global or holistic method of validation that Graphoanalysis contains some validity as a system. The fact, however, that both tables contain sets in which scores have been perfect suggests that some Graphoanalysts and some criterion matchers can in combination succeed well.

It is important to deal with three statistical questions which might be raised concerning data of this type: (1) Is the N "inflated"? (2) Does the lack of "independence of events" in evaluating chance guessing in situations of this type affect the statistical interpretations? (3) Does the skewness of the chance distributions appreciably affect results?

First, the claim of a possible inflated N would assert that the true N is not the number of "trials" at matching a graphoanalytic description to a known personality but rather the number of sets of data. The idea would be that the number of trials or of matchers merely multiples the same basic data, as if one wanted to know the thickness of the human skull and determined it by a thousand measurements of one skull. Here the N would not be 1,000 but one.

In our special instance we are not **presently** interested in what proportion of Graphoanalysts can write personality profiles from handwriting samples — profiles which can be recognized by people who know the subjects — or in what proportion of people who know the subjects are able to recognize them from the sketches. We are interested only in whether this can be done at all by one or more Graphoanalysts in combination with one or more persons who know the subjects. Thus our correct N is the total number of trials or times such a match is attempted.

Secondly, the lack of independence of events in a matching study of this type — which means that when one match has been made, the possibilities for the remaining trials in a given five-subject series are reduced and the probabilities are therefore changed — does technically require a correction which increases the standard error of the chance-expected probabilities. In practice this proves to be a very small amount in most situations. This is easily illustrated in evaluating the chance factor in calling the ESP cards, which are also based on probabilities of 1:5 (five symbols whose order is to be matched by the subject). Early criticisms made a big issue of this lack of independence of events, but the statisticians found it an insignificant factor, amounting to only .04 in the formula for the standard error of chance expectation in ESP runs: $2.04 \sqrt{N}$ where N = number of runs. Since the data of Table I are equivalent to two ESP runs, we have used this correction in computing the standard error for these data. Obviously insignificant in determining the reliability of differences from chance expectation in our obtained data, we have ignored it in Table II.

Third, the skewness of the chance distribution — the fact that with probabilities of 1/5 the "hits" can go only to zero below the chance expectation of one, whereas they can go four above to five — theoretically affects the standard error. Here again, however, the practical effect is slight.

The best confirmation of the view that these factors do not appreciably affect the results of our study is in empirical chance-matching to parallel the experimental data. To this end we performed by pure chance (matching shuffled numbered cards to numbers ordered one through five) 25 replications of the data of Table I. The results followed very closely chance expectation, yielding chance variations slightly higher than the theoretical probability of 1/5, as would be predicted from the afore-mentioned sources of error variance, but results which do not come anywhere close to those of our experimental data, even in the most deviant replication. Further, there were only four "5" (or perfect) matching scores in 25 replications, whereas there were three such scores in the pilot study (Set A) and one each in Sets C and D. We feel that this is adequate evidence that our findings cannot be accounted for by the assumption that they are the product of chance variation.

While this experiment is only a first step in the validation of Graphoanalysis by the global or holistic method, we offer its paradigm as a fruitful approach for further research. Attention should now be turned to questions of the characteristics of Graphoanalysts and of matchers who can perform consistently at above-chance level and to demonstration of this consistency in replications of the paradigm.

REFERENCES

Crumbaugh, J. C. (1970). Quoted comment. *Behavior Today, 1*(13), 4.

International Graphoanalysis Society, Research Department. (1970). *An annotated bibliography of studies in handwriting analysis research.* Chicago.

Weinberg, G. H. , Fluckiger, F. A. & Tripp, C. A. (1962). The application of a new matching technique. *Journal of Projective Techniques, 23,* 221-224.

NOTES

1. This chapter is an abridged version of an article which is reprinted with permission of the publisher from Crumbaugh, J. C. & Stockholm, E. (1977). Validation of graphoanalysis by "global" or "holistic" method. *Perceptual & Motor Skills, 44,* 403-410.

16

VALIDATION OF GRAPHOLOGY THROUGH THE USE OF MATCHING METHOD BASED ON RANKING

BARUCH NEVO and HAY HALEVI

Summary

MATCHING MODELS are offered as a possible solution to some of the major methodological problems presented in the research on validities of graphology. Past studies based on matching procedures are briefly summarized and their weaknesses outlined. An improved variation — matching based on ranking — is presented, together with a report on two empirical studies conducted by the authors in which such a procedure was instituted. Results show that raters can match persons known to them with graphological reports of those persons, with a probability greater than chance. Combined with previous findings, these results suggest that there is a strong case for the statement that handwriting does contain some information with regard to the personality of the writer.

Introduction

After nearly one hundred years of investigating the psychodiagnostic value of handwriting behavior, and after almost two hundred years of the practical application of graphology, it is still unclear whether these methods are — or could be — valid. Many of the validity studies are vulnerable to methodological criticism. (For methodological comments and reviews regarding problems in graphological research, see: Fluckiger, Tripp & Weinberg, 1961; Wallner, 1965, 1975; Michel, 1969; Lockowandt, 1976; Rafaeli & Klimoski, 1983.) The most common criticisms can be phrased as follows:

1. The graphologist should not have access to information regarding the writer, except age, sex and handedness. Moreover, handwriting samples which are neutral as to content are preferable to samples which disclose personal information about the writer.

2. When asked to evaluate diagnostic statements which purport to describe them, people tend to be naive and susceptible to suggestion. Therefore, the criterion against which the graphological report is validated should be neutralized from personal effects. Special attention should be paid to the detection and (if possible) prevention of the "Barnum Effect."

3. Expecting simple linear relations between individual isolated graphometric indicators ("signs") and personality/behavioral variables is unrealistic because graphology does not operate in a linear pattern.

4. Graphologists who participate in validation studies should not be requested to undertake practices which contradict their professional standards, such as rating subjects on variables with which they are not fully conversant or rating **all** subjects even though not every handwriting is open to analysis, thus violating the "default option." It would be more appropriate for the graphologist to work in a more "natural" way, with the researcher adjusting his method accordingly.

The first two arguments are usually adopted by "non-believers," while the latter two are held by scholars to whom the present validity coefficients are underestimates of the true picture.

Is there any model which may satisfy both parties concerned? A design which has the potential for being accepted as methodologically sound by "believers" and "non-believers" alike?

A promising step in this direction was taken by Powers (1933), who was the first to introduce matching procedure into this area. Powers asked three groups of raters to match ten handwriting samples of ten actual people unknown to the raters with ten personality sketches of the same people: college students, faculty members and graphologists. Out of a possible ten correct matches, each group obtained the following number of correct matches: 143 college students — 1.77; 25 faculty members — 1.80; 17 graphologists — 2.41. The expectancy for each group was 1.0. All figures are statistically significant (p < .001). The scripts in Powers' study were copies of a standard passage and the personality sketches were made in collaboration by three psychologists, at least one of whom was intimately acquainted with the writer.

Since 1930, two other "holistic" matching studies have been published. Eysenck (1945) had fifty patients at a mental hospital copy a personality questionnaire on uniform paper, in order to obtain specimens of their handwriting. A graphologist was then asked to match each patient's handwriting with a personality sketch as well as with his case history and his score on a non-verbal ability test. The 50 handwritings were randomly divided into ten groups of five scripts each. The graphologist was required to match within each group. The expected number of "hits" from this experiment is 1.0. The observed result was an average of 2.4, a figure which is highly significant statistically (P < .01).

Another matching study was published by Crumbaugh and Stockholm in 1977. In this study, the researcher selected five subjects who were all known to three people. He obtained a standard handwriting sample (one page of copied book material) from each of these five subjects. These were then sent to graphologists who had no knowledge of the subjects, and who were requested to write concise single page reports of the personality which produced each script sample. The five reports were then coded and submitted independently to each of the three people who knew all five target persons. The three raters were asked to match the five target persons. The three raters were asked to match the five reports with the five names. Their responses were used as data for the analysis of this study. This procedure was replicated six times (18 matches altogether). The expected number of chance "hits" per matcher is 1 (out of five.) The actual number of chance "hits" achieved by matchers in this study averaged 1.72 and the result was significantly different from chance level (p < .01).

All three studies summarized above suffer from two shortcomings:

a) The pairings are not independent; a correct match increases the probability of another correct match.
b) The simple matching design does not allow for intermediate values of the matching outcome: a single match is either a "hit" or a "miss," "1" or "0." This situation does not accurately reflect the full spectrum of the raters' hesitations.

In this series of studies, a variation of the matching method has been applied, so that these two drawbacks will be overcome. The two studies are presented in the next section.

STUDY 1 (HALEVI, 1964)

Seven undergraduate students (A, B, . . . G) presented class notes to the researcher, who erased any clue which could lead to the identification of the writer. The researcher then presented the seven handwriting samples to a graphologist, asking him to write a report in his own style on each of the writers. The seven reports ($\overline{A}$, $\overline{B}$, . . . $\overline{G}$) were then presented to seven raters ($\grave{A}$, $\grave{B}$, . . . $\grave{G}$), considered by each writer (A, B, . . . G) respectively to be a person who knew him well. Each rater was then asked to read all seven reports and then match and **order** them according to closeness of fit to the one person he knew. The results are presented in Table I.

TABLE I

Graphological Reports Ranked by Raters According to Their Closeness of

Fit to Target Persons (Halevi, 1964)

	$\overline{A}$	$\overline{B}$	$\overline{C}$	$\overline{D}$	$\overline{E}$	$\overline{F}$	$\overline{G}$
$\grave{A}$	1	4	3	7	6	2	5
$\grave{B}$	1	3	6	4	7	2	5
$\grave{C}$	7	4	1	2	5	6	3
$\grave{D}$	3	4	6	1	7	2	5
$\grave{E}$	4	7	1	3	5	6	2
$\grave{F}$	6	5	2	7	4	1	3
$\grave{G}$	4	3	1	7	6	5	2

Explanation: The number "1" in the upper left hand cell means that rater $\grave{A}$ nominated report $\overline{A}$ as the best fit to A as he knew him. Report $\overline{F}$ (same line, sixth place to the right) was chosen by him as second best and so on.

Halevi developed a statistical technique for determining the level of significance of the specific distribution of the ratings in the diagonal being different from random (Halevi, 1965). According to Halevi's technique, the probability of Table I occurring by chance is $P < .001$.

STUDY II (NEVO, 1982)

Ten undergraduate students were each asked to bring to class a handwriting sample (one page of copied material from Genesis) from a person they knew very well (A, B, . . . J). The scripts were distributed among ten student graphologists, each of whom independently wrote one graphological report ($\overline{A}$, $\overline{B}$, . . . $\overline{J}$) based on these scripts. The ten reports were then presented to each of the undergraduate students ($\grave{A}$, $\grave{B}$, . . . $\grave{J}$), who matched and ordered them according to their closeness of match to the target person.

The entry values in the cells, which should be interpreted in the same way as in Table I, were as follows: 2 (for cell $\grave{A}\overline{A}$), 3 (for cell $\grave{B}\overline{B}$), 8 (cell $\grave{C}\overline{C}$), 1,1,7,6,5,3,1 (for cell $\grave{J}\overline{J}$). Employing Halevi's statistical technique, it was found that the probability of these results occurring by chance is $P < .05$.

DISCUSSION

The purpose of this article was to learn how close a graphological analysis of handwriting can come to the image of the real person as perceived by people who knew him well.

In the two studies reported above (and the three studies described earlier) it was found that graphological reports match impressions held by other people better than chance. The two studies vary a great deal: one study was executed in the sixties, the other in the eighties; the specific schools of graphology which were involved differ considerably. The similarity of the findings in spite of these variations, and the fact that the Israeli results resemble the American and British, strengthens the generalizability of the conclusion.

It seems quite safe to state that it is impossible to accept the authenticity of the findings of this series of studies and still claim that handwriting does not reflect **anything** of the writer's personality.

The question is, how strong is the phenomenon? Significant as the results of the matchings are, it does not seem that the validity of graphological analysis was proved to be very high. On the basis of these findings, the practical application of graphology as a single psychodiagnostic tool **cannot**, in fact, be recommended: too many "misses" are involved and the probability of getting a distorted personality description is too high.

Also, it should be noted that the findings do not provide any direct support for the common practice of employing graphology as a personnel selection tool — simply because the studies were not designed to investigate that question.

But if we accept the idea that **some** personal information is conveyed through a person's handwriting, then we may wish to plan future research in that area. Questions such as — What kind of personal information is projected through handwriting? What are the best techniques for extracting this information? What overlap is possible between graphology and more traditional projective techniques? In what way is graphology unique and how could it be integrated into a more complete psychodiagnostic frame? "Legitimization" of graphology as a possible subject of scientific study can promote interesting research in a long neglected area.

REFERENCES

Crumbaugh, J. C. & Stockholm, E. (1977). Validation of graphoanalysis by global or holistic method. *Perceptual and Motor Skills, 44,* 403-410.

Eysenck, H. J. (1945). Graphological analysis and psychiatry: An experimental study. *British Journal of Psychiatry, 42,* 70-81.

Fluckiger, F. A., Tripp, C. A. & Weinberg, G. H. (1961). A review of the experimental research in graphology 1933-1960, *Perceptual and Motor Skills, 12,* 67-90.

Halevi, H. (1964). *Studying graphology via matching technique,* unpublished master's thesis, Hebrew University of Jersualem.

Halevi, H. (1965). An alternative approach to the method of correct matching, *Psychometrica,* 30, 67-90.

Hartford, H. (1973). *You are what you write.* New York: Collier Books.

Lockowandt, O. (1976). Present status of the investigation of handwriting psychology as a diagnostic method, *Catalog of Selected Documents in Psychology, 6,* 4-5.

Michel, L. (1969). Empirische Untersuchungen zür Frage der Übereinstimmung und Gültigkeit von Veurteilungern des Intelliktuellen Neveaus aus der Handschrift, *Archiv für die Gesamte Psychologie, 121,* 31-54.

Nevo, B. (1982, February), Application of matching technique to the study of graphology. *Scientific Aspects of Graphology,* Symposium conducted at the University of Haifa.

Powers, E. (1933). Matching sketches of personality with script. In: Allport, G. W. & Vernon, P. E. (Eds.). *Studies in expressive movement,* Chap. 10. New York: Hafner.

Raphaeli, A. & Klimoski, R. J. (1983). Predicting sales success through handwriting analysis: An evaluation of effects of training and handwriting sample content, *Journal of Applied Psychology, 68,* 211-217.

Wallner, T. (1965). Graphologie als Objekt Statistischer Untersuchungen, *Psychologische Rundschau, 16,* 282-298.

Wallner, T. (1975). Hypotheses of handwriting psychology and their verification, *Professional Psychology, 6,* 8-16.

PART IV

METHODOLOGICAL CONSIDERATIONS

17

VALIDATION OF GRAPHOLOGY:
A PROPOSED RESEARCH DESIGN

BARUCH NEVO

Summary

A POSSIBLE MODEL for validation studies in graphology is presented. The unique features of its holistic design are as follows:

a) The graphologists are allowed to analyse and report in the style which they find most suitable for their purposes.
b) The required sample size is small.
c) A control group of psychodiagnosticians is employed as a baseline.

These characteristics of the proposed research are expected to fill certain gaps which were detected in the past in graphological research.

Introduction

In the previous two chapters, evidence was brought to support the validity of graphology. However, a major problem with the aforementioned matching studies is the lack of a baseline to which the graphology results could be compared. In addition, the graphologists were not offered the option not to respond to a certain handwriting sample. A third weakness concerns the matchers. In most of the validation studies of graphology, the raters (or matchers) were people other than the writers. Regrettably, self-assessment was never carried out.

In this chapter, we would like to outline an "ideal" design for the study of validation of graphology which has the potential of being accepted as methodologically "clean" by experimentalists and graphologists alike and which will take care of the above-mentioned flaws.

METHOD

Subjects

16 males, aged 20-35, right-handed; each one should have a psychologist who has known him for at least six months. One may therefore assume that the subjects will be patients, colleagues, spouses, students or good friends of the psychologists.

Graphologists

Three highly qualified and experienced graphologists.

Psychodiagnosticians

Three highly qualified, clinical psychologists who specialize in psychodiagnostics.

Raters

Sixteen (or fewer) psychologists who have been personally acquainted with one or more of the subjects for at least six months.

Procedure

Each subject will be tested by a battery of psychological tests considered to be "standard" (by psychodiagnosticians) in the locality of the research — for example: Individual intelligence scale, Bender-Gestalt tests, Draw-a-Person, T.A.T., Rorschach (or Holzman), MMPI. He or she will then provide standard written materials extracted under standard conditions: copied material, dictations, signature.

The handwritten materials will then be given to the three graphologists, each one of whom will be asked to write a full graphological report of no more than one typed page, on each one of the 16 subjects. They will be instructed to include in their report some standard topics, such as the subject's cognitive abilities, his social orientation, emotions, personality traits, etc. They should employ their normal approach and style of report. The three graphologists will work independently of each other, and of any external source of information. Each graphologist will be permitted to skip 1-2 cases on whatever basis he chooses.

The three psychologists will follow exactly the same procedure, except that they will base their reports on the test protocols.

At this stage, only 10 subjects' files in which all 6 reports exist (3 graphological reports and 3 psychodiagnostic reports) will remain. The rest of the research will be carried on with these 10 files only. (The other 6 files are those of subjects who were omitted by any one of the graphologists or psychodiagnosticians.)

We come now to the task of the raters. Each rater will perform the same task 6 times. Each time he will receive a series of 10 reports (for instance, those which were written by graphologist no. 1), and will be asked to read them carefully. His next step will be to choose the one report he views as the best-fit to the personality of "his" subject. Out of the remaining 9 reports he will again choose the best-fit description; and so on, until a full rank-order of the 10 reports' closeness to the subjects' personality will be reached. A few days later he will receive the second series of 10 reports (e.g., of graphologist no. 2); all in all he will repeat the same procedure 6 times. A rater should rate each of the 6 tasks independently of each other and independently of the other raters' products.

The 10 subjects will be asked to serve as raters and to perform the same task (as the raters), but instead of matching reports with "subjects," they will try to rank-order the reports with themselves. The fact that the subject is forced to rank-order the reports and not just to rate his satisfaction with each one of them, protects the design from a potential "Barnum Effect."

Statistical Analysis

The basic unit for data analysis will be a 10 x 10 table, similar to that shown in Chapter 16. The numbers in the table will be the ranks given by the rates. Number "1" in a diagonal cell means correct identification of subject by his psychologist (rater), via the graphological (or psychodiagnostical) report. "2" is still a good approximation, etc. Each row represents the ranking of 10 reports carried out by the rater. It should be remembered that the reports, when presented to the raters, do not carry any identification signs.

Although this is **not** a representative sample of the general population, the main question in the proposed study is not directly concerned with people but with a technique and its efficiency. At this stage it will be sufficient to learn whether or not **good** graphologists can diagnose accurately **certain** people and whether or not they can do it better than good psychodiagnosticians. The researchers should ensure that the sample is not too homogenous (turning the ranking into a very difficult task) or too heterogenous (turning the ranking into a trivial task). But besides that, we do not see how the findings—whether they support graphology or not—can be attacked on the grounds of biased sampling.

18

RELIABILITY OF GRAPHOLOGY: A SURVEY OF THE LITERATURE

BARUCH NEVO

Summary

A N ATTEMPT is made to summarize the findings concerning the reliability of graphological indices. Three groups of indices (graphometric measures, graphoimpressionistic characteristics, graphodiagnostic scales) and two types of reliability (stability and interrater agreement) are described. Six "cells" are defined by these two facets, and the literature is categorized in accordance with these "cells" and systematically surveyed. It is concluded that the effort expended on studying that area till now is not sufficient and that whatever knowledge we have acquired so far is not enough. However, generally speaking, the reported level of reliability, especially for graphodiagnostic scales, is low and calls for improvement. Several methods which have a potential for increasing reliability are discussed.

Introduction

A basic principle of psychometrics states that the validity of a predictor has an upper boundary enforced by its reliability (Anastasi, 1982; Cronbach, 1984). In other words, a variable which cannot be reliably measured cannot be expected to correlate with external criteria and is therefore destined to be ineffective for practical purposes. In this chapter an attempt will be made to summarize the findings concerning the reliability of handwriting indices. Failure to prove that handwriting variables are, or can be, reliably assessed, must lead to the immediate and inevitable termination of the application of graphology in selection, placement and diagnosis. If, on the other hand, the level of reliability is satisfactory, then, and only then, empirical research of the validity issue may start.

253

Types of Graphological Indices

Surveying the literature, one can group the variables which were studied into three categories:

(a) Graphometric measures (e.g., letter size, letter shape, margin width, space between lines). These measures are based on exact measurements.

(b) Graphoimpressionistic characteristics (e.g., roundness, rhythms, decorativeness, pressure). These variables are rated somewhat subjectively.

(c) Graphodiagnostic scales (e.g., ego strength, emotional instability, stubbornness, need for order). Ratings of these variables are based on interpretation, which greatly depends on the graphologist's experience, the school of thought to which he belongs, and so on.

A fourth kind of product which can be extracted from a handwriting sample is a global personality description, drawn by the graphologist. Even though this kind of product is, in practical life, more popular among graphologists than types (a) and (b) above, the question of its reliability has not been investigated and therefore will not be reported here. Some comments will be made, however, later on.

Types of Reliability

Two major types of reliability are relevant to our case: stability and interrater agreement. Stability means consistency of measurements of handwriting samples produced on different occasions, with different writing instruments, different contents, etc. Interrater reliability means agreement between graphologists when dealing with the same scripts.

The product of these two facets — types of graphological indices and types of reliability — is a 3 x 2 table, whose six cells should be studied. In the following paragraphs, we shall summarize the findings regarding reliability, by utilizing this 3 x 2 scheme.

GRAPHOMETRIC MEASURES

Stability

Harvey (1934) asked 20 female students to copy a typed paragraph of medium length. Two months later, a similar paragraph was dictated to them under speed conditions. Sixteen graphometric indices were measured for every script. The median value of the sixteen correlations was 0.77.

Fischer (1964) employed a similar design but with a one week interval, achieving slightly higher correlations (median r = 0.84). A series of studies executed in the sixties, report on even higher coefficients of correlations (around 0.90) between two sets of graphometric measures, extracted from the same handwriting sample; this design is called split-half procedure. (Fischer, 1962; Timm, 1967; Prystav, 1969).

Kimball (1974) asked 80 school children from the sixth grade to copy a paragraph from a book twice, at an interval of five weeks. He then measured no less than 81 graphometric indices for every script. Now, Kimball defined a criterion for "change" — a difference of 10% between the absolute values of the two measurements. Out of 80 children, 78 received a "score" of 73 points or more, where each point represented one unchanged index.

In contrast to the particularistic approach, whereby every index is treated separately, Lockowandt & Keller (1975) employed the **global** approach. They collected handwriting samples from 120 children between the ages of 10-13. After a period of two years, they returned and took samples from the same children. They then asked six graphologists and ten laymen to identify and match the original pairs. On the average, both groups of raters had a success rate of more than 75%. The author of this chapter replicated this study several years later. Nevo asked 15 people to copy out one page from Genesis Chapter I. A week later, the same people were asked to copy out one page from Genesis Chapter II, but this time, they were asked to use a different writing instrument and to carry out their mission at a different time of day. Fifteen raters were then asked to match the pairs. For technical reasons, they had to rely on photocopies of the original scripts, a fact that made their task even more difficult. Eleven raters made 15 correct matches — 100%. Two raters had 13 correct matches. The other two raters achieved 11 correct matches.

Interrater Reliability

Birge (1954) measured five graphometric indices in 50 scripts. He then explained the procedure to his secretary and she repeated the measurements independently. The range of correlations for the five variables was 0.94-0.99.

Kimball (1974) gave 32 handwriting samples of sixth grade school children to two raters, who measured 81 graphometric indices. The average correlation between the two graphologists for the 81 variables was 0.73. Perron and de Gobineau (1957) gave two handwriting samples to six graphologists, and instructed them how to rate the scripts on a 12-point Epilepsy Scale. One point was counted for each specific graphometric sign appearing in the script. The raters worked independently, and the average interrater correlation was 0.90.

The author of this chapter gave 15 handwriting samples (copied from Genesis Chapter I) to two raters, who measured eleven graphometric variables. The range of the correlations was 0.85-0.99, with a median of 0.95.

It is interesting to note, however, that when a comparison of the absolute means of the two raters was made, significant differences were found for some of the variables! In other words, high correlation does not necessarily rule out the existence of significant differences in the base-rate of the measurement of each rater. Only after intensive training and a more detailed specification of the measuring operations did these differences disappear in a replication study.

GRAPHOIMPRESSIONISTIC CHARACTERISTICS

The empirical evidence in the following two "cells" is very scarce.

Stability

Prystav (1969) rated the writing pressure of 56 scripts on an ordinal scale of four categories. Six weeks later, he repeated the rating on another set of specimens, extracted from the original group of people. The correlation between the ratings was 0.90.

Writing pressure must be an easy characteristic to rate, because for other graphoimpressionistic variables, such as "lively-rigid," "curvy-straight," Prystav reported a range of correlations of 0.15-0.47, when the ratings were made on two parts of the same handwriting sample. Timm (in Lockowandt, 1976) employed a similar design and found an average value of $r = 0.73$. It is difficult to understand from the study reports, the reason for these large differences between the coefficients of reliabilities.

Interrater Reliability

Wallner (1961, 1962) asked five graphologists to rate 100 scripts on a 7 point scale of a complex graphoimpressionistic characteristic (Rhythmic flow — "ablaufrhythmus") and achieved an average interrater correlation of 0.59. Other characteristics produced similar results. Paul-Mengelberg (personal communication) successfully trained a team of raters who reached an interrater reliability range of 0.70 — 0.85 when rating graphoimpressionistic variables such as roundness, instability, aesthetics.

GRAPHODIAGNOSTIC SCALES

Stability

Our survey of the professional literature did not bring to light any published studies in this category.

Interrater Reliability

Galbraith and Wilson (1964) had 100 students copy a standard text of 85 words. Three graphologists rated the handwriting samples on five graphodiagnostic (personality) scales (i.e., attention to detail, dominance, self-awareness, perseverance, stubbornness). The median correlation across pairs of graphologists and across the five scales was 0.78.

Brandstatter (1969) asked two graphologists to rate 84 handwriting samples of girls aged 13-16, on 24 graphodiagnostic scales. The average correlation (across 24 scales) was 0.71.

Prystav (1971, a,b) gave 50 handwriting samples to ten graphologists and asked them to rate the scripts on 10 graphodiagnostic scales. Out of 450 possible inter-correlations, 335 were significantly higher than zero.

Vine (1974) asked 63 raters to rank six handwriting samples as to (a) extroversion (b) neuroticism. The raters were students who received special training for their task. The average Kendall coefficient for extroversion was 0.60 and for neuroticism, 0.31.

Hofsommer et al. (1965) asked three graphologists to rate leadership (on a 7 point scale) in 322 foremen, on the basis of their handwriting. The average inter-correlation among pairs of graphologists was 0.74. This figure dropped to 0.62 when clerical ability was evaluated (by the same graphologists) and even lower (to 0.39) when technical ability was the graphodiagnostic scale.

Wallner (1962) gave 89 handwriting samples to six graphologists, asking them to rate the writers on 12 scales (e.g., personal tempo, perceptual ability, emotional instability). Out of 180 inter-correlations, 167 were found to be significantly positive.

Flug (1981) asked three graphologists to rate 58 candidates for banking jobs, on several scales, relevant to their future positions in the bank. Handwritten curricula vitae were used as the basis for the rating. Each scale consisted of five points. The average inter-correlation between the pairs of rates on the general scale — "predicted future performance as a bank employee" — was 0.30.

In a study performed by Ramati (1981), six graphologists were asked to rate handwritten curricula vitae of 65 cadets in an officers' training course of the Israel Army, as to their chances of completing the course successfully. The average inter-correlation (among six graphologists) was 0.36. The corresponding coefficient for six laymen (who rated the same samples for the same criterion) was 0.15.

Rafaeli and Klimoski (1983), who studied the predictive validity of graphological ratings in the area of salesmanship, asked two graphologists to rate 32 scripts on nine personality scales (e.g., social confidence, sales drive, empathy). The range of the nine interrater correlations was 0.22 to 0.59, with an average of 0.41.

Bar-El (1984) gave ten handwriting samples (1-2 pages of an essay on a topic chosen by the writer) to eight graphologists. They were asked to rate each sample according to fourteen 9-point personality scales (e.g., dominance, tolerance, femininity). For each scale, the median inter-correlation (among the eight raters) was calculated. The range of the 14 medians was 0.33-0.64, with the "median of the medians" being 0.51. When the procedure was repeated with six laymen, the "median of the medians" was 0.18.

DISCUSSION

Returning to our 3 x 2 table, we can now see that in some cells, empirical evidence is lacking. Further research will certainly contribute to our knowledge in these "blank" areas. However, a general picture does emerge:

- The range for most of the reported reliabilities of graphometric measures is approximately 0.70-0.90.
- The reliability range for the majority of graphoimpressionistic characteristics is 0.40-0.80.
- The corresponding range for graphodiagnostic scales is 0.30-0.60.

Differences between the coefficients reported in the various studies should be attributed to differences between the specific variables under consideration, the type of training given to the raters prior to the actual rating, and to differences between the specific conditions under which the various experiments were carried out.

When compared with the reported reliability level of psychometric tests, the above-mentioned figures (especially those of graphodiagnostic scales) are low. It seems that graphology can gain so much from an "investment" in clearer definition and better standardization of graphological indices. However, when compared with personality questionnaires, and especially when compared with projective techniques, the reliability of graphology does not seem inferior. If we now approach the question of validity, it seems that the (low) reliability level cannot be the sole reason for zero-order validity coefficients — if and when such coefficients are found. The reliabilities reported in this summary are simply not **so** low. A possibility which has not been properly explored is the expected increase of reliability resulting from combining independent ratings of several raters. Such a procedure may indirectly influence (positively) the predictive validity of graphological indices. Another technique which should be considered is to increase the number of scripts (per writer) which are used as the basis for the graphological assessment.

As mentioned earlier, the level of concordance between total or global graphological reports of the same persons was never studied. Powers (1933), describes an experiment in which he gave the same handwriting sample to five graphologists, who wrote five reports, independently. On page 191, Powers compares these reports and concludes that they correspond quite well with each other. However, the way in which he made the comparison is not clear and his statistical techniques are not standard. Cantril and Rand (1935) report on "good agreement" between 34 (!) graphologists who were asked to classify six scripts into six given pure "personality types." But again, essential details regarding the methodology and statistics of their research are missing. The author of this chapter believes that the best way to assess concordance between, let us say, two graphologists, is to ask psychologists to match up two sets of graphological analyses based on the same **n** scripts, each one prepared by one of the graphologists. If the global personality descriptions are essentially the same, the psychologist must be able to match the pairs. Until now, no such study has been carried out. Once again, we see here a situation where lack of empirical evidence prevents us from drawing conclusions regarding an important topic.

Generally speaking, the recommendation arising from this chapter is that much more research is needed on the subject of reliability of graphology.

REFERENCES

Anastasi, A. (1982). *Psychological Testing* (5th ed.) New York: Macmillan.

Bar-El, N. (1984). *Interrelations among graphological judgments, psychological assessments and self-ratings of personality.* Unpublished master's thesis. Tel Aviv University.

Birge, W. R. (1954). An experimental inquiry into the measurable handwriting correlates of five personality traits. *Journal of Personality, 23,* 215-223.

Brandstatter, H. (1969). On diagnosing integration of personality from handwriting. *Psychologische Rondschen, 21,* 159-172.

Cantil, H. & Rand, H. A. (1935). An additional study of the determination of personal interests by psychological and graphological methods. *Character and Personality, 3,* 72-78.

Cronbach, L. (1984). *Essentials of psychological testing.* (4th ed.) New York: Harper and Row.

Fischer, G. (1962). *Die faktorielle Struktur der Handschrift.* Doctoral dissertation. Vienna University.

Fischer, G. (1964). Zur faktorielle Struktur der Handschrift. *Zeitschrift experimentelle angewissen Psychologie, 11,* 254-280.

Flug, A. (1981). *Reliability and validity of graphology in personnel selection.* Unpublished master's thesis. Hebrew University, Jerusalem.

Galbraith, D. & Wilson, D. (1964). Reliability of the graphoanalytic approach to handwriting analysis. *Perceptual and Motor Skills, 19,* 615-618.

Harvey, O. L. (1934). The measurement of handwriting considered as a form of expressive movement. *Character and Personality, 2,* 310-321.

Hofsommer, W., Holdsworth, R., & Seifert, T. (1965). Problems of reliability in graphology. *Psychologie und Praxis, 9,* 14-24.

Kimball, T. D. (1974). The systematic isolation and validation of personality determiners in the handwriting of schoolchildren. *Dissertation abstracts International, 34,* 6450-6451.

Lockowandt, O. (1976). The present status of the investigation of handwriting psychology as a diagnostic tool. *JSAS: Catalog of Selected Documents in Psychology, 6*(1), 4.

Lockowandt, O. & Keller, C. H. (1975). Beitrag zur Stabilität der Kinderhandschrift. *Psychologische Beiträge, 17,* 273-282.

Perron, R. & De Gobineau, H. (1957). Study on identification and diagnosis of epilepsy by means of handwriting analysis. *Travail Humain, 29,* 323-338.

Powers, E. (1933). Studies in Graphology. In G. W. Allport & P. E. Vernon (Eds.). *Studies in expressive movement* (Chap. 9-11). New York: Hafner Publishing Co.

Prystav, G. (1969). *Beitrag zur faktoren analytischen Validierung der Handschrift.* Doctoral dissertation. University of Freiburg.

Prystav, G. (1971). (a) Reliabilität graphometrischer schriftbeschrebung (Teil I: Merkmalsebene). *Zeitschrift für Menschenkunde, 35,* 70-94.

Prystav, G. (1971). (b) Reliabilität graphologischer Beurteilungen. (Teil II: Interpretationsebene). *Zeitschrift für Menschenkunde, 35,* 95-110.

Rafaeli, A. & Klimoski, R. (1983). Predicting sales success through handwriting analysis: an evaluation of the effects of training and handwriting sample content. *Journal of Applied Psychology. 68,* 212-217.

Ramati, T. (1981). *Reliability and validity of graphology as a tool for the selection of officers in the Israel Defense Forces.* Unpublished master's thesis. Tel Aviv University.

Timm, U. (1967). Graphometrie als psychologischer Test? *Psychologische Forschung, 30,* 307-356.

Vine, I. (1974). Stereotypes in the judgment of personality from handwriting. *British Journal of Social and Clinical Psychology, 13,* 61-64.

Wallner, T. (1961). (a) Bemerkungen zu W.H. Mullers Untersuchungen über die Objektivität von Anmutungsqualitäten in der Handschrift. *Psychologische Beiträge, 5,* 586-596.

Wallner, T. (1961). (b) Experimentelle Untersuchungen über die Reliabilität direkt metrisch messbarer Handschriftvariablen. *Zeitschrift für Menschenkunde, 25,* 49-78.

Wallner, T. (1961). (c) Reliabilitätsuntersuchungen an metrisch nicht messbaren Handschriftvariablen. *Zeitschrift für Menschenkunde, 25,* 1-14.

Wallner, T. (1962). Neue Ergebnisse experimenteller untersuchungen über die Reliabilität von Handschriftvariablen. *Zeitschrift für Menschenkunde, 26,* 257-269.

NOTES

(1) Many of the European references for this chapter were hard to obtain. The author would like to thank Prof. O. Lockowandt of Bielefeld University for granting access to his extensive library and for putting at the author's disposal his own important manuscript, "The Present Status of the Investigation of Handwriting Psychology as a Diagnostic Method." (Lockowandt, 1976.)

19

THE A PRIORI CASE AGAINST GRAPHOLOGY: METHODOLOGICAL AND CONCEPTUAL ISSUES

MAYA BAR-HILLEL and GERSHON BEN-SHAKHAR

Summary

BESIDES EMPIRICAL considerations, there are various methodological and theoretical arguments which strengthen or weaken the prospects of finding a consistent relationship between features of handwriting and personality traits. Although handwriting has many characteristics which make it an attractive candidate for serving as a means of personality assessment, a closer look casts serious doubt on the plausibility of inferring traits such as honesty, responsibility, loyalty, etc., from purely graphological analysis. There are two sources for such doubts. The first is specific to graphology — the absence of a theory to account for how a tie between personality traits such as honesty and graphological features might come about. The second refers more generally to any attempt at predicting behavior — the fact that it is often insufficiently consistent across situations. That being so, attempts to validate personality assessments empirically can hope for limited success at best, irrespective of which predictor is being used. In general, predictions, of human behavior are successful only to the extent that the behavior sample on which the prediction is based occurs under highly similar conditions to those in which the predicted behavior would occur. This is rarely the case with respect to handwriting. The a priori case for graphology being weak, strongly convincing empirical results are necessary to overrule it. To date, even weakly convincing results are hard to find.

Introduction

Motivation for Testing

From time immemorial, people have wondered about the true nature of their fellow men, and have looked for cues that would reveal that nature to them. On the simple level, we size people up on the basis of their appearance, voice, etc. At the other end of the scale lies the domain of **psychological testing.**

Psychological tests come in many shapes and colors. They can differ as to goal (e.g., achievement versus aptitude), scope (describing the entire person versus predicting only one trait), by elicitation method (e.g., projective techniques versus questionnaires), by evaluation method (e.g., holistic intuitive evaluation versus closed scoring manuals), etc. But their common denominator is the desire to uncover or discover an unobservable truth about another from more readily available and observable behavior samples.

It is hardly necessary to explain the motivation for such endeavors. On the personal level, knowledge about others has important implications for one's own behavior and decisions. In modern industrialized societies, the ability to diagnose and predict people's behavior and their enduring patterns of traits and characteristics, acquires immense economic and societal significance that transcends the personal level.[1] Selection and classification of people for people for allocation of resources and duties (e.g., jobs, educational opportunities, therapeutic interventions, etc.) can be made immeasurably more efficient — or more congenial and fair — if the abilities and qualities of the potential candidates can be assessed or predicted.

Prevalent methods of psychological testing typically require information which can be obtained at most within a few hours, and which is relatively easily accessible. Methods relying on information that can be assessed even without the knowledge or cooperation of the testee are even more desirable.

Two Domains of Psychological Testing

Psychological tests can be loosely divided into tests of ability and tests of personality. In ability testing, the prototype of which is the IQ test, the first systematic attempt of modern times, undertaken by the French educator, Alfred Binet, at the turn of the century, was successful. Binet's idea was simple: If you want to detect intellectual brightness or dullness, ask questions of the kind that you think bright people are more likely than dull people to answer correctly, and score people by their success with such questions. This basic idea still characterizes much of intelligence testing.

This success story is in marked contrast with the story of personality testing. Whereas validity coefficients for ability tests typically range around .4 to .6, personality tests seldom enjoy validities of over .2 to .3.[2] Yet the attempts to assess personality systematically have a history even longer than that of intelligence assessment. Some methods are encountered today only in tales of old, as in the biblical story of Gideon selecting warriors according to how they drank water from a flowing stream (Judges, Ch. 7, Verses 1-8). These stories may have no basis in fact, but the methods they describe highlight a truth that still holds today: anyone can, and many do, invent their own idiosyncratic personality test.

A small inventory that we drew shows an amazing variety both of established and of esoteric "tests," some of which seem to have little to recommend them beyond the fact that they obviously show individual differences among people. The tests are based on: time and place of birth (astrology and numerology), line patterns on the palm (palmistry), patterns of bumps on the skull (phrenology), body characteristics (somatotype theory), patterns in externally produced configurations of cards (Tarot readings), color preferences (Luscher color test), dreams, word associations, responses to representational or abstract visual stimuli (e.g., the Thematic Apperception Test), free-hand drawings (e.g., Draw-a-Person tests, etc.), patterns of individual differences in responses to ability tests (e.g., IQ tests), etc. To this list might be added common sensical cues such as biographical details, as well as style of dress, manner of speech, etc. Indeed, the limit to what can potentially be used as a guide to the inner self seems to be set largely by the limits of imagination — and audacity.[3]

Various kinds of rationale underlie personality tests. Some seem to be based on face validity — the judgment that test items really measure what they are supposed to. Typical here are, for example, the various pulp magazine questionnaires designed for self-diagnosis of psychological properties such as assertiveness, femininity, extroversion, etc.

Other tests are based on some notion of representativeness (Nisbett & Ross, 1980): the items may not be sampled directly from the content universe of interest, but they bear some kind of resemblance to it. Typically, the information gathered by these tests lends itself readily to description by adjectives suitable to or suggestive of personality description as well, and so when the test results show property X, it is taken as an indication that the subject has property X.

Other tests are simply based on the empirical observation that certain traits convey. Thus, if individuals that are independently known to differ on some dimension of interest (e.g., normal versus psychotic; extrovert versus introvert; career oriented versus family oriented; etc.) are found to respond in a systematically different manner to some questions or tasks, then the latter differences can be exploited for diagnostic purposes when the former are not known. Such, for example, is the rationale underlying the Minnesota Multiphasic Personality Inventory (MMPI), or the Strong Vocational Interest Blank. For example, "Masculinity-femininity measures traditionally have been constructed empirically so that on each item the response scored 'masculine' is the one that is endorsed by most males while the one scored 'feminine' is the one favored verbally by the majority of females" (Mischel, 1976, p. 141).

Naturally, tests can combine more than one rationale.

From a strictly scientific point of view, of course, the acid test for any proposed personality test is to put it to an empirical test. To be valid, it is not sufficient that a test be based on an appealing rationale. It has also actually to work.[4] It is extremely difficult to generate the kind of evidence that conclusively and rigorously demonstrates a test's validity. Decades of research have led to the conclusion that some of these difficulties are inherent in the construct being assessed by these tests—i.e., personality. This has led to skepticism about the very possibility of the naive kind of personality assessment that is based on the model of ability testing. The case of graphology can serve very nicely to demonstrate some of these issues and difficulties.

What Is Graphology?

Various Uses of Handwriting Analysis

Handwriting analysis is carried out for many purposes besides character assessment. In the forensic sciences it may be used to establish the identity of the writer, or the authenticity of the sample: in the medical sciences it may be used to diagnose drug effects (e.g., Hirsch, Jarvik & Abramson, 1956; Legge, Steinberg & Summerfield, 1964) or intoxication (e.g., Rabin & Blair, 1953); for the developmental sciences, writing provides a fascinating example of an acquired finely tuned motor skill; etc. The present paper, however, pertains solely to attempts to predict **behavior** or derive **personality descriptions** from such analysis, and we shall limit the term "graphology" (as contrasted with the more general term "handwriting analysis") to this specific endeavor. Our critique of this endeavor should not be taken as an indictment of other forms of handwriting analysis, any more than a validation of handwriting analysis for those purposes should be taken as evidence for its validity as a personality test.

Two Meanings of "Graphology" [5]

Personality assessment by graphology can be taken to refer both to the principle of the endeavor (i.e., the **potential** use of handwriting analysis for personality assessment), and to the actual field as defined by the manuals and practices of its adherents and experts. This distinction is important, since there is no single dominant theory or method of graphology, nor a central textbook. Hence, it is entirely possible, in principle, that one graphological theory be highly valid while another is not, or even that all existing graphological systems be invalid although the potential for a valid system is hidden in the features of handwriting. Our discussion will not be addressed to any specific graphological method, but rather will deal largely with issues relevant to the enterprise in its entirety. Nonetheless, the absence of a general consensus among graphologists is noteworthy, since it is one of the methodological concerns in this area. It reflects the state of the art, and has direct bearing on some of the issues which we shall consider. Thus, this chapter will combine a methodological critique of graphology as it is standardly practiced with an outline of the methodological concerns facing any graphological — or other — attempt at personality assessment.

Since graphology can, in principle, proceed via the extraction of any kind of information from any kind of handwritten text, it is instructive to list those aspects of graphology that characterize most prevalent methods, so that we shall have something concrete to examine.

Input

In general, graphologists prefer handwritten samples that were not generated specifically for the purpose of being analyzed, and are spontaneous and expressive rather than the result of copying some text or of writing down from memory some standard text such as a poem or a pledge of allegiance. They prefer several samples produced at various times and under various circumstances to a single specimen, and a text of some length. They require a writing tool that is sensitive to factors such as pressure and speed, such as a pen, and caution against analyzing a photostatic handwritten sample. They are happier with a sample that includes the writer's signature. Advance knowledge of the writer's sex and age is deemed crucial and many require, in addition, information about the writer's nationality, and a brief medical and educational history. Handedness seems to be required too, though many manuals neglect to list it. Other information does not seem to be a firm prerequisite, but graphologists appreciate some background social and cultural facts about the writer, and in practice often know much more than that, including the reason that the graphological analysis is sought.

Some of these requirements are self-explanatory. Naturally, if pressure and speed are important graphological cues, one wants them maximally reflected in the handwritten sample; other cues might have different implications if they are standard in the writer's graphological community, or are idiosyncratic. However, the request for age and sex is rather odd, because rarely have we seen graphological manuals stratified according to these variables.[6]

Output

The typical graphological analysis addresses itself in a global fashion to all aspects of the writer's personality, and its result is usually presented in the form of a free-style characterization of the entire personality. The methods whereby graphologists work vary a great deal, and need not concern us here.

THE A PRIORI CASE FOR GRAPHOLOGY: FACE VALIDITY

On the face of it, handwriting analysis looks like an excellent candidate for personality assessment. Unlike palmistry, astrology, etc., the analysis relies on an actual sample of individual behavior. Indeed, the behavior is self-generated and expressive of its producer (Allport & Vernon, 1933).

Handwriting is also very rich in features and attributes which afford it the requisite scope for expressing the richness of personalities. Indeed, handwriting is as unique as personalities. Moreover, people can be more or less similar on various dimensions of handwriting, just as they can be more or less similar on various dimensions of personality. Like personality, handwriting exhibits both individual differences and shared structure.

Furthermore, handwriting is a stable characteristic of the individual (Fluckinger, Tripp & Weinberg, 1961) which nevertheless shows development over time. It more or less retains its recognizable identity across writing media — not only pen versus pencil, but also page versus blackboard and even, to a lesser extent, mirror writing, writing with the non-dominant hand, etc. Since these employ totally different muscles, it has lead to some calling handwriting "brainwriting" (e.g., Saudek, 1929). Similarly, chances in writing circumstances (e.g., taking a dictation, copying a text, writing a complex essay, jotting down a shopping list), and in moods of the writer, seldom hinder us from recognizing a familiar handwriting, even if it underwent some changes due to these changing circumstances. This allows handwriting to reflect persisting cross-situational components of personality as well as those that are more occasional and transient. From a pragmatic point of view, just about anyone who is likely to undergo a personality test can write. A sample of handwriting is obtainable cheaply and quickly, and does not even require the consent or cooperation of the contributor. And, if handwriting analysts are to be believed, attempts to alter one's handwriting in order to foil the analyst are seldom successful, because the skilled analyst can either detect the attempt at deceit, or even see through it (Osborn, 1929). Finally, graphology seems not to be limited in terms of what it can divulge about the inner person. It claims to be able to detect attributes for which no other tests exist — most notably, honesty. Indeed, handwriting allegedly divulges the whole personality.

REEXAMINING THE A PRIORI CASE FOR GRAPHOLOGY

The previous section highlighted various factors that argue, on a priori grounds, for the suitability of handwriting as a basis for personality assessment. There are, however, serious flaws in the a priori case for graphology. In this section we wish to point them out, and question both graphology's claim that handwriting potentially reveals the writer's personality, and graphologists' claim that state-of-the-art graphology has already figured out the key to the correspondence between personality features and those of handwriting. Some of the points we shall raise are based on circumstantial evidence. They are offered, however, not as proof of the invalidity of graphology, but just to emphasize that its apparent a priori advantages are no substitute for an empirical validation.

i. How plausible is the connection between personality and handwriting? With respect to some traits, a connection is quite plausible. For example, sloppy handwriting suggests a sloppy writer; stylized calligraphy indicates some artistic flair; bold, energetic script conjures an image of a bold, energetic personality; etc. To the extent that these inferences are valid, they are relatively easy to explain. Writing sloppily is an actual behavioral instance of sloppiness, artistic flair may well mean, among other things, an inclination to adopt a stylized handwriting, and a high level of energy would naturally find expression in one's motor movements, writing included. Such inferences are commonsensical and would seem to require no particular expertise.

We hasten to clarify that we are not asserting that any such connections actually exist, merely that we would not be arguing the case against graphology if its claims were restricted to the assertion of such connections. But graphology claims to be able to derive from handwriting much more — traits such as honesty, insight, leadership, vulnerability, responsibility, warmth, analytical capacity, musicality, sadistic inclinations, promiscuity, loyalty, etc. What reason is there to believe that traits such as these find any kind of expression in any graphological features? With respect to some, there is even no reason to believe that they are expressed in any kind of motor movement — and features of the body movement are only loosely correlated with writing movements, if at all (Allport & Vernon, 1933). Indeed, if a correspondence were to be empirically found between graphological features and such traits, it would be a major theoretical challenge to account for it. Other correspondences posited by some graphologists would, if they actually existed, be nothing short of miraculous. For examples: Sadism is expressed by sharply pointed end strokes (Friedenhain, 1959); suicidal tendencies are expressed by a signature and stroke that turns back upon the capital initial, crossing over it (Singer, 1969); the angular writer can be expected to be "firm, strong-minded, hard, uncompromising, tense, and tending to lack in ability to 'feel' " (Paterson, 1976); pregnancy can be detected from the way a woman writes letters with "bellies," such as the Hebrew Gimel (Koren, 1983); etc.

To be sure, science often makes use of signs whose relationship to what they indicate is far from intuitively obvious: spectograms, carbon dating, etc. But these relationships are anchored in theory and sustained by evidence, rather than being based exclusively on common association or representation (see Nisbett & Ross, 1980, on folk medicines). None of the examples above was supported by research.

ii. Are there enough constraints in graphological analysis? The very richness of handwriting can be its downfall, especially if one compounds it by analyzing several different samples from the writer. Unless the graphologist makes firm commitments to the nature of the correspondence between handwriting and personality, one can find ad hoc corroboration for any claim. Moreover, when adopting an empiricist approach, one can then always find some variable on which some difference between two distinct populations (as defined by some trait) is significant.

iii. How robust is the connection between personality and handwriting features? Graphologists' insistence on one particular writing instrument to the exclusion of others, on several writing samples taken at different times rather than just one, and on original texts rather than copied texts or photostats, is curious in the light of claims of relative constancy, especially since the a priori intuitions supporting graphology which were listed above operate on a much wider range of texts than those graphologists find acceptable. It may well be the case that some handwriting samples reflect personality better than others, but the insistence on particular kinds of handwriting samples is not supported by any account of why personality factors would express themselves in one and not in another, or by empirical demonstrations that these differences really do make a difference. As matters stand presently, it appears that from a graphological viewpoint, handwriting is actually extremely sensitive to extraneous influences that have nothing to do with personality.

iv. Is there consensus among graphologists? A survey of expository books on graphology show a great deal of idiosyncracy and divergence. For example, the "modern" trend seems to be an increased reliance on global, holistic features of the handwriting, but many still use something akin to a "dictionary" of signs with fixed meanings. The absence of reliability between graphologists sets severe limitations on the validity coefficients that can be obtained. None of the proposed methods are based on serious research. Clearly, it is not sufficient to establish the plausibility of some connections between handwriting and personality; the specific details of the nature of this connection must be worked out.

"Mission Impossible": Why All Personality Tests Have Low Validities

In the previous section, we focused critically on some of the factors that seem to favor graphology, on a priori grounds, as compared to other popular methods of personality prediction, giving it some "scientific" plausibility. In the present section, we wish to focus on some of the factors that impede **any** personality test from having high predictive accuracy. These have nothing to do with the specific nature of the graphological enterprise, but they do apply to graphology as an instance of a general class. If the previous sections focussed on the suitability of handwriting as a **means** for personality assessment, the present section focusses on the **end** towards which personality tests are reared, namely the prediction of behavior, pointing out the obstacles to this goal.

Traits Versus Situations

Personality traits are not directly observable. Rather, they are constructs inferred from behavior. One of their chief functions is to serve as a way of organizing and systematizing an individual's various behaviors in a manner that accounts for differences among people and enables prediction within people. Although most psychological theories — including naive ones (i.e., those of lay people) — assume that people behave more or less consistently over situations and time, a vast amount of empirical research has shown that there is less consistency in behavior than these theories would lead us to expect (e.g., Mischel, 1976). Since "behavior is **situation-specific** — [i.e.,] more dependent on the nature of the specific situation in which it occurs than on enduring traits or response tendencies in the person . . . [then] it is not very useful to characterize people in broad trait terms ('impulsive,' 'dependent,' and so on) because individuals show variability and discrimination in their behavior. Whether a person acts 'impulsively' depends to a great extent on the particular conditions she or he confronts" (Hilgard, Atkinson & Atkinson, 1983, p.413). In other words, it is not possible to predict with much accuracy how a person would behave in a new situation from knowing how the person has behaved previously. Indeed, "it has been found that normal people tend to show considerable variability in their behavior even across seemingly similar conditions" (Mischel, 1976, p.159). The fact that people tend to overattribute the causes of others' behavior to their dispositions and underattribute them to situational forces was labelled **the fundamental attribution error** by Ross (1977; 1978).

It follows from the above that if we wish to predict how people will behave in a certain situation, it is helpful to know how they have previously behaved **in the same sort of situation.** This is the approach taken today by assessment centers. This approach brings candidates for some position or job to a center where their performance is intensively and individually watched under conditions which attempt to simulate those under which they will actually be operating in the position or job. Although this prediction method is considerably more costly and time-consuming than standard personality tests, it reflects the growing realization that shortcuts simply fail to do the job. Whether or not a paper and pencil questionnaire — or a face-to-face interview — or analysis of projective tests opens a window to the real underlying personality, revealing the real inner-self, it does not allow the prediction of actual behavior — which, ultimately, is the real variable of interest — with anything approaching satisfactory accuracy.

In a sense, graphological analysis is a move in exactly the opposite direction from the principle guiding assessment centers. It is an attempt to infer from how people behave in a single context — and one which is not a prototypical behavioral context — what kind of people they really are. It relies on a supreme article of faith that the characteristics of such behavior, as they are expressed in handwriting features, are indicative of the personality as a whole, and therefore of the entire range of an individual's behavior. It is a holographic notion of personality, and flies in the face of much of the evidence in the field.

The reasons why cross-situational behavioral consistency is so low have been discussed at length elsewhere (e.g., Mischel, 1976; Nisbett & Ross, 1980). Here we shall briefly mention a few.

First, behaviors and personality traits do not correspond one-to-one. Indeed, the same trait can cause a whole range of different behaviors and even opposing ones (e.g., some shy people when in a party shrink from social contact, withdrawing quietly, while others might drink a lot to overcome shyness, becoming loud and boisterous). And many different traits, even contrasting ones, can result in the same behavior (e.g., some of those who are loud and boisterous in a party are uninhibited extroverts, while others are timid introverts covering up and over-compensating). Second, two different people, even when put in the same situation extensionally and even if they (are assumed to) possess the same trait, may behave differently, if the situation assumes a different subjective or phenomological meaning for them. Third, some traits are applicable to a person without there even being much of an expectation of cross-situational consistency. For example, it is sufficient that a person be occasionally dishonest, or occasionally original, to deserve the trait name (Tversky, 1985). Fourth, traits may designate latent dispositions that are not realized in behavior because of lack of opportunity, incentive, etc. Thus, "inability to withstand temptation" would only manifest itself in the presence of temptation of sufficient magnitude.

Reasons such as this make it difficult to infer from traits what a person's behavior would be like, even assuming that the traits are correctly diagnosed and applied. The person reading a graphological character analysis however, has a distinct sense that an integrated, whole personality has been put together, and that he now actually knows the person described. Moreover, it might give one a sense of being able to account for and explain observed behaviors. At the same time, however, it is of little help in **predicting** behavior.

This may explain the reluctance of many graphologists to have their work evaluated against specific behavioral or other observable criteria. Most graphologists, for example, decline to predict the sex of the writer from the handwriting, insisting that handwriting only reveals psychological, rather than biological, gender (e.g., Crépieux-Jamin, 1926). While common sense would agree that some women are masculine and some men are effeminate, it would be somewhat perverse to argue against the presumption that most women must be feminine and most men masculine. That would seem to render the terms rather empty of empirical content (recall the quote from Mischel, 1976, which we quoted above). Furthermore, even lay people can diagnose a writer's sex from handwriting correctly about 70% of the time (e.g., Goodenough, 1945), whereas the diagnosis of "dominance" versus "non-dominance" (often taken to be the equivalent of masculinity-femininity) is no better than chance (e.g., Eisenberg, 1938; Middleton, 1939). It would therefore seem reasonable to expect graphologists to be willing—and able—to predict a writer's sex from handwriting. That they refuse to do so reflects, under a charitable interpretation, their preference for predicting deep-lying unobservables to their observable correlates and perhaps even a disavowal of the relevance of behavioral criteria to the evaluation of their assessments.

WHY DOES GRAPHOLOGY APPEAR TO WORK?

The popular appeal of graphology rests on two bases. One is its face validity, or the a priori factors favoring it. The other is the fact that people who have had some experience with graphological analysis are usually positively impressed. In other words, graphology "works." This is called **personal validation** and is, subjectively, an extremely powerful evidential source. Unfortunately, a sense of personal validation is rather easy to impart, and by means that have little if anything to do with true validity. Indeed, many of these means are no more than cheap gimmicks. Hyman (1977) lists some of these tricks and methods. Prior to becoming a cognitive psychologist, Hyman himself enjoyed a brief career as a cold reader (i.e., a character reader who has little if any advance information about the client prior to the actual reading). This puts him in a position to combine his personal experience and familiarity with the tricks of the trade with insights anchored in psychological research.

"The Barnum Effect"

One powerful way to make strangers believe that you know all about them is to give them a charcter reading composed of certain statements that — though vague, contradictory, or universally true — are considered by just about all people to be uniquely descriptive of themselves. Indeed, in one study (Forer, 1949), people who thought that a certain personality sketch was written specially for them by a psychologist on the basis of a personality test gave the sketch a rating of over 4 on a 5-point scale ranging from 1 (poor fit), to 5 (perfect fit). In fact, the sketch given all of them was the same standard and uniform one. This effect has since been replicated in scores of classrooms in many countries and over many years, including by one of the present authors, who does it routinely in Introductory Psychology classes with much the same results (see also Hyman, 1977; Snyder and Shenkel, 1975).

Snyder did a series of studies which uncovered some of the factors that enhance this effect (Snyder, 1974; Snyder and Shenkel, 1975). An important factor is that the client be prepared in advance to believe that the reading is done uniquely for him or her, using a method of some repute, or one in the validity of which the client is a priori willing to believe. Hyman (1977) developed a recipe for the ideal stock spiel. It consisted of a combination of "about 75% desirable items, but ones which were seen as specific, and about 25% undesirable items, but ones which were seen as general. The undesirable items had the apparent effect of making the spiel plausible" (p.31). Many however (e.g., Freud, 1933), have noted that telling the client what he or she wants to hear is very effective, even without adding the subtle touch of not being totally

complimentary. Flattery, it has often been observed, will get you every-
where. When clients voluntarily solicit the opinion of a character reader,
some of the important conditions are automatically met. (The "Barnum
effect" takes it name from a quote from P.T. Barnum of Barnum and
Bailey's Circus fame, that "there's a sucker born every minute.")

"Cold Reading"

The stock spiel, effective as it is, can be improved upon if the reader
has an opportunity to interact with the client and is sufficiently sensitive
and observant. It is then possible to give a reading which not only
sounds uniquely descriptive of the client, but actually is, since it incorporates specific elements picked up before or during the reading. One
effective method is to begin with vague generalities and let the client's
reactions direct you to truth. Typically, the naive client will not only
steer you in the right direction, but will be actively engaged in interpreting whatever the reader is saying in a manner that would make it meaningful and sensible in terms of the client's personal history and concerns.

Graphological Character Readings

Hyman does not list graphology in his paper, but it is easy to see
how his tips can be readily applied by the graphologists who in addition, enjoy other advantages that enhance personal validation and that
do not typically accrue to cold readers. First, they often have "hot" —
namely, truly relevant and diagnostic — information prior to their
character reading, for example, when a graphologist is asked by some
firm to assess the suitability of candidates for potential employment on
the basis of handwritten autobiographical sketches submitted by the
candidates. Such sketches can lead to predictions of modest validity
simply by virture of the bio-data they contain, as well as other non-
graphological attributes of the text (see e.g., Ben-Shakhar, Bar-Hillel
& Flug, 1985). Indeed, an autobiographical sketch is the typical
handwritten sample used in these circumstances. The client may well
receive a sense of personal validation — from output that has little, if
anything, to do with graphological analysis, though that is what it pur-
ports to be.

Second, large scale clients of graphologists, such as firms and organizations, are seldom in a position to evaluate the reading given by the
graphologists against the truth. In other words, a criterion may be com-

pletely unavailable, for many reasons: some candidates are simply rejected at the graphologist's recommendations, other predictions have no clear observable correlates, etc. Even here, however, clients can get a sense of personal validation simply because a proficient graphologist can give a reading that simply sounds good. The character sketch may be rich or credible or familiar enough that it checks not with any specific piece of reality but simply with one's notion of what people are like.

Why Does Personal Validation Work?

Graphology, we have argued, appears to work because personal validation is mistakenly substituted for empirical validation, although it is an illusory and fallacious validity measure. Why, however, does personal validation work? Hyman argues persuasively that the astute cold reader goes beyond reliance on people's gullibility or suggestibility. On the contrary, the cold reader enlists their active intelligence as problem solvers and as natural inference makers to assist him. A "reading succeeds just because it calls upon the normal processes of comprehension that we ordinarily bring to bear in making sense out of any form of communication. The raw information in a communication is rarely, if ever, sufficient in itself for comprehension. A shared context and background is assumed. Much has to be filled in by inference. The good reader, like anyone who manipulates our perceptions, is merely exploiting the normal processes by which we make sense out of the disorderly array of inputs that constantly bombard us" (Hyman, 1977, p.33). It is precisely when someone deliberately tries to distort our perceptions and inferences, that the need to distrust naive intuition and arm oneself with proper methodological safeguards becomes essential. The validity of graphology cannot be left to the judgment of uninformed and undisciplined intuition since, unfortunately, the field has been infiltrated by malicious manipulators, as well as by those who are as much victims of the fallacy of personal validation as their clients. Stripped of the veneer of personal validation and of naive a priori considerations, graphology cannot at present claim the status of a scientifically based method of personality assessment. Happily for its proponents, however, this status is not inherent, but can be acquired by merit. Science need not, should not and cannot, prove the impossibility of the graphological enterprise. It is graphology that needs to establish its feasibility and status as a scientific enterprise.

REFERENCES

Allport, G. W. & Vernon, P. E. (1933). *Studies in expressive movement.* New York: The Macmillan Company.

Ben-Shakhar, G., Bar-Hillel, M. & Flug, A. (in press). A validation study of graphological evaluation in personnel selection. In B. Nevo (ed.) *Scientific aspects of graphology: A handbook.*

Crépieux-Jamin, J. (1926). *The psychology of the movements of handwriting.* (translated and arranged by L. K. Given-Wilson). London: Routledge.

Eisenberg, P. (1938). Judging expressive movement: I. Judgments of sex and dominance feelings from handwriting samples of dominant and non-dominant men and women. *Journal of Applied Psychology, 22,* 480-486.

Fluckiger, F. A., Tripp, C. A. & Weinberg, G. H. (1961). A review of experimental research in graphology, 1933-1960. *Perceptual and Motor Skills, 12,* 67-90.

Forer, B. R. (1949). The fallacy of personal validation: A classroom demonstration of gullibility. *Journal of Abnormal and Social Psychology, 44,* 118-123.

Freud, S. (1933). *New introductory lectures on psychoanalysis.* New York: W. W. Norton.

Friedenhain, (1959). F. *Write and reveal.*

Goodenough, F. L. (1945). Sex differences in judging the sex of handwriting. *Journal of Social Psychology, 22,* 61-68.

Hilgard, E., Atkinson, R. & Atkinson, R. (1983). *Introduction to psychology* (8th edition). New York: Harcourt, Brace & Jovanovitch.

Hirsch, M. W., Jarvik, M. E. & Abramson, H. A. (1956). Effects of LSD-25 and six related drugs on handwriting. *Journal of Psychology, 41,* 11-22.

Hyman, R. (1977). "Cold reading": How to convince strangers that you know all about them. *The Zetetic,* 18-37.

Koren, A. (1983). *Graphology.* Tel Aviv: Massada. (in Hebrew).

Legge, D., Steinberg, H. & Summerfield, A. (1964). Simple measures of handwriting as indices of drug effects. *Perceptual and Motor Skills, 18,* 549-558.

Middleton, W. C. (1939). The ability of untrained subjects to judge dominance from handwriting samples. *Psychological Record, 3,* 227-238.

Mischel, W. (1976). *Introduction to personality.* New York: Holt, Rinehart and Winston.

Nisbett, R. E. & Ross, L. (1980). *Human inference: Strategies and shortcomings of social judgment.* Englewood Cliffs, N.J.: Prentice Hall.

Osborn, A. S. (1929). *Questioned documents.* (2nd edition). Albany: Boyd Printing Company.

Patterson, J. (1976). *Interpreting handwriting.* New York: David McKay Company.

Rabin, A. & Blair, H. (1953). The effects of alcohol on handwriting. *Journal of Clinical Psychology, 9,* 284-287.

Ross, L. (1977). The intuitive psychologist and his shortcomings: Distortions in the attribution process. In L. Berkowitz (ed.) *Advances in experimental social psychology, 10,* New York: Academic Press.

Ross, L. (1978). Some afterthoughts on the intuitive psychologist. In L. Berkowitz (ed.) *Cognitive theories in social psychology.* New York: Academic Presss.

Saudek, R. (1929). *Experiments with handwiting.* New York: Morrow.

Schmidt, F. L., Hunter, J. E., McKenzie, R. C. & Muldrow, T. W. (1979). Impact of valid selection procedure on work-force productivity. *Journal of Applied Psychology, 64,* 609-626.

Singer, E. (1969). *The graphologist's alphabet.* London: Duckworth & Co.

Snyder, C. R. (1974). Why horoscopes are true: The effects of specificity on acceptance of astrological interpretations. *Journal of Clinical Psychology, 30,* 577-580.

Snyder, C. R. & Shenkel, R. J. (1975). The P.T. Barnum effect. *Psychology Today, 8* (3), 52-54.

Tversky, A. (1985). Personality traits: Scope and attribution. (unpublished manuscript).

NOTES

1. For example, Schmidt, Hunter, McKenzie & Muldrow (1979) estimated the economic value of valid procedures for selecting computer programmers at hundred of millions of dollars per year, based on a job life expectancy of ten years and present market conditions. There is every reason to believe that the figures may be as high with respect to other occupations as well.

2. It is more appropriate to evaluate correlations in terms of percentage of explained variance, obtained by squaring the correlation. Hence, the former is four times as good as the latter, not two.

3. Shortly after Ronald Reagan became president of the USA, a journalist asked him why he always kept a jar of multi-colored jelly beans on his desk. The president answered that he used it as a kind of personality test on some of his visitors. He would offer them some of the candy, and observe their response. Some took a handful, some took a single candy, and some took none at all; some chose only beans of one color, or avoided those of one color, while others were less discriminating; some chewed the candies slowly, others sucked on them; etc.

4. There are also difficulties inherent in tests that work empirically without any theoretical understanding of how it is that they do, but this is usually a temporary state of affairs, and we shall not be concerned with it here.

5. The term "graphology" should be kept distinct from the term "graphoanalysis," which is the trademarked name of a particular American school of graphology.

6. It could also serve merely to guide — or ensure — the graphologist in making judgments that are age and sex appropriate, or to protect the graphologist from the need to predict so readily verifiable — or refutable — a variable.

20

SOME INFORMAL EXPLORATIONS AND RUMINATIONS ABOUT GRAPHOLOGY

LEWIS R. GOLDBERG

Summary

THIS CHAPTER poses some questions regarding existing procedures and proposes some new ideas for research design in graphology. Several "classical" topics are discussed:

- Cross-Cultural comparisons of handwritings.
- Identification of sex of the writer through his/her handwriting.
- Intra-graphologist reliability.
- Correspondence between graphological and psychological ratings of the same people.

Some empirical evidence regarding these issues is provided, and methodological considerations are presented.

An experimental setup for cooperation between a graphologist and a researcher is described.

THE IDENTIFICATION OF NATIONALITY

It all began in a bar, in a small city in the very north of Holland, a country in which I was spending a sabbatical year as a Fulbright Professor. I had traveled to each of the six major universities in the Netherlands during the course of the year and had met there the major Dutch psychologists, one of whom was drinking with me in this dark, crowded bar near the University of Groningen. We were drinking Dutch gin, called Genever. It is very strong, very fragrant, and its effects are quite wonderful.

In the early hours of the morning, the psychologist made me a wager: "I bet I can tell the difference between an American and a European just

from their handwriting." For ten years my colleagues and I had been studying judgment and decision making — using the forecasts and predictions of
clinical psychologists, physicians, personnel directors and stock market
analysts (Goldberg, 1968). As a result, I was convinced that no one could
always predict anything, much less whether a person was a European or
an American from his or her handwriting. So I called his bet.

When the bet was finalized, however, it was that he could differentiate between the handwriting of Americans and Europeans **at a statistically significant level.** Nonetheless, I set out to prove he was wrong. I
picked a short Latin phrase, Latin being a base language for both Dutch
and English, which I typed on a 3 x 5 inch card. I then asked persons in
the Netherlands — a motley sample of ages, sexes, sizes, and hair colors
(or lack thereof) — to copy that phrase onto another card, first as quickly
as they could, and then on a second card at their natural writing speed.
Thus, for each Dutch subject I had a fast and regular handwriting specimen of a Latin phrase.

Upon my return to Oregon, I did the same thing again, with the
same card, under the same conditions. I tried to match, as well as I
could, the characteristics of the people I had sampled in the Netherlands
with the ones in the United States. I now had 100 handwriting samples,
half from Europeans and half from Americans. Roughly half were from
males and half from females; and half were written quickly and half were
written slowly.

At this point I decided to see whether Americans could make this sort
of differentiation with any accuracy. To this end, I enveigled about
twenty of my colleagues into sorting the cards into two piles, those they
thought were produced by Americans and those they thought were produced by Europeans. What were my expectations? I guessed that the
range of correct predictions would be between 40 and 60% with a mean
around 50% — a nice chance distribution. But the actual distribution
didn't look like that at all. The person who did the worst got 56% correct. The person who did the best got 90% correct. And I realized with a
sickening thud that I was out a good bottle of Scotch. For if the average
American schlunk can do this task with a median accuracy of 70%, then
certainly a brilliant Dutch psychologist, one who thinks he has special
expertise in doing this, is going to do better than 50% at a statistically
significant level. So I kissed the bottle of Scotch good-bye and decided to
have some fun.

For each of the 100 handwriting specimens — 50 from Americans and
50 from my Dutch sample — I found the percentage of people who correctly identified it. Table I presents the results of this stage. Then, I selected the hardest 25 American ones and the hardest 25 European ones,

and sent this sample of 50 cards to my friend. To my surprise, he got 77% correct, which is significantly different from 50%. While he would have received his bottle of Scotch no matter how well he did, he won his bet even on the tough ones. That got me interested in the study of handwriting as a discipline.

TABLE I

Differentiation between Dutch and American Handwriting:

Distribution of the Accuracy Proportions for the 100 Handwriting

Samples (N = 20 Judges)

Proportion of Judges Identifying the Sample Correctly	Dutch Samples	American Samples	Combined Samples
1.00	3	1	4
.95	2	7	9
.90	5	4	9
.85	5	6	11
.80	3	3	6
.75	7	8 *	15 *
.70	6 *	1	7
.65	5	6	11
.60	4	3	7
.55	2	2	4
.50	0	3	3
.45	1	2	3
.40	2	1	3
.35	0	0	0
.30	3	2	5
.25	2	0	2
.20	0	1	1
	--	--	---
Total	50	50	100

* Median Handwriting Sample

THE IDENTIFICATION OF SEX

Handwriting analysis has never been all that popular in the U.S. It has, however, been extremely popular in Europe, especially in Germany. There are many handwriting schools, most of which have theories about the relationship between handwriting and personality. Indeed, some persons have argued that our handwriting not only reveals our personalities but also that it can inform us about past and future events in our lives.

The literature, however, reveals one strange anomaly. As background, note that those who want to do scientific research on handwriting are stuck with the problem of finding characteristics of people against which they can validate the handwriting inferences — characteristics which are unambiguous, for which there clearly is no doubt. And, as you might guess, the single most popular criterion is whether the person producing the handwriting is a male or a female. Since this is a reasonably clear criterion, reports of two or three dozen studies have been published in English — and for all I know dozens more in other languages — in which either graphologists or others were asked to predict biological sex from handwriting specimens (e.g., Gesell, 1906; Downey, 1910; Kinder, 1926; Newhall, 1926; Broom, 1929; Young, 1931; Eisenberg, 1938, Goodenough, 1945).

The results of those studies are easy to summarize. In all studies in which the base-rate of males and females is half and half, so chance accuracy is 50%, judges range from about 2/3 to 3/4 correct. Virtually everybody does better than chance, but few do better than 80% correct. The average value over all studies is very close to that in my study of Dutch versus American handwriting, namely 70% correct — 20% more than one would get by chance, and 30% less than if one got them all correct.

Now there's something here that's important to think about. If you had to classify all the individual differences we observe around us in terms of their importance and impact on our lives, I doubt if you could think of an individual difference more potent than sex. That is, whether or not we assume great genetic differences between males and females, there is no question that at the phenotypic level, males and females look different and are treated differently. Indeed, there are a host of sex-linked attributes, some of which appear to be genetically determined, and many of which we assume to be the result of societal practices. So, if there's any individual difference that should be easy to predict, it ought to be biological sex. And if it turns out that you can only do that with 70% accuracy, then you already know something about the likely predictability of more difficult, more subtle, and less important kinds of individual differences.

Moreover, in those studies of the differentiation of the sexes by handwriting which have included non-graphologists as well as graphologists, there are typically no differences between the accuracy of the experts and that of the rest of us. That again ought to make us pause. Because if there is something to these graphological systems, those who use the system ought to be more accurate than the person in the street. In the cases of the studies of sex, they do not seem to be so.

COLLABORATING WITH A PROFESSIONAL GRAPHOLOGIST: STUDYING INTRA-RATER RELIABILITY AND VALIDITY

Fascinated by the literature on handwriting analysis, and fresh from a series of studies of clinical judgment and decision making of experts in a variety of professional fields (e.g., Goldberg, 1968), I set out to study the judgment of a professional graphologist. I picked a graphologist who had been in practice for a long time, and who claimed to have sold her services to stores to detect dishonest employees, to police and sheriff's departments, as well as to individuals who simply wanted to learn more about themselves. I had been at her house when she conducted a handwriting analysis of someone I knew very well, someone whom she had just met for the first time. While I was not struck by the accuracy of her predictions, I was amazed by their specificity. Unlike some "cold readers" (Hyman, 1977), she did not deal in generalities. She thought she could make very detailed descriptions of people's personalities.

I engaged her in the following collaboration. I proposed that we study her predictions to see what she could do best. Since it was unlikely that she could make every kind of judgment equally well, perhaps we could find out what she was able to do well and what she was able to do less well. She agreed. So began a three-month odyssey, during the course of which she came to our research institute three or four days a week, for which she was well paid. She was given her own office at the institute, with a tape recorder. It was a very comfortable setting, very relaxed and casual, yet professional in the sense that she could do her own thing.

To describe this study adequately, I have to go back a bit in time to outline an earlier study of mine which made this one possible. For years I'd been interested in improving teaching methods at the college level. But, what kind of teaching techniques work best for college students? After a number of studies (Goldberg, 1964, 1965), I had come to believe that there is no one method which works best for everybody, but rather that there is likely to be an interaction between characteristics of the learner and the best method of teaching him or her. And so, three colleagues and I engaged in one of the largest studies ever done of trait-by-treatment interactions in a college setting (Goldberg, 1972). We studied roughly 1,000 University of Oregon students, each of whom was taught by one of four different kinds of teaching methods. All of these students completed a very extensive battery of psychological tests, questionnaires and inventories. Since we wanted to measure achievement in the course in a variety of ways, we included on the final examination both an objective multiple-choice test and two open-ended essay questions. That is, every student wrote two essays under somewhat speeded conditions, and of course in their own handwriting.

Now those handwriting samples were absolutely perfect for a study of graphology, because they were **not** written under conditions where the person knew that his or her personality was going to be analyzed. They were written during a final examination. They are probably as natural handwriting samples as one can find. There is only one problem with them. They contain content, and that content could be used to make inferences about the author's personality. (Parenthetically, to control for that content, we typed the essays and had people make judgments from the typed essays, judgments which we then compared with those made from the handwriting samples. Since this control study is not important in this context, no more will be said of it here.) However, our professional graphologist said that she never read the essays for content. So maybe that was not such a serious problem.

To select a task for the graphologist, we spent a day together examining each of the tests, inventories and questionnaires that were available. For each kind of data, I asked her to estimate how well she thought she could predict it. Some things she thought she could predict well, whereas others she thought she couldn't. For example, she was not willing to predict the sex of the subject from his or her handwriting. But, she said, she could predict quite accurately how subjects would describe themselves. And so she made her predictions only on the basis of those data that she thought she could predict accurately.

Actually, she did two tasks. The first is one she does every day. She would get a handwriting sample; stapled over the name of the person who wrote the essay was a code number (e.g., 001-M, [or F], for male [or female]). Her first task was to dictate into the tape recorder everything that she could say about the person who produced this handwriting. It was free and open-ended, with no restrictions whatsoever. (We asked her to do that because we wanted independent judges to rate the transcripts that she produced, to see how much agreement they would have with each other, as well as how much agreement they would have with the subjects' own assessment of themselves.)

Her second task, the most important, was to complete a questionnaire in which she was asked to predict as accurately as she could how the subjects had described themselves. Included in this questionnaire were 22 of the items from the Adjective Check List (ACL), 10 traits representing scales from the California Psychological Inventory (CPI) and 22 of the Basic Interests measured by the Strong Vocational Inventory Blank (SVIB). We engaged two non-graphologists to do the same job. We gave them the exact same handwriting specimens, and asked them to complete the same questionnaire. So, we obtained free descriptions from the expert, plus her actual predictions. And we had predictions from college students who said they knew nothing about handwriting analysis. It took the graphologist about one hour to analyze each handwriting sample; the college students less than half as long.

Now, psychologists are not only crabby and grumpy, but they are also shady. After the graphologist had completed her analyses of a dozen or so handwriting specimens, I began giving back to her the same samples again on a random basis, always correctly identified in terms of sex, but now with a new code number. So, handwriting specimen 007-M might come back to her on some subsequent occasion—like a month later—as handwriting specimen 039-M. For 21 of the essays, I collected her judgments on two occasions, thus enabling an analysis of intra-rater reliability.

After nearly a dozen of these test-retest protocols had been rerated by the graphologist, she came into my office, quite excited, and said: "I've seen this handwriting before." I replied, as calmly as I could, "Of course. I wanted to see how reliable you are, and therefore I have to give you from time to time the same specimens on a second occasion." And she said, "Oh, that's fine. I just didn't want you to think that you had fooled me, because I never forget a handwriting specimen."

Well, it's unreasonable to expect anyone to remember all the handwriting that they have seen, any more than it's reasonable to assume that one is going to remember all the faces that one has seen. So it's not surprising that she may have seen quite a number of retest specimens without realizing that they were the same. That's **not** what's important. What is important is her test-retest reliability. Without at least some reliability one cannot have validity. Reliability constrains validity; it provides an upper limit to accuracy. If one says on one occasion that a person is dominant and on another occasion that this person is submissive, regardless of whether the person is dominant or submissive, one is going to be right half the time and wrong half the time. So, if one is **completely** unreliable, one cannot have other than a validity coefficient of zero.

TABLE II

Reliability Analyses for Three Judges and for Male and Female Targets:

The Percentage of Consistent Responses on Retest vs. the Percentage

Expected by Chance

| | Expert Judge | | Non-Expert Judges | | | |
| | | | Judge J | | Judge M | |
	Males	Females	Males	Females	Males	Females
Obtained % Consistent	.67	.67	.67	.73	.71	.72
Chance % Consistent	.61	.59	.64	.64	.59	.60
Difference	.06	.08	.03	.09	.12	.12
Number Test-Retest Pairs	286	384	288	384	352	320

It turned out that, across all of her judgments on repeated occasions, she had stability coefficients near zero. That is, given the exact same handwriting specimen on the second occasion, she did **not** make the same predictions as she had done on the first occasion, in spite of the fact that she swore up-and-down that she would always make the same predictions from the same handwriting. And so, as a consequence of that unreliability, she had no validity. Table II summarizes the reliability data for the graphologist and the two non-graphologists, and Table III presents the mean validity coefficients for the three judges.

TABLE III

Validity Analyses for Three Judges and for Male (N=76) and Female (N=94) Targets: Mean Correlations between the Judges' Predictions and Each of Three Types of Criteria

	Expert Judges		Non-Expert Judges			
			Judge J		Judge M	
Criteria	Males	Females	Males	Females	Males	Females
22 A.C.L Items	.01	.00	.01	-.01	.08	.01
10 C.P.I. Scales	.03	.04	.03	-.01	-.01	.08
22 S.V.I.B. Scales	.01	.02	-.01	.00	.06	-.03

NOTE: The criteria included 22 items from the Adjective Check List (e.g. aggressive, contented, faultfinding, hurried, moody, precise, quiet, sarcastic), the traits measured by each of 10 scales from the California Psychological Inventory (e.g. dominant, sociable, responsible, self-controlled, tolerant, intelligent, flexible, feminine) and 22 interests measured by the Basic Interest scales of the Strong Vocational Interest Blank (e.g. adventure, art, mathematics, music, nature, sales, science, teaching, writing).

METHODOLOGICAL CONSIDERATIONS

Now that's only one expert and one must be careful about making inferences about all graphologists from so small a sample. But to the best of my knowledge, none of the graphological systems widely available in the United States and Europe has been scientifically validated. Which is not to say, by the way, that there may not be anything in one's handwriting. What I would take from the limited research, and from my own research with one graphologist, is that graphological predictions should be taken with many grains of salt. "Experts" are likely vastly to overrate their own abilities. The scientific evidence linking aspects of handwriting with personality characteristics is at the moment still in its infancy. The few links that exist are ones that **you** can see as easily as an expert. For instance, people who write with large, wide, sweeping letters probably differ on the average in at least some other ways from people who write with little, tiny, cramped letters. You can observe that; anybody can.

That is, although the link between handwriting and personality is probably very weak, it is not zilch. There is probably a low-magnitude relationship between our style of writing and such broad traits as introversion-extroversion. By "low" I mean that if we could accurately classify people as introverts and extroverts, and if we had half introverts and half extroverts in this sample, our predictions about them from their handwriting would probably be correct about 70% of the time or less. Not 50%, but not 100%. If I am right, one important question is: Why do so many people, both the experts who perform the art and the consumers of that "expertise," believe so strongly? I suspect that there are at least four reasons why we appear to be so gullible.

The first is a myth that every aspect of behavior is a sign, or clue, to everything else, if only we could decode it. Just as we think of our genetic code as written into every cell of our body, so we have this belief that each bit of our behavior can reveal our psychic code. That belief was given its most forceful expression by A. Conan Doyle in his Sherlock Holmes novels. Sherlock takes a very small and seemingly trivial bit of behavior, and then tells enormous amounts about the person from that small detail. Fascinating, but probably rubbish! Yet we believe it and it leads us to think that some handwriting system must be accurate.

Another myth: we think that because experts have seen thousands of cases, they have to be right. But it is not how many cases they have seen that's important; it is the nature of the feedback they get about the inferences that they make. How immediate is it? How easily can it be connected to the cues from which the inference was made? In the case of professional experts (be they psychiatrists, clinical psychologists, graphologists, astrologists, or whatever), feedback is often nonexistent; and when it does come, it comes at a time so far removed from the actual making of the inference that they can't use that information to improve their judgment processes.

Our gullibility comes also from another major myth, namely that called personal validation: "If it works for me, it must work equally well for others." The problem here is that what we **want** to work may actually **seem** to do so (just like the placebo effect in medicine) even when it doesn't. There have now been many dozens of studies that demonstrate that the information in a false "test report" (often the same report is given to all subjects) comes to be believed as highly personalistic and incredibly accurate by a large majority of the individuals exposed to it (e.g., Forer, 1949; Sundberg, 1955; Stagner, 1958; Ulrich, Stachnik & Stainton, 1963; Manning, 1968; O'Dell, 1972; Snyder, 1974, 1978; Layne & Ally, 1980; Lackey, 1981; Zaren & Bradley, 1982).

A final myth is one called illusory correlation. It has to do with judging the probability — the likelihood — of events, not on the basis of the actual experiences we have, but rather on the basis of our expectations about what that probability ought to be. If somebody says to us, in looking at projective test material, "I see eyes, big eyes, staring at me," we think to ourselves, "Ah, that person must be paranoid." Or someone says, "I seek buttocks," and we think, "He must be a homosexual." Indeed, even if we experimentally construct materials, as Chapman and Chapman (1967, 1969, 1971) have done, in which eyes are **not** associated with paranoid symptoms, and buttocks are **not** associated with homosexuality, people still "see" what they expect to see (Golding & Rorer, 1972). Such expectations lead us both to be gullible ourselves and to assume too much expertise among others.

Since this saga began in a bar, perhaps it is appropriate to end it there. For much of what I've said so lightly in tone has a sober underside to it. The past decade or two has brought vast changes to our intellectual landscape, stimulated in part by the fundamental work on judgmental biases of Tversky, Kahneman, and Fischoff. All of that work has now been summarized in a brilliant gem of a book by Nisbett and Ross (1980). So, if we must repair to a bar, let it be a clean, well-lighted place. That will permit us to read (or re-read) that book. And then to ponder its many implications for us all.

REFERENCES

Broom, M. E. (1929). Sex differences in handwriting. *Journal of Applied Psychology, 13,* 159-166.

Chapman, L. J. & Chapman, J. P. (1967). Genesis of popular but erroneous psycho-diagnostic observations. *Journal of Abnormal Psychology, 72,* 193-204.

Chapman, L. J. & Chapman, J. P. (1969). Illusory correlation as an obstacle to the use of valid psychodiagnostic signs. *Journal of Abnormal Psychology, 74,* 271-280.

Chapman, L. J. & Chapman, J. P. (1971). Associatively based illusory correlation as a source of psychodiagnostic folklore. In L. D. Goodstein & R. I. Lanyon (Eds.), *Readings in personality assessment,* 558-589. New York: Wiley.

Downey, J. E. (1910). Judgments on the sex of handwriting. *Psychological Review, 17,* 205-216.

Eisenberg, P. (1938). Judging expressive movement: I. Judgments of sex and dominance-feeling from handwriting samples of dominant and non-dominant men and women. *Journal of Applied Psychology, 22,* 480-486.

Forer, B. R. (1949). The fallacy of personal validation: A classroom demonstration of gullibility. *Journal of Abnormal and Social Psychology, 44,* 118-123.

Gesell, A. L. (1906). Accuracy in handwriting, as related to school intelligence and sex. *American Journal of Psychology, 17,* 394-405.

Goldberg, L. R. (1964). The effects of six teaching conditions on learning and satisfaction in a televised college course. *Psychology in the Schools, 1,* 366-375.

Goldberg, L. R. (1965). Grades as motivants. *Psychology in the Schools, 2,* 17-24.

Goldberg, L. R. (1968). Simple models or simple processes? Some research on clinical judgments. *American Psychologist, 23,* 483-496.

Goldberg, L. R. (1972). Student personality characteristics and optimal college learning conditions: An extensive search for trait-by-treatment interaction effects. *Instructional Science, 1,* 153-210.

Golding, S. L. & Rorer, L. G. (1972). Illusory correlation and subjective judgment. *Journal of Abnormal Psychology, 80,* 249-260.

Goodenough, F. L. (1945). Sex differences in judging the sex of handwriting. *Journal of Social Psychology, 22,* 61-68.

Hyman, R. (1977). "Cold reading:" How to convince strangers that you know all about them. *The Zetetic, 1,* 18-37.

Kinder, J. S. (1926). A new investigation of judgments on the sex of handwriting. *Journal of Educational Psychology, 17,* 341-344.

Lackey, D. P. (1981). A controlled test of perceived horoscope accuracy. *The Skeptical Inquirer, 6,* 29-31.

Layne, C. & Ally, G. (1980). How and why people accept personality feedback. *Journal of Personality Assessment, 44,* 541-546.

Manning, E. J. (1968). "Personal validation": Replication of Forer's study. *Psychological Reports, 23,* 181-182.

Newhall, S. M. (1926). Sex differences in handwriting. *Journal of Applied Psychology, 10,* 151-161.

Nisbett, R. & Ross, L. (1980). *Human inference: Strategies and shortcomings of social judgment.* Englewood Cliffs, NJ: Prentice-Hall.

O'Dell, J. W., (1972). P.T. Barnum explores the computer. *Journal of Consulting and Clinical Psychology, 38,* 270-273.

Snyder, C. R. (1974). Why horoscopes are true: The effects of specificity on acceptance of astrological interpretations. *Journal of Clinical Psychology, 30,* 577-580.

Snyder, C. R. (1978). The "illusion" of uniqueness. *Journal of Humanistic Psychology, 18,* 33-41.

Stagner, R. (1958). The gullibility of personnel managers. *Personnel Psychology, 11,* 347-352.

Sundberg, N. D. (1955). The acceptability of "fake" versus "bona fide" personality test interpretations. *Journal of Abnormal Psychology, 50,* 145-147.

Ulrich, R. E., Stachnik, T. J., & Stainton, N. R. (1963). Student acceptance of generalized personality interpretations. *Psychological Reports, 13,* 831-834.

Young, P. T. (1931). Sex differences in handwriting. *Journal of Applied Psychology, 15,* 486-498.

Zaren, A. S., & Bradley, L. A. (1982). Effects of diagnostician prestige and sex upon subjects' acceptance of genuine personality feedback. *Journal of Personality Assessment, 46,* 169-174.

21

USES OF GRAPHOLOGY IN PERSONNEL MANAGEMENT

ANAT RAFAELI

Summary

HANDWRITING ANALYSIS is being used as an aid for personnel management by an increasing number of organizations. Nevertheless there is a dearth of information about the merit of graphological assessments for personnel practices, or even of the issues that managers employing this technique ought to be aware of. The present chapter considers critical issues about employing inferences based on handwriting analysis in personnel administration.

A brief review of the very limited literature available on this specific application of graphology is presented. This is followed by an analysis of basic measurement questions, as well as ethical and legal questions about such use of the technique. Specifically, the questions of reliability and validity are addressed from the perspective of personnel assessments. The appropriate procedure for establishing the validity of personnel assessments is outlined and potential variables that may moderate the reliability or validity of graphological inferences are considered.

Introduction

The management of personnel repeatedly calls for assessment of individuals. New employees need to be selected, senior employees promoted, and poor performers fired. A variety of methods have been proposed to facilitate such decisions. But optimal tools for collecting information about applicants and employees are few and far between. Thus, novel ways of addressing old problems are always in demand. Handwriting analysis has recently been suggested as a potential aid for personnel management.

In Europe, 85% of all companies reportedly include graphology in their hiring procedures. American organizations are less likely to implement this technique for personnel selection, although handwriting is routinely employed for identification purposes (e.g., by banks). It has, however, been reported that more than 3,000 American firms currently retain handwriting analysts as personnel consultants (International Management, July, 1979).

The present chapter will discuss critical issues about the application of graphological judgments to administration. Following a brief review of the literature, the personnel management perspective on major measurement questions (i.e., reliability and validity of graphological inferences, and the effects of moderating variables on graphological judgments) will be reviewed. The ethical questions that accompany all personnel management techniques will then be discussed with respect to graphology. It is important to start, however, with a brief review of the (albeit limited) literature on the topic at hand — the use of graphology in personnel management.

Graphology offers several advantages to the personnel manager; the assessment procedure is quick; it does not actively involve the employee; graphology is usually less costly than a complex battery of psychological tests; and assessment materials (i.e., script samples) can be collected anytime, anywhere, by anyone.

Graphology offers inferences about a wide spectrum of individual attributes; Curr-Briggs, Kennett and Patterson (1971) for example, classify five categories of retrievable information::

a. temperament - nervousness, complacency, phlegmatism, depression, self-confidence, etc.
b. mental traits - intelligence, intuition, reasoning, memory, analytical ability, etc.
c. social traits - introversion, extroversion, independence, egoism, humor, stubbornness, dominance, etc.
d. work traits - leadership, trustworthiness, reliability, precision, etc.
e. moral traits - selfishness, jealousy, wickedness, generosity, etc.

If even a subgroup of these attributes can be validly inferred from a sample of script, this technique may have the potential to facilitate diverse personnel practices that require assessments, such as selection of employees from a pool of applicants, placement of newly hired employees, promoting employees or counselling problematic employees.

An extensive review of the literature about inferring personal qualities through handwriting analysis is available elsewhere (Klimoski & Rafaeli, 1983). Hence the present review will focus on studies on graphology in work settings. Available research on this issue is quite limited. Reliability findings are mostly satisfactory. This is true for internal consistency of graphological signs (Birge, 1954; Wallner, 1975), for consistency between two samples of script of the same writer (Sonneman & Kernan, 1962), and for inter-rater reliability (Galbraith & Wilson, 1964; Prystav, 1971; Rafaeli & Klimoski, 1983). No research data is available on the reliability of employment decisions (e.g., hiring or placement) made on the basis of graphological inferences.

Little is known about the relationship between graphology and work criteria (i.e., validity of handwriting inferences). The new studies which examined the issue and had relatively acceptable methodology yielded conflicting results. Thus, Sonneman & Kernan (1962) and Drory (see Ch. 11) found positive and statistically significant relations between graphological ratings and success on the job. Rafaeli and Klimoski (1983) reported non-significant results, and the two other studies (Zdep and Weaver, 1967; Jansen, 1973) reported some valid and some invalid predictions by graphologists. No valid conclusions can be drawn from such a limited number of studies, which entailed such a diverse set of jobs and criteria. But this chapter does make two recommendations: first, that additional studies are in place on the applicability of handwriting analysis to personnel decisions, second, that managers should heed questions about this measurement technique. The next section will review the relationship of major measurement questions to uses of graphology in personnel management.

MEASUREMENT QUESTIONS

Several questions are essential in a discussion about graphology as a measurement strategy for personnel recommendations, notably the reliability and validity of graphological predictions, and effects that may moderate them.

Reliability

Reliability of graphological assessments for personnel management encompasses a diverse set of issues: stability of the behavior tested, stability of interpretations, and stability of personnel recommendations.

1. Reliability of the Behavior Tested

Any psychological test is ultimately a sample of behavior; in using graphology as a test, writing is the sampled behavior. The first reliability question is therefore to what extent individuals' handwriting is stable over time.

2. Reliability of Handwriting Interpretations

This issue comprises three separate questions:

2.1 Inter-judge reliability: Do graphologists agree on inferences from the same handwriting sample?

2.2 Reliability over time: the consistency of judgments across different samples of handwriting provided by the same writer at different points in time.

2.3 Reliability across content: the consistency of graphologists' judgments from different samples of handwriting which describe a different content.

The reliability of the behavior tested and the reliability of handwriting interpretations are general questions about the technique, and are addressed elsewhere in the book. It is, however, important to emphasize that these forms of reliability should be verified with respect to attributes that are unique to the personnel administration context, that is traits that are commonly assessed by graphologists making personnel selection recommendations. A limited amount of research has addressed the question of inter-graphologist agreement on personnel assessments. Hofsommer, Holdsworth & Seifert (1965) asked three graphologists to rate 322 foreman on leadership ability (using a seven-point scale). They report highly significant agreement among graphologists, with an average correlation of $r = 0.74$. Rafaeli & Klimoski (1983) collected two script samples for each of 103 real estate agents and had graphologists rate the scripts on attributes with particular relevance to this job category. A satisfactory level of consensus was found. Thus findings tend to be positive, but additional research on this question is necessary before managers can assume that graphological ratings are reliable across graphologists.

The question of script content is particularly relevant to personnel management applications because job application letters or life descriptions (biographies) are often used by organizations for generating script inferences. These sources may offer information that a non-graphologist could use for making recommendations. In the case that content affects the inferences it is essentially a source of error, lowering the reliability of assessment. If contents have no effect, this is another indication of test-retest reliability.

The only study to examine systematically the issue of content was conducted by Rafaeli & Klimoski (1983). Using a sample of professional graphologists and naive subjects, and a set of standardized data (script) gathering procedures, they compared the reliability and validity of graphological inferences based on neutral and traditional script content. The former were descriptions of houses, the latter were autobiographical in nature. They concluded that script content had little effect on the graphologists' assessments. Again, additional research is essential.

3. Reliability of Personnel Recommendations

When assessing the reliability of a selection or placement device, it is essential to document that the same individual, across different points in time, will receive the same recommendations from the graphologist or the manager making such recommendations. This is similar to the distinction between the employment interview process, and the interview outcome (Arvey & Campion, 1982). When Sue's handwriting is used to evaluate her for an administrator's job, for example, the reliability question here is whether she is recommended for the job and whether she would receive the same recommendation at another time or by another judge. This is a different question from the reliability of specific behavioral or personality ratings that she receives.

Personnel recommendations made on the basis of graphological inferences are perhaps the essence of using graphology in personnel management. It is known that the validity of such recommendations is bound by their reliability (Anastasi, 1976). Before we can discuss whether Sue's appointment to the administrative position was a valid decision we need to confirm that this was a stable (rather than random) decision. This part of the reliability question has not been examined in the past; it is of critical importance both to researchers and to managers. But the reliability question here applies to the personnel decision maker, most commonly the manager who uses graphological ratings to make a decision. Thus, this is an important reliability question, and one worthy of further attention, which applies to consumers of graphology rather than to graphologists.

Validity

When graphology is applied toward different ends, a central question is the accuracy of the inferences and the predictions based upon them. When testing tools for their applicability to personnel selection, we question whether they can predict if a person is suited to the job, and whether they can predict if he or she will be successful. The intent here is to outline the basic issues associated with establishing such validity.

The Rating Process

The importance of a thorough job analysis for a valid selection strategy can not be over-emphasized. General testing standards have long required job analysis to precede all selection efforts (Division of 1/O Psychology, APA 1980; Tenopyr & Oeltzen, 1982). This important guideline should not be overlooked with respect to handwriting analysis as a selection tool. Only to the extent that graphological predictions are on dimensions identified in a valid and reliable job analysis can they be expected to be valid.

Most applied graphologists present their assessments in a non-structured essay type form, which is similar to clinical reports. There is no consistent set of personal characteristics that all subjects of graphological analyses are rated on. A valid comparison of different individuals on the same characteristic is therefore difficult, if not impossible. The development of common, valid rating scales, to be employed in assessing all applicants for the same job is essential to eliminate the effects of various judgment errors, and to ensure valid selection and placement decisions.

The Validation Process

Of utmost importance in a discussion of the validity of graphological inferences for personnel administration are the procedures used and the criteria employed for testing the validity. A variety of procedures can be employed in establishing validity. Of particular relevance to graphology and personnel assessment is criterion-related validity, that is, the extent to which a selection technique is predictive of, or correlated with, important elements of job behavior. In this strategy, performance on the assessment exercise is checked against on the job performance. The job performance is called the criterion, and it can comprise units of output, supervisors' ratings, sales results, etc. The professional procedure to follow in establishing criterion-related validity is deceptively easy. Cascio (1978, p.89) summarizes it as follows:

1. Measure candidates for the job.
2. Select candidates without using the results of the measurement procedure.
3. Obtain measures of the criterion performance at some later date.

The validity coefficient is then the correlation between the predictor measures (stage 1) and the criterion indicants (stage 3). When applied to graphology this procedure calls for:

1. Collecting graphological assessments on a pool of applicants; these assessments are to be kept separate from all other selection information.
2. Selecting employees for the job based on any criteria other than graphological recommendations.
3. Collecting indicators of individual performance on the job at a later date.

A host of pitfalls are inherent in this procedure. First, the procedure is quite costly. It calls for paying graphologists to generate recommendations which will not be put to active use, and managers often resist this seemingly unnecessary expenditure. but once graphology is actually used to screen applicants, by definition people who were rated low by graphologists will be excluded from the validation procedure. Yet the detection of people rated low (or unacceptable) by the assessment technique is a crucial component of a valid selection test. Only such separation as described above can ensure that "restriction of range" (Cascio, 1978) does not bias the results of a validation effort.

A second problem has been labeled "contamination" of the criterion. This typically occurs at stage 3 — the collection of the criterion data. The most common, and most easily accessible criterion is supervisors' ratings of employees' performance. For such ratings to serve as valid criteria they have to be completely independent of the predictor, in our case the graphologists' input, even after selection decisions have been made.

A common argument posited by managers employing graphological recommendations is: "I have been using graphological assessments for ten years and it has provided me with the best group of employees." This may be true for a particular manager. But it cannot be known what the situation would have been if he or she had not relied on graphological recommendations. Nor is it known how good objectively this "best group of employees" actually is. In other words there is no evidence for or against graphology that can be generalized from this manager's past experience to his, or any one else's future use of graphology.

A third complex problem embedded in establishing predictive validity is the problem of the criterion, that is, the index of performance used by manager's or researchers to test the truthfulness of graphological assessments.

The Criterion

The general problem of selecting valid criteria for validating personnel assessment techniques has been discussed extensively by others (e.g., Schmidt (1976), Guion (1976), Schmidt & Kaplan (1971) and Campbell, Dunnette, Lawler & Weick (1976). The present review cannot encompass the many details of this issue. I will therefore only summarize critical points for managers and researchers of graphology; it should be emphasized that this summary cannot replace a thorough review of the criteria development process.

The emphasis in selecting criteria must be placed on critical aspects of performance. Once these are determined, the construct validity of their measures have to be ascertained, because the predictive ability of graphology should not be belittled by inappropriate criteria.

Smith (1976) outlines five requirements of a good criterion:

1. It should be relevant to the desired goals of the individual or the organization.
2. It should not be contaminated, that is it should not contain any variance that is unrelated to the stated goals.
3. It should not be deficient, that is it should not overlook some important aspects of the above goals.
4. It should not be biased.
5. It should not be trivial.

The process of selecting and validating criteria calls for careful, professional attention. Actual job performance is subject to many influences, some of which are not within the employee's control. Such contaminating effects should be monitored and controlled in the process of a validation effort. The development of good (valid and reliable) criteria is no less important to constructive personnel management than the development of predictors.

Predictive vs Concurrent Validity

The concurrent validation strategy is often used as a substitute for predictive validity. This strategy is based on predictor and criterion and criterion data collected at the same time, from present employees. In us-

ing this strategy it is assumed that if workers who score high on the predictor (graphology) are also rated high on the criterion (job performance) then the technique is valid, and the same relationship should
hold for job applicants. Concurrent validity is the only form of validity
check that has been employed with respect to graphology. Zdep &
Weaver (1967), Rafaeli & Klimoski (1983) and Drory (1984) all collected script samples and criterion data at the same time: Jansen (1973)
states that for his study some scripts were "obtained from company files,"
but "if there was not suitable script available, the employee was asked to
provide a script in the form of an essay on topic of his own" (p.98). Thus
his was also essentially a concurrent validity assessment.

The problem with any generalizations from concurrent validation results is that the effects of motivation and job experience on validity are
ignored (Guion, 1965). It has been demonstrated empirically that individuals who are secure in their job, and realize that performance on a
test will not affect their job standing, are not motivated to the same degree as are applicants for jobs (Jennings, 1953).

It is also inappropriate to assume that experienced sales employees,
for example, who have been selling for several years, respond to a personality assessment test (such as graphology) in the same way that new
applicants for sales jobs would.

Moderating Variables in Graphological Applications

Most studies on handwriting analysis employ a similar design:
scripts are collected from a sample of employees, graphologists analyze
these scripts and the graphologists' inferences are compared to certain
criteria of the writers' job performance. The similarity in the basic procedures, combined with discordant results, suggests that issues not specifically addressed in such studies play an important role in determining
the predictive validity of handwriting analysis. Four components of the
practice of graphology may distort or moderate the validity of this technique: the writer, the analyst, the job and the organizational context.

Graphologists often set several prerequisites for providing analyses:
(1) that they be allowed freedom in their examination of specimens of
handwriting; (2) that natural, adequate and honest specimens of script
be used; (3) that mature subjects be employed, whose sex, nationality
and handedness are known to the graphologist (Cantril, Rand and Allport, 1933). It has been argued that an adequate specimen is one that is
spontaneously written in ink, on unlined paper, and includes a signa-

ture. Some graphologists claim that several samples of script from the same writer are desirable. Finally, knowing the writer's cultural and social background is thought desirable, but as Sonneman (1950) suggests, "cannot be considered an absolutely indispensable datum" (see also Meyer, 1931; Link, 1973; Patterson, 1976). These prerequisites suggest several important questions about effects that could moderate graphological recommendations.

Ghiselli (1956) suggested that individuals should be differentiated according to their predictability on various tests. Since Ghiselli's proposal, many studies have searched for individual moderators of employment interviewing. Meta-analysis techniques employed by Schmidt & Hunter (1981) as well as Callender & Osborn (1980) found that individual and group moderators of objective tests, notably handwriting analysis, have yet to be explored.

It is plausible that there are individual or group differences in the degree to which handwriting is a reliable and valid reflector of job performance. This has been found to be the case in many testing vehicles: sex, age and race have been found to moderate the extent to which certain tests are valid (Cronbach, 1984) and several authors have found that the applicant's sex bore a significant influence on interview decisions (Ferris & Gilmore, 1977; Simas & McCarrey, 1979; Cann, Siegfried & Pearce, 1981).

It has been stated that sex of the writer cannot be validly inferred from scripts (Lester & McLaughlin, 1976; Lester, McLaughlin & Nosal, 1977). But the role of sex as a moderating variable, that is, its effects on the graphologists' methods or their inferences, has not been examined.

Furthermore, an extensive literature has explored sex differences in analytic abilities and attribution judgments (Maccoby & Jacklin, 1974). It has not been determined whether male or female graphologists employ different analytic techniques or make different attributions in the process of analyzing a script sample.

Finally, the interaction between the sex of the interviewer and the interviewee has been found to have an influence on interview decisions. For example, male interviewers typically give male interviewees higher ratings than female interviewees, while most females do not discriminate in this way (Arvey & Campion, 1982). A similar pattern could be operating in graphological judgments. Although the graphologist is not physically observing the applicant, he or she is constantly aware of the applicant's sex and this may be biasing his or her thought processes.

Other individual attributes may also be important determinants of the extent to which handwriting is a valid selection device. The role of age and handedness information, which is required for graphological analyses, as moderating variables, should be explored. Other potential moderators may be locus of control, introversion (Eysenck, 1961), and social desirability (Crowne & Marlowe, 1964), all of which have been found to be associated with the degree to which people openly express their thoughts and feelings. We do not know the proportion of men and women writers in any of the reliability or validity studies cited above, nor that of left-handed writers, old writers, etc. Differences in composition of the samples may be one source of the inconsistent results between the various studies.

A final important variable may be the graphologist's experience and knowledge of graphology, specifically his or her experience in applying graphology to personnel recommendations. Rafaeli & Klimoski (1983) did not find a difference between graphologists' predictions and students' predictions. But their graphologists had had very little experience with employment decisions, and both graphologists and non-graphologists in their study were unable to produce valid predictions. Thus familiarity with the specific applications of graphology as a selection tool, not only with general graphological principles, may be a prerequisite for valid employment predictions.

Graphological traits may also be more descriptive of some job traits than of others. Different jobs have different requirements. It is not immediately clear with what types of jobs one could expect a stronger link between handwriting and job performance. One speculation may be that performance on jobs that require more manual dexterity (such as welding), or where writing in longhand is important (such as stenographer) will be more closely related to graphological attributes. This is clearly just speculation at this point.

ETHICAL AND LEGAL ISSUES

Personnel administrators in the Eighties have to concern themselves with the ethical and legal implications of any actions they take. Particularly in the U.S., a variety of laws and regulations monitor and prohibit employment discrimination. Most important of these is Title VII of the 1964 Civil Rights Act which prohibits employers from discriminating on the basis of race, religion, color, sex, or national origin. Other laws protect the aged, the handicapped, and special classes of veterans. Two powerful agencies (Equal Employment Opportunity Commission and Office of Federal Contract Compliance Programs) have been established to enforce this legislation.

A thorough presentation and discussion of such federal laws regarding employment discrimination is presented by Arvey (1979) and Modjeska (1980), and is not within the domain of the present review. Similar regulations and enforcement agencies exist in other countries — for example, the 1948 Race Relations Act and the 1975 Sex Discrimination Act in England (Murg & Fox, 1978).

The legal requirements are but one reason why managers are concerned about the social implications of their personnel practices. The social responsibility of a person making decisions about other people's futures should be the driving force in this respect. Before employing graphological recommendations, managers should be educated about them and should ascertain that such recommendations do not unfairly discriminate among applicants.

The requirement of most graphologists to know the writer's age, sex and handedness is perhaps a hazard in this respect. Consciously or not, a graphologist may employ a different set of criteria when rating women vs. men on dimensions of initiative, aggressiveness or social skills, for example. A fair (non-discriminating) assessment practice would require that the criteria employed in generating graphological predictions be independent of the writer's sex.

Moreover, the graphologist is typically aware of the particulars of the job for which a writer is being evaluated. The graphologist's stereotypes may influence ratings in a discriminatory manner. Women may be rated lower when assessed for managerial positions, for example. Or older applicants may be rated lower for dynamic, upwardly mobile positions, regardless of their objective abilities.

The graphologist may or may not be aware of such stereotypes, or of their effects. This is immaterial. In either case, practices that discriminate among individuals on the basis of variables that are not related to job performance are unfair and should be avoided.

No research is available on these questions. It is not known whether there is any systematic relationship between writers' biographic attributes (e.g., age, sex, race, handedness) and employment recommendations or decisions based on handwriting analysis. It seems that managers and psychologists are either oblivious to the issue, or they assume that graphological predictions are not discriminatory. At this point we cannot argue whether such assumptions are valid or not. We can say a word of caution about them.

An extensive amount of unfair discrimination has been documented in other selection settings, particularly in situations where the assessor is aware of the applicants' sex, age or race, such as the employment interview (Arvey & Campion, 1982). Since graphologists are also actively reminded of such information there is room for concern, and reason to require tests of non-discrimination from managers employing graphological recommendations.

Two questions serve as bench-marks for discriminatory practices:

1. Is the practice related to real job or organizational requirements?
2. Does an employment practice have unequal or adverse impact on a certain sub-group of the population?

A practice is unethical and illegal if both questions are unfavorable (Ivancevich & Glueck, 1983). The first bench-mark question is essentially that of the validity of the technique: this was discussed extensively earlier. But it should be reiterated that clear, specific job descriptions and unambiguous, operationally defined rating scales, are essential components of a validation process.

A variety of formulas have recently been suggested for statistical assessments of the extent to which a measure is discriminatory (Ledvinka, 1979; Bartlett, Bobko, Mosier & Hannan, 1978). The goal of effective personnel management should be to eliminate discrimination on any basis that is not directly related to job performance.

Two other issues pose ethical and possible legal concerns for users of graphological assessments, although they are secondary to the concerns about employment discrimination.

First there is a threat of invasion of individuals' privacy. Curr-Briggs et al. (1971) noted that one of the advantages of graphological assessments is that applicants do not have to be informed at the time of writing, that a sample of script they are providing will be used to evaluate them. Granted, this is likely to reduce the probability of faking. But employees have an undisputable right to be aware of procedures and criteria employed in the process of evaluating them. Any attempt by managers to deceive applicants or current employees is unethical.

Finally, consumers of graphology in personnel management may soon be confronted with applicants' and employees' demands for "open testing procedures." Open testing refers to the test takers' rights to extensive information about the test and its scoring. The following standards have been called for with regard to the use of ability testing for personnel decisions (Roskind, 1980, pages 5-6).

1. Prior to testing, each applicant would be informed in writing as to the purpose and reliability of the test and applicants' right to receive test results.

2. After the tests are scored, and upon the applicants' request, they will be notified of their scores on the various tests, the passing score etc.

This bill of test takers' rights has been dubbed "open testing" or "truth in testing." The appropriateness of such policies is quite controversial among testing professionals and personnel administrators (Sparks, 1980; Lefkowitz, 1980). But such legislation exists in at least two of the largest and most progressive American states (New York and California). Similar legislation was recently considered at the federal level in America (Wicklund, 1980).

If graphology is considered a "test," at some point takers of this test may demand such rights. For example, they may want to know where they have gone wrong and what specific criteria were employed in rating them. Managers and graphologists should be prepared with qualified answers to such questions. And managers and graphologists have to consider what effects the dissemination of such information will have on the utility of graphological assessments.

REFERENCES

Anastasi, A. (1976). *Psychological testing* (4th ed.) New York: Macmillan.

Arvey, R. D. (1979a). *Fairness in selecting employees*. Reading, Mass: Addison Wesley.

Arvey, R. D. (1979b). Unfair discrimination in the employment interview. *Psychological Bulletin, 86,* 736-765.

Arvey, R. D. & Campion, J. E. (1982). The employment interview. A summary and review of recent research. *Personnel Psychology, 35,* 281-322.

Bartlett, C. J., Bobko, P., Mosier, B. & Hannan, R. (1978). Testing for fairness with a moderated multiple regression strategy. *Personnel Psychology, 31,* 233-241.

Birge, W. R. (1954). An experimental inquiry into the measurable handwriting correlates of five personality traits, *Journal of Personality, 23,* 215-233.

Callender, J. C. & Osborn, H. G. (1980). Development and test of a new model of validity generalization. *Journal of Applied Psychology, 65,* 543-558.

Campbell, J. P., Dunnette, M. D., Lawler, E. E. & Weick, K. E. Jr. (1970). *Managerial behavior, performance and effectiveness,* New York: McGraw Hill.

Cann, E., Siegfried, W. D. & Pearce, L. (1981). Forced attention to specific applicant qualifications: Impact of physical attractiveness and sex on applicant biases. *Personnel Psychology, 34,* 65-76.

Cantril, H., Rand, H. A. & Allport, G. W. (1933). The determination of personal interests by psychological and graphological methods. *Character and Personality, 2,* 134-143.

Cascio, W. F. (1982). *Applied Psychology in Personnel Management* (2nd ed.). Virginia: Reston.

Cronbach, L. J. (1984). *Essentials of psychological testing.* San Francisco, CA: Harper & Row.

Crowne, D. & Marlow, E. (1964). *The approval motive.* New York: Wiley.

Curr-Briggs, N., Kennett, B. & Patterson, J. (1971). *Handwriting Analysis in Business,* Associated Business Programs. London.

Drory, A. (1984). *The Validity of Handwriting Analysis in Predicting Job Performance.* Unpublished Manuscript. Department of Industrial Engineering and Engineering Management, Ben Gurion University of the Negev. Beer-Sheva, Israel.

Edson, R. K. (1971). Graphoanalysis vs. graphology. *The Journal of Graphoanalysis, August,* 11-12.

Eysenck, H. J. (1967). *The biological basis of personality.* Springfield, Illinois: Charles C Thomas.

Ferris, G. R. & Gilmore, D. O. (1977). Effects of mode of presentation, sex of applicant and sex of interviewer on a simulated interview decisions. *Psychological Reports, 40,* 566.

Galbraith, D. & Wilson, D. (1964). Reliability of the graphoanalytic approach to handwriting analysis. *Perceptual and Motor Skills, 19,* 615-618.

Ghiselli, E. E. (1956). The placement of workers: Concepts and problems. *Personnel Psychology, 9,* 1-16.

Guion, R. M. (1976). Recruiting, selection, job replacement. In: Dunnette, M. D. (ed). *Handbook of industrial and organizational psychology.* Chicago: Rand McNally.

Guion, R. M. (1965). *Personnel testing.* New York: McGraw Hill.

Hakel, M. D. (1984). Employment interview, in: Rowland, K. M. & Ferris, G. R. (Eds.) *Research in personnel and human resources management,* Boston, Mass.: Allyn & Bacon.

Hofsommer, W., Holdsworth, R. & Seifert, T. (1965). Problems of reliabilty in graphology. *Psychology and Praxis, 9,* 14-24.

Ivancevich, J. M., Glueck, W. F. (1983). *Foundations of personnel.* Plano, Texas: Business Publications.

Jansen, A. (1973). *Validation of graphological judgments.* Paris: Mouton.

Jennings, E. E. (1953). The motivation factor in testing supervisors. *Journal of Applied Psychology, 37,* 168-169.

Klimoski, R. & Rafaeli, A. (1983). Inferring personal qualities through handwriting analysis. *Journal of Occupational Psychology, 56,* 191-202.

Ledvinka, J. (1979). The statistical definition of fairness in federal selection guidelines and its implications for minority employment. *Personnel Psychology, 32,* 551-562.

Lefkowitz, J. (1980). Pros and cons of truth in testing legislation. *Personnel Psychology, 33,* 17-23.

Lester, D. & McLaughlin, S. (1976). Sex deviant handwriting and neuroticism. *Perceptual and Motor Skills, 43,* 770-773.

Lester, D., McLaughlin, S. & Nosal, G. (1977). Graphological signs for extraversion. *Perceptual and Motor Skills, 44,* 137-138.

Levy, L. (1979). Handwriting and hiring. *Dun's Review.* 72-79.

Link, B. (1973). A graphological method for personnel selection. *Annals of the American Association of Handwriting Analysts, 3,* 42-46.

Maccoby, E. E. & Jacklin, C. N. (1974). *The psychology of sex differences,* CA: Stanford University Press.

Meyer, J. S. (1931). *How to read character from handwriting.* New York: Blue Ribbon Books.

Modjeska, L. (1980). *Handling employment discrimination cases.* New Jersey: The Lawyers' Cooperative Publishing Co.

Murg, G. E., & Fox, J. C. (1978). *Labor relations law: Canada, Mexico and Western Europe.* New York: Practising Law Institute.

Patterson, J. (1976). *Interpreting handwriting.* New York: David McKay Company.

Prystav, G. (1971). Reliability of interpretation in handwriting psychology. *Schweizersche Zeitschrift für Psychologie und Ihr Anwendungen, 30,* 320-322.

Rafaeli, A. & Klimoski, R. J. (1983). Predicting sales success through handwriting analysis: An evaluation of the effects of training and handwritten sample content. *Journal of Applied Psychology, 68,* 2.

Roskind, W. L. (1980). Deco vs NLRB, and the consequences of open testing in industry. *Personnel Psychology, 33,* 3-16.

Schmidt, F. L., & Hunter, J. E. (1981). Moderator research and the law of small numbers. *Personnel Psychology, 31,* 215-232.

Schmidt, F. R. & Kaplan, L. B. (1971). Composite versus multiple criteria: A review and resolution of the controversy. *Personnel Psychology, 24,* 419-434.

Schmidt, N. (1976). Social and situational determinants of interview decisions: Implications for the employment interview. *Personnel Psychology, 29,* 79-101.

Simas, K. & McCarrey, M. (1979). Impact of recruiter authoritarianism and applicant sex on evaluation and selection decisions in a recruitment interview analogue study. *Journal of Applied Psychology, 64,* 481-493.

Smith, P. C. (1976). The problem of criteria. In Dunnette, M. D. (ed). *Handbook of industrial and organizational psychology.* Chicago: Rand McNally.

Sonneman, U. & Kernan (1962). Handwriting analysis — A valid selection tool? *Personnel, 39,* 8-14.

Sparks, P. (1980). Open vs secure testing. *Personnel Psychology, 33,* 1-2.

Tenopyr, M. M. L & Oeltzen, P. D. (1982). Personnel selection and classification. *Annual Review of Psychology, 33,* 581-618.

Wallner, T. (1975). Hypotheses of handwriting psychology and their verification. *Professional Psychology, 6,* 8-16.

Wicklund, G. A. (1980). Truth in testing congressional hearings. *Personnel Psychology, 33,* 33-39.

Zdep, S. M. & Weaver, H. B. (1967). The graphoanalytic approach to selecting life insurance salesman. *Journal of Applied Psychology, 51,* 295-299.

22

TESTING GRAPHOLOGY: IS GRAPHOLOGY A TEST?

(Or: The Future of Graphology Within the Context of Psychological Testing)

ELCHANAN I. MEIR

Summary

THIS CHAPTER examines whether graphology meets the definition of a "test" as a standardized and objective measure of human behavior. The definition is broken down into its components — standardization, objectivity, measurement and comparison — and graphology is examined in accordance with each component. In addition, reasons are suggested for the low predictive validity of graphological ratings. A general outline for the future development of graphology — within the context of psychological testing — is proposed.

Definition of a Test

A test is a standardized and objective measure of human behavior or characteristics which is administered for purposes of comparison.

This definition of "test" is in agreement with scientific terminology (e.g., Anastasi, 1982; Cronbach, 1984) and popular meaning (e.g., Oxford Dictionary).

If the examination of handwriting (i.e., graphology) meets the above definition, follow-up studies are required to examine the validity of this "test" against various criteria. The usefulness of a test, as we all know, is determined by the relationship of the test scores, on the one hand, to an external criterion measured later on, on the other hand — in other words, its predictive validity. If, however, graphology does not conform to our definition, it might better be classified along with intuition, arts,

311

etc. Let us examine graphology in accordance with the components of the definition.

Standardization

For their judgements, graphologists require a handwriting sample written on a blank sheet. So far, they agree. However, there seems to be no such agreement as to whether the written text should or should not be emotionally loaded for the subject. Thus, some graphologists agree to assess the writer's personality on the basis of a free composition, others employ copied material, but many require the subject's handwritten curriculum vitae. Standardization would also mean a fixed number of scripts, set as a desired minimum. These standards should be accepted and implemented by all graphologists, as a common basis.

Objectivity

The second component in the definition of a "test" requires agreement among raters — in other words, inter-rater reliability. In the case of graphology, this should include: (1) agreement among graphologists on the quality and quantity of certain symbols in the handwriting; (2) agreement on the interpretation of these symbols. The evidence as to the objectivity of graphology in both respects is not impressive and it limits the potential validity. Very few studies have focused on the rater's training process, but it is clear that intensive training can contribute to the improvement of inter-rater reliability. Reliability coefficients which now lie in the range of 0.4-0.6 might be raised to 0.5-0.8, thus raising the reliability barrier for validity.

Measurement

This component of the "test" definition requires differentiation between subjects. One must admit that handwritings differ in various respects, such as letter size, pressure, angle of writing, organization on the page, etc. But is there any agreement regarding which **variables** should be measured? The situation now is that every graphologist has his own list. In order to improve measurement, two groups of variables should be outlined: (1) graphometric indices, i.e., measures of size and height, margin width, etc.; (2) graphoimpressionistic indices, i.e., basic rhythms, roundness, order and cleanliness, elaborateness, etc. The big question is, of course, can the majority of graphologists agree on the content of these two lists?

Comparison

The fourth component of the "test" definition, the comparison—which is the purpose of the measurement—exists in graphology, as in all other measurements of human characteristics. The comparison might be among candidates or of a single subject in comparison with an ideal case or distribution. Comparisons could be executed much more easily if **norms** existed. Unfortunately, this is not the case with graphology to date.

It can thus be concluded that graphology **does** in some cases conform to the definition of a test, but that this depends on the extent to which it meets the standards set out above.

Predictive Validity

Ghiselli (1973) summarized thousands of studies on the predictive validity of psychometric tests when he wrote: "the grand average of the validity coefficients for all tests for all jobs taken together is 0.39 for training criteria and 0.22 for proficiency criteria. . .(and) maximal validity coefficients are 0.45 for training criteria and 0.35 for proficiency criteria" (pp. 476-477). In the scientific literature, as a general rule, graphology fails to reach that level of predictive validity.

Why does graphology fail to show the validity level of the common psychometric test? I believe that the reason lies in the neglect of important methodological consideration. The variance in assessments of handwriting can be separated into eight sources:

a) The variance between the people assessed;
b) Variance between symbols of the same kind on the same page—the inconsistency of the data;
c) Variance between symbols which are believed to indicate the same personality characteristic;
d) Variance between the subject's writing samples under different test conditions;
e) Variance due to differences in the content of written tests, which might cause various emotional reactions;
f) Variance between test and retest;
g) Variance between graphologists (raters)—the objectivity of the handwriting analysis;
h) Error variance.

Validity depends on the proportion of the error variance to the total variance. As long as the other variance sources are not minimized, poor validity coefficients can be expected.

Strictness with regard to the test situation (e.g., text and writing implement) and data analysis (e.g., sampling of letters, words, and lines to be scored) would improve the chances of graphology demonstrating high validity.

Conclusion

In order to qualify as a psychological test, several changes should be made in the graphological test.

a) The handwriting input and the conditions under which the sample is collected must be defined in a more standardized way.
b) The variables which are measured and rated should be clearly defined and the measurement (or rating) operations should be made explicit.
c) More serious attention should be paid to the training of raters.
d) Norms for the population should be defined.

If all these changes are carried out, we may see the start of a new era in graphology.

REFERENCES

Anastasi, A. (1982). *Psychological Testing.* New York: Macmillan.

Cronbach, L. J. (1984). *Essentials of Psychological Testing.* New York: Harper.

Ghiselli, E. E. (1973). The validity of aptitude tests in personnel selection. *Personnel Psychology, 26,* 461-477.

APPENDIX

THE GRAPHOLOGY OF EXISTENTIAL ADJUSTMENT

I. ODEM

Summary

THEORY AND practical knowledge have established that there is no simple one-to-one correlation between a graphic sign and a trait of the writer's personality. Various systems involving the association of graphic syndromes (a group of graphic signs) with a single trait of the writer's personality have been proposed to cope with this difficulty; conversely, it has been shown that a single graphic sign can reflect more than one trait.

This chapter will introduce a graphological typology, based on consideration of the process of handwriting itself. Nine graphological syndromes, which correspond to nine types of existential adjustment will be defined. In the analysis of any handwriting, one examines the interaction between the potencies (types) that constitute the basis of the writer's existential adjustment. This system also includes an original psychogram which graphically displays the proportions and tendencies of the types constituting the specific personality. It is the author's belief that this method offers a new contribution to graphological research in general. The main purpose remains, however, the systematic application of the "Nine Types of Existential Adjustment" to the problem of understanding human relations, thereby shedding new light on the old controversy on how to achieve a correct individual diagnosis and its practical employment in a variety of areas, such as vocational guidance, marital compatibility, etc.

315

THE GRAPHOLOGY OF EXISTENTIAL ADJUSTMENT

*Evolution is a change from the incoherent, the indefinite homogeneity--to coherent, defi-
nite heterogeneity, with constant adjustment of inner and outer relations.*

Herbert Spencer

Let me begin by defining graphology as a discipline in which the process of personal existential adjustment is studied and diagnosed from the
individual's handwriting.

Writing is behavior. It is executed by movements that form letters revealing the mode of the writer's individual existential adjustment. Like
any other manifestation of behavior, graphic behavior is activated by a
motive force driving the personality to accomplish some purpose, either
conscious and preplanned or unconscious and arising at the spur of the
moment. The graphologist assumes that at the origin of this chain of interactions, consisting of motivation-drive-behavior-writing, there exists
an essential purpose that the writer is trying to realize — mainly, his personal survival.

Basically, therefore, what we are dealing with is the individual expe-
riencing the primary purpose of his existence. This process requires the
unceasing adjustment of the writer's personality to the changes taking
place both within himself and in his external circumstances.

The Components of Graphic Adjustment

Experience has shown that the performance of any writing, even
when it involves something so trivial as making a comma or period, is
conditioned by at least three factors: motivation, coordination, and
graphotechnics. Let us therefore review briefly the nature and effect of
each of these factors.

1. Motivation is used here to mean all mental experiences, such as
wishes, anxieties, conflicts, frustrations, repressions, and the like. These
mental experiences set the personality in motion. That is, they function as
the driving force of graphic self-expression, which directly manifests the
nature of the experience involved. The graphic expression thus obtained
both depicts and describes the situational behavior which is characteristic
of the particular writer's personality. It is this last which is at the core of
graphology as a psychodiagnostic tool. However, the diagnosis of motivation can only be undertaken after the subject's coordination and the
graphotechnical conditions have been duly examined by the analyst.

2. Coordination of the nervous and muscular systems is a prerequisite condition for the execution of writing movements. It is well known that any disturbance in neuromuscular coordination will cause defects in an individual's writing movements. In such cases the disturbed graphic image that is obtained may obscure the motivational image and thereby mislead the handwriting analyst in his evaluation of the subject's character. It is therefore indispensible for the graphologist to make certain, before he sets out to analyze a subject's handwriting, that no coordinational disturbance has interfered with graphic performance.

3. Graphotechnics comprises all of the purely technical aspects involved in the execution of any writing. These include the type and quality of pen employed; the quality and size of the paper; the manner in which the pen is held in the writer's fingers; the angle of inclination of the pen in relation to the paper; the angle at which the paper is placed in relation to the edge of the table; the quality of the surface beneath the page (whether soft or hard, smooth or rough); the relationship of the height of the chair to the table; the conditions of illumination; the subject's posture and physical ambience (e.g., writing against a wall, or while standing or travelling). All of these and similar technical factors affect graphic performance. It is not surprising, therefore, that persons wishing to disguise their own handwriting will often resort to such simple devices as changing the angle at which they normally hold their pen, or at which they ordinarily place a sheet of writing paper. In any event, the analyst must be clear about any graphotechnical circumstances that may have interfered with or altered a subject's handwriting, so as to avoid errors of judgement in evaluating the writer's character.

Under normal circumstances, when performance is unhindered by either graphotechnical or coordinational problems, a person's writing movements become unconsciously integrated in the expression of his mental state, and disclose the nature of the motivation represented in his graphic behavior.

The Crux of Graphic Adjustment

The process of graphic adjustment involving the interaction of the three factors that were just considered is determined by the **potencies** of the writer's personality. These potencies remain latent until that infinitesimal fraction of time in which they assume a manifest form in the **angle of writing.**

I cannot stress strongly enough the importance of this particular graphic component, which has been assigned only minor importance in the literature of all the schools of handwriting analysis. After over three decades of exhaustive investigations, I am convinced that the angle of writing is the primary point of departure for determining the nature of a writer's personal existential adjustment in his graphic expression.

This conclusion, arrived at empirically, as well as my own experience in the psychodynamic interpretation of handwriting, is responsible for my having established the angle of writing as the key to my **graphological typology of existential adjustment,** which I offer here as an original method of studying the human personality on the basis of the evidence furnished by handwriting. It seems to me, moreover, that my graphological typology resolves two crucial methodological problems that lie at the very root of graphodiagnostics.

The Rationale of the Graphological Typology of Existential Adjustment

As I have observed, the threefold process of adjustment, consisting of motivation, coordination, and graphotechnics, which establishes the angle of writing, is determined by the specific nature of the individual writer's potencies. However, before undertaking a detailed account of my method, I should like to elucidate a number of basic concepts, whose application I shall subsequently demonstrate.

By the term **potency,** I mean an inherent functional ability having a propensity to produce a homogeneous set of phenomena which together constitute a typical mode of personal conduct and manner of doing things, of impressing others and expressing oneself, of acting and reacting.

I should like to stress that the word "potency" was carefully chosen to convey the sense that a person is merely prone to behave in a certain way — that is, he is more frequently than not inclined to perform his actions homogeneously, or in a manner typical of the **dominant** potency in his personality. However, this propensity is by no means inevitably made manifest by action, or given visible graphic form. What is required, therefore, is a yardstick to assess to what extent, and by what means, a given potency has been realized; in other words, to assess the extent and manner of change, for better or worse, in the process of an individual's existential adjustment.

In my graphological method, the writer's personality is conceived of, and interpreted, in terms of the psychodynamic interaction of various potencies; and the nature of these interactions accounts for the types of existential adjustment that make up the writer's personal style or manner of existence in a variety of areas (See Fig. 1).

Our consideration of the interactions among potencies opens the way for establishing the nature of the heterogeneous existential adjustment of the individual, both psychodynamically and graphologically. That is, what has been hitherto regarded as an interaction of complementary and contradictory traits of personality is to be conceived of, according to my graphological typology, in terms of types or potencies that go to make up a personality whose nature is heterogeneous.

The Factors

The blank page is the external physical field within which the writer's graphic activity takes place. The act of writing involves a threefold relationship consisting of:

1. **The objective thesis,** which is determined by the size and quality of the paper that define area and boundaries of the external conditions at the writer's disposal.
2. **The subjective antithesis,** which is an expression of the individual writer's "self" as he guides his pen with his own hand and fingers across the neutral and impersonal surface of a blank page, and leaves the imprint of his distinct and personal style of behavior and manner of existence.
3. **The existentially adjusted synthesis,** which is incorporated in the written page as a whole.

Two additional factors have to be considered in connection with the external field within which the act of writing is performed:

a) The writer's **free choice** of the size and quality of paper, guided by his personal preference or needs in a manner similar to his free choice of neighborhood, home, place of employment, and the like.
b) **Constrained adjustment,** which may occur when the writer is deprived of the possibility of choosing the surface he would prefer to write on. Thus, under pressure of time or circumstance, a writer may resort to a small card or scrap of paper, instead of exercising his real personal preferenc. Being unable to extend the physical field on which he is writing, he is compelled to adjust his writing in order to satisfy the demands of his personal mode of graphic expression. In these circumstances, however, the writer's adjustment of his graphic expression takes place under the influence of an inner compulsion.

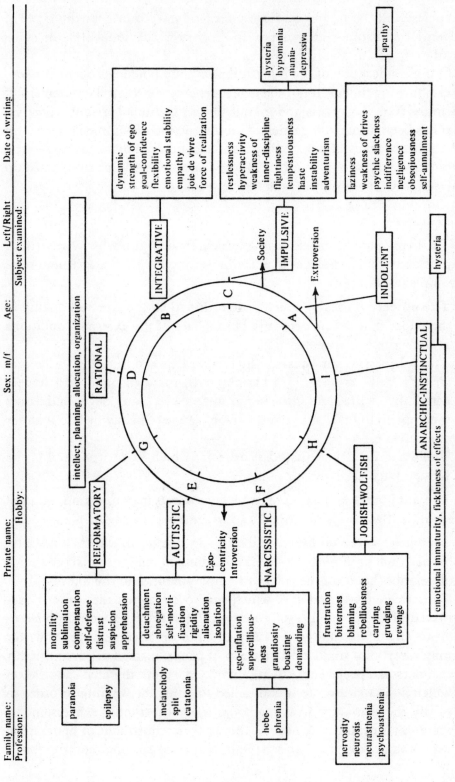

Figure 1. Psychogram illustrating the proportions and tendencies of the various types, which go to make up the specific personality.

This general distinction between free and constrained adjustment is ramified when we come to examine handwriting in a more essential way.

The Threefold Adjustment in Graphic Performance

Three types of graphic adjustment are involved in an individual's self-recorded image on the written page: **dynamic adjustment, formational adjustment,** and **organizational adjustment.**

Dynamic adjustment in writing is primarily responsible for the execution of writing movement. The qualities of writing movement may be characterized as being quick or slow, flexible or rigid, smooth or coarse, restrained or wild, strong or weak, lively or cramped, etc. The particular characteristics of the writer's movements are responsible for the dynamic aspect of his existential graphic adjustment.

Formational adjustment is conditioned by the standard forms of written characters. These are prescribed by the writer's society or culture, and are universally imposed on all persons who are members of the same community. An individual's formational adjustment of his handwriting may be distinguished as being rounded or angular, standard or unique, simple or stylized, original or commonplace, and so on. All of these qualities, insofar as they relate to the shape of letters, represent the writer's adjustment to **communal** requirements regarding letter forms. The way in which one shapes one's letters testifies to one's ability and readiness to accept or deter to the official standard, and reveals the extent, manner, and means of one's effort to conform in one's personal behavior and conduct to the social conventions that are part and parcel of one's existence as a member of a community.

The writer's **organizational adjustment** is discerned in his manner of arranging all of his graphic marks (i.e., letters, punctuation marks, dots, underlinings, overlinings, etc.) in relation to the surface of the page.

This arrangement or organization is determined by the height and width of the letters; the width of spacing between letters, words, and lines; the direction of the lines; and the width of all four margins of the page. The organization of handwriting is individually distinguished in terms of qualities such as ordered or disordered, crowded or dispersed, whole or broken in paragraphs, filled-up or empty, flooded or airy, systematic or casual, and so on. The writer's characteristics in this category show the extent of his conformity or lack of conformity to the standard of letter magnitude and spacing in accordance with the degree of his graphic organizational abilities.

The Three Images of Handwriting

Handwriting consists of three images that function together inseparably: **movement, space,** and **form.** The degree of their interrelatedness depends on the proportions to which they function mutually in respect not only of the writing sample as a whole, but of the individual letters as well. This tripartite interdependence is rooted in a fundamental law of our psychophysical nature, which is reflected in human behavior.

Table I

Wholeness of the Writing - Personality as a Whole		
The Three Images of Writing - The Three Aspects of Personality		
Movement Image	Form Image	Space Image
Dynamic Aspect	Formal and Formative Aspect	Organizational Aspect
Base Layer (depth)	Intermediate Layer	Head Layer
Vitality	(adjacent to feeling)	(adjacent to logic)
Motivation	Formation of Self	Self-determination
Dynamics	Refining, Exhibiting	Regarding Environment
Temperament: Cold/Hot	Covering, Faking	Self-Discipline in respect of Social Background
Emotionality	Aesthetic Sensitivity (Art)	Scale, Consideration of Checks
Activity/Passivity	Social Ethics (Civilization)	Self-Control, Order, System
Pleasure/Pain Principle (Freud)	Preconscious or Conscious Principle of Reality	
Self: Genotype (Jung)	Phenotype: "Persona"	
Relations of Strength/ Weakness of Restraints/ Drives	Plastic: Formed or Amorphic	Intellect: Objective, One-sided
	Originality/Formality/Routine	Initiative: Perspective, Confusion, Splitting
Restraints/Drives	Developing/Simulating	
Synthesis		

Let us first consider the issue graphically. Writing necessitates moving a pen along a path consisting of a letter or stroke that occupies a certain space. Inherent in every movement is its distinctive shape. However, in the case of handwriting, the writer is supposed to make his letters conform to an accepted standard. Whether a particular writer observes or disregards that standard is something to be determined by an examination of his writing. But such personal differences in individual handwriting do not alter the fundamental fact that the form of a letter occupies a location that is both defined and circumscribed by the writing movement.

Of the three images of handwriting, only the bare space retains its independence as something distinct from the personal influences of action and shaping, which create the vital symbiosis that takes place when an individual's action (movement) shapes his conduct (form) within a social environment (space). Or, to put the matter succinctly: No writer acts in a vacuum, and no form comes into existence without action.

Every individual's writing involves these three images, and the differences found in the writing of various persons depends on the character and degree of stress an individual bestows upon each of these images.

Three Types of Experiences and Their Interaction in Existential Adjustments

The graphic expression of the writer's existential adjustment is conditioned by the interaction of three types of experience: **tactile, motoric, and visual.**

The writer's **tactile experience** is conveyed through the manner in which he brings his pen into contact with the surface of the paper. The varying degrees of lightness or heaviness of touch disclose a writer's delicacy and susceptibility, or their opposite, in his adjustment to the material surface upon which he is writing. The tactile experience is always present, and is the primary condition of the art of writing: it is the prerequisite of the writer's control of the meeting between the point of his pen and the paper, and must be present for a graphic record to be made by him. The nature of his tactile experience will reveal whether the writer's existential adjustment is self-confident, outgoing, joyful, intuitively creative — or, on the contrary, apprehensive, introverted, depressive, and repressed.

The writer's **motoric experience** is expressed by the distinctive character of his writing movement — that is, by his writing tempo (quick or slow — and writing pressure (weak or strong, even or uneven); by the size of his letters; and by the direction of expansion (upward, downward, leftward, rightward, slantwise).

The **visual experience** of the writer involves two factors:

(a) **formational control**
(b) **organizational control**

In the case of formational control, to the extent that the writer is concentrating on the proper shaping of his letters, he maintains visual contact and control of his writing movements, thereby guiding and adjusting the movement of his hand to execute the required form of the letters. This visual control results in a variety of letter shapes, ranging from very pedantically formed letters to formations so negligently executed as to be illegible. Formational control is an index of such personal qualities as artistic sensitivity, creative imagination, memory of forms, perseverance in executing forms, firmness of aesthetic and/or moral principles, and sometimes hesitancy, reluctance or compulsive inability to make one's existential adjustment conform to the formal code of behavior established by the community.

Regarding organizational control of visual experience, individuals differ in accordance with their personal visual sensibilities and preferences in respect of space. These are determined by factors such as aesthetic inclination, the wish to facilitate the physical activity of writing, considerations of organizational efficiency, and the like. Moreover the ability to organize presupposes the possession by the writer of certain personality traits, and these may be classified according to the following categories:

1. Intellectual: This involves the faculty of coherent thinking that allows for a systematic arrangement of ideas in an intelligible order.

2. Ethical: Communal life is controlled by law, in other words by an organized body of rules. Although these rules do not always entirely coincide with ethical principles, they are adjusted so as to regulate and maintain the requirements of justice in a variety of areas with respect to the individual's privileges and duties in the life of the community. Hence it is not surprising that the handwriting of persons like judges, lawyers, educators, moralists, and social reformers tends to reveal the qualities of organization appropriate to disciplined rational thought arranged in logical sequence.

3. Technological: Any scheme—whether the design of a machine or device, or a city plan, or the plan of a military campaign—consists essentially of an organized chain of ideas and technical details whose order is arranged so as to suit the specific requirements of the scheme's purpose.

The common denominator of the preceding categories in the writer's visual control is his effort to adjust and organize his various needs in a way that best facilitates his personal existence.

4. Psychopathological: Paradoxical though it may seem, there are instances in which extraordinarily well-organized handwriting is the product of an insane mind. The existence of such cases requires that the graphologist take precautions to minimize the possibility of misinterpreting "nice organization" when it in fact represents the sort of pathological systematization that is sometimes associated with psychotic (paranoid) or neurotic (exhibitionist) modes of existential adjustment.

5. Criminal: "The end justifies the means," is a proverbial maxim. In practice it is not unusual to meet up with examples of wonderfully well-organized handwriting, exhibiting the most impressive attributes, and then to discover that they were produced by highly sophisticated swindlers who have managed convincingly to endow their handwriting with classic qualities of organization and formal embellishment. Nevertheless, apart from the socio-ethical issues involved in such cases, the criminal organization of handwriting shares with other varieties of organization the same primary motivation of living personality striving to achieve existential adjustment.

The Two Graphic Planes of Existential Adjustment

The tactile, motoric, and visual experiences discussed earlier, which are involved in the writer's existential adjustment, function on two distinct and different graphic planes:

(1) the plane of **objective execution;**
(2) the plane of **subjective experience.**

The plane of objective execution represents the working level, and is determined by the **horizontal** or oblique platform beneath the sheet of paper upon which the writing is performed. From the writer's standpoint, this plane is the physical field of his writing activity. Indeed, it is the drive for activity that plays the dominant role here. However, when considering the writer's personal activity, his subjective relationship to it must be taken into account — particularly in regard to writing with an acute angle, and occasionally in regard to writing with an obtuse angle, insofar as writing movement is free from influence or uninhibited by constraints. On the primarily objective plane of execution, handwriting attests to the writer's traits in respect of work, such as industriousness, ambition for advancement, pursuit of achievement, perseverance in carrying out his tasks and duties. This category of operative features is invaluable in the vocational guidance of the writer's existential adjustment.

The primarily **subjective plane of experience** is entirely independent of the objective plane represented by the platform beneath the page. On this plane the writer experiences the page upon which he writes as the real space of his actual feelings and behavior. For instance, the base of the written line may represent the ground on which he stands, or a footpath along which he walks as he turns his face upward toward the sky. The starting (or left) side of the page is experienced by him as the inner world of his intimate feelings emanating from his past, whereas the closing (the right) side of the page is experienced by him as his external environment and his ability to cope with it in the future. What is inherently involved here is the individual writer's attitude toward his own self. Consciously or unconsciously, the writer clings to his personal outlook, which he is unable — either temporarily or entirely — to disassociate from the anticipations of his ego or the demands of the task he has to perform. Such subjective experience is closely bound up with the right angle of writing, and sometimes with the obtuse angle in the case of curbed movement, artificial shaping of letters, and pedantic organization of writing on the page. In this case, the writer is evidently trying to display his abilities and skills in the best light, with the intention of enhancing his personal prestige and social standing. In so doing, he clearly concentrates on what is regarded as demonstrating such personal qualities as a strong sense of responsibility and the will to get things done: disinterested dedication to the task; unquestionable integrity in carrying out one's duty: the pursuit of perfection of performance; prudent and careful planning of one's actions in advance. However, these and the like positive characteristics often merely cloak negative traits such as the egocentric pursuit of personal advantage, narcissism, conceit, pretentiousness, alienation, detachment, solitariness, inconsiderateness, disregard of the rights of others — to name but a few of the unnumerable shades and nuances of the means and strategems of the personality's existential adjustment.

Basic Graphic Adjustment and its Derivatives

Basic graphic adjustment is first of all differentiated by three angles of writing: the **acute angle,** the **right angle,** and the **obtuse angle.** These are each qualitatively determined by the specific experiences of the plane and image involved in their execution.

1. The **acute angle** is first of all characterized by the facility with which it is executed with respect to motoric coordination. This is proved by the fact that the overwhelming majority of people write with their right hand. This relative effortlessness of execution not only facilitates the writer's discharge of energy (libido), so that his writing movements are free, easy, and uncurbed, but it also takes the strain off his visual experience because of the great range of acute angles available to him (approximately $30° - 85.°$

Briefly then, the acute angle of writing may be qualified in the following ways:

a) **Motorically** it is easily and conveniently executed, and allows for continuous writing activity with the least amount of fatigue.

b) **Visually** it alleviates the strain of controlling the descending strokes, whose acute angle may be varied broadly.

2. The execution of the **right angle** is primarily conditioned by restraint exerted by visual control, since recording a vertical stroke obviously requires a concentration of attention in order to prevent the descending stroke from slanting to the right or left. The extremely narrow range of options in deviating from the vertical (between $85°$ and $95°$) makes for a psychic situation of constraint that only adds to the motoric difficulties involved in the execution of the required movements.

To sum up, therefore, adjustment associated with the right angle requires:

a) Visually, a control that ranges from rational concentration to compulsive fixation.

b) Motorically, an allocation of energy that ranges from realistic (either practical or theoretical) and purposeful to mentally stagnant, with the energy being blocked and movement impeded or suppressed.

3. The **obtuse angle** of writing is an odd phenomenon by any standard among right-handed writers, and is never presented as an example to be emulated by elementary school pupils. An obtuse angle of writing in the case of right-handed persons can be interpreted in no other way than as expressing an exceptional personal preference arising from a variety of motivations. The underlying reasons for such a choice may range from emotional immaturity to pretentiousness. In the latter case, the writer's contrived stylization and the distinctive and unusual effect conveyed by the obtuse angle of writing stem from his pretentions to ori-

ginality and his consequent urge to create the impression of personal uniqueness. This misleading impression sometimes serves to compensate for the writer's personal shortcomings, frustrations, and grievances. Not infrequently, however, the obtuse angle is strongly indicative of a personality given to calculated exploitation of other people's confidence for selfish purposes.

Producing an obtuse angle of writing involves:

a) **Visually,** a formational and/or organizational control that ranges from the most extreme severity of control to a loss of control so complete as to be beyond the writer's capacity to reimpose.

b) **Motorically,** an extreme exertion in which the discharge of the writer's energy is distorted, resulting in a twisted movement and/ or deformation of letter forms.

So far, the qualitative significance of the three angles of writing, as they bear on basic graphic adjustment, have been treated only in very general terms. In order to deal with the great variety of modes of existential adjustment, we have to inquire into the uses that the individual writer makes of the qualities attributed to each of the three angles. In other words, we must consider how and to what purpose the individual writer applies the specific qualities of the angles in the process of his existential adjustment. To do so will require a minute account and differentiation for what I call the nine "potencies" or types of existential adjustment, each of which I have designated respectively by one of the letters in the alphabetical sequence **A-I.**

Differentiation of the Nine Potencies (A-I) of Existential Adjustment

The **acute-angle** writer is primarily motivated by the **dynamic** aspect of his personality, with **movement** being the predominant image projected by his writing. The application of the facilitating characteristics of the acute angle of writing to the process of existential adjustment is differentiated in terms of Potencies A-C in the following manner;

POTENCY A is associated with the **indolent type** of existential adjustment, which is distinguished by such qualities as passivity, weak concentration, avoidance of exertion, a tendency to vacillate effortlessly in idle daydreaming, sluggish motivation and a feeble drive for self-realization, weak will-power in regard to self-control, carelessness in coping with the requirements of daily existence, negligence concerning the formal rules of the community, low self-esteem bordering on apathy.

In short, Potency A represents an indifferent existential adjustment of a person who is physically lazy and mentally unconcerned about pursuing any goal or seeking any justification for his personal survival. Essentially Type-A lives by inertia: he exists merely because he happens to be alive.

POTENCY B represents the integrative type of existential adjustment, characterized by a dynamic motivation combined with mental flexibility, emotional warmth, and an empathizing attitude in social relations. All of these traits function together to produce a harmonious joie de vivre.

This "upbeat" presentation of the Type-B writer should be no means be taken to signify that his integration is invariably constant and always satisfies his personal wishes and expectations. The salient mode of Type B's existential adjustment is qualified by the periodicity of cyclical biophysical changes, which he experiences in so wide a range as to allow him dynamically to harmonize his personal behaviour in respect of the fulfillment of the three fundamental and indispensable requirements of living that are represented by the Adlerian "three S's": Subsistence, Sex, and Society.

The Type-B writer is energetic by his very nature. In keeping with his strong drives he likes and needs to be involved in productive activity of some kind, and is untiring in his quest for diversity, innovation, and reinvigorating experiences. Although Type-B remains essentially true to his predominantly emotional nature — to his sympathies and antipathies — he does his best to encourage friendly relations and cooperation. He is a "good mixer," and by virture of his natural frankness and practical wisdom is able quickly to discover the proper orientation in dealing with people and to find the appropriate manner in which to perform his tasks and duties.

Briefly, the Type-B writer's existential adjustment draws on his sound self-confidence and natural optimism in matters pertaining to self-realization and useful participation in communal life.

POTENCY C is characteristic of the **impulsive type** of existential adjustment, and may be easily discerned. It is recognized not only by its outstanding feature of sheer extravagance of action, but also by outbursts of wild and far-flung movements that defy the standard letter forms and upset the layout of the written page as a whole.

The tempestuous motivation of the Type-C writer breaks down the restraints imposed by self-control. As a result he is frequently deceived by the hasty impressions he forms, and is driven into taking hot-headed, imprudent and irresponsibly venturesome actions. The proverb, "More haste, less speed," describes his unpremeditated manner of doing things. Notwithstanding his excess exertions — or, more accurately, because of his unbridled oscillation between his depressive impatience in the face of obstacles — Type-C is given to suddenly losing interest in his goals and giving them up completely.

Despite his best intentions and lofty ideas, the Type-C writer's behavior is unaccountable from one action to the next. Unexpected turns of behavior constitute the rule of his conduct. He may struggle for justice with great moral fervor while losing sight of the unjustifiable distress and pain he causes to others in the process.

To sum up, therefore, the impulsive existential adjustment of the Type-C writer functions as a restless and zealous self-involvement that often takes the form of improvisations born of whim and caprice. This may result in creative work or productive enterprises. On the other hand, he may put his undertakings at risk by involving himself in activities that violate the law.

The **right angle** is predominant among Type D, E, and F writers; it stands on the alert in an upright tension that graphically depicts the concentrated determination of his efforts to maintain his central position, and reveals his selfhood as an independent entity among the "great crowd," as it were, that occupies the written line. In this way the right-angle writer expresses his personal unwillingness, emotional unpreparedness, and at times mental inability to communicate and mix with other human beings.

The motivation of such centering on the self in the right angle of writing may derive from a spiritual, moral or intellectual strength that focuses the writer's personal energies on a particular central idea or undertaking that is at the core and crux of the writer's existential adjustment. Moreover, this graphic self-centering may express a range of attitudes, from D (rational self-control) to E (mystical aloofness, solitariness originating in personal detachment), right down to F (profitable self interest).

At this juncture, the manifestations of the right angle of writing should be differentiated in relation to Potencies D, E, and F.

POTENCY D is characteristic of the **rational type** of existential adjustment. The Type-D writer is the embodiment of homo sapiens — the very exemplar of the prudent, thinking man, whose powers of self-control keep him from making hasty decisions and, even more, prevent him from acting precipitously and in an unpremeditated fashion. Painstaking analysis and meticulous and scrupulous planning precede his conduct and action. Type-D's consciousness of responsibility binds him to act in a systematic manner and with great vigilance — and not merely in order to ensure thoroughness in performing his tasks and duties; he also feels it incumbent upon himself to look after the details and organization of his work before submitting it in its finished form to his superiors.

The right angle of writing is experienced by Type-D as a concentrated effort at self-control, which he maintains in order to preserve a rational independence in his mode of thought, his personal judgments, and his manner of reaching decisions. He is a law-abiding person with no pretensions to a talent for invention, nor any claim to revolutionary ideas concerning communal existence in regard to either public service or political affairs. He rather prefers to take the well-trodden path of traditional experience. His general adjustment is largely conservative in nature. His style of performance is characterized by cautious regulation of his acts and of the steps he takes in carrying out an action. His aim in this is to reduce the likelihood of error. And when occasionally he is found to have made a mistake, the error is very rarely slipshod. The Type-D writer likes to be in control of the reasons behind his way of viewing both things and people. His attitude is therefore one of objective correctness and honest appraisal in which feigned politeness and diplomatic maneuverings play no part. His uprightness and principled behavior is in the main accompanied by cautious trustfulness, which he holds to steadily, despite occasional exploitations of this trait by others.

In sum, the existential adjustment of the Type-D writer is regulated by ethical principles, a practical order of prudence, and a personal independence of a reliable kind.

POTENCY E is representative of the **autistic type** of existential adjustment, which functions as a self-centered detachment from the conventional reality that is governed and run by the sane majority.

The components of the homogeneous graphic syndrome of autistic writing reveal a predominantly constricted ego (in the Freudian sense), and a deeply entrenched dogmatism that the E-Type writer assumes provides him with a secure anchor for his high-flown puritanical precepts, which cloak his mentally divided manner of coping with the need to adjust his needs and conduct to the insistent, and to him disagreeable, demands of the environment.

The Type-E writer may be a profound and sharp-witted polemicist and an acute hair-splitter. Nevertheless, because of his fixated preconceptions, he is captivated by his own convictions to the point of self-assured confidence in the righteousness of his inner world, in which he is wholly engrossed. This characteristic prevents Type-E from looking squarely at the facts and daily reality without illusions.

Type-E's self-absorption is a mistaken and misleading solution by which he tries to compensate for his difficulties of communication with the world at large. Moreover, rather than weigh himself down by a sense of guilt over his own shortcomings and alienation, he prefers escapism as the more agreeable alternative. This he practices and conceals by appealing to lofty maxims about "eternal wisdom" that transcends ordinary human understanding. His truths are sanctimoniously given out by him with a show of unblemished personal perfection and splendid isolation.

The Type-E writer may occupy his inquisitive mind with exact sciences like mathematics, physics, and chemistry. However, his recognition of the validity of scientific facts is inadequate to affect his fixated self-centeredness sufficiently so as to allow him to communicate freely with his social environment.

To conclude: Type-E's existential adjustment is distinguished by a pattern of behavior that ranges from the asocial to the antisocial, and is burdened by an excess of frailties as well as being fraught with perils, which are either turned against himself in a variety of self-punishing ways or in pathological cases, become dangerous to the public.

POTENCY F indicates a **narcissistic type** of existential adjustment, which is characterized by an excessive self-love egocentrically inflated to the point of being insatiate and which is frequently associated with pretentious vaingloriousness. As is indicated by the homogeneous graphic syndrome, Type-F's inflated self-love protects at its root an inhibition that is very likely the result of a frustrated youthful love affair.

The inflated psychological self-aggrandizement of Type-F goes hand in hand with an aggravated susceptibility to injuries to his self-esteem, characteristic of the fantasizing self-adoration of youth (aged 17-22, approximately), and from which he has so far failed to emerge. This trait constitutes a serious impediment to his transition to a mentally more mature stage in his romantic life.

The Type-F writer often claims for himself admirable attributes such as brilliant intelligence, a broad range of artistic talents, warm and deep concern for public welfare, and a noble readiness to devote his initiative and energies to the cause of social justice and equality. However, underneath all of this, Type-F (more often than not a woman in her climactic stage of life) nostalgically cherishes fantasies that have remained unfulfilled. To compensate for this emotional failure, Type-F indulges in self-pity that takes the form of gluttony, by which he pampers himself, seeking relief in a soothing corpulence. In his egocentric self-admiration he regards his unutilized talents as being nothing less than the community's failure and loss. Type-F's real tragedy, however, resides in his **inhibited** existential adjustment, which results in his deprivation of relationships or friendships, leaving him abandoned at the wayside as the endless stream of life passes him by. These are the circumstances to which he is condemned, unless he is able to transmute his unhappy experiences into some kind of creative work. But because of his excessive vanity and his cherishing of self-indulgent comfort, he is unprepared to make the sort of strenuous effort that is required to realize the talents to which he lays claim. He prefers, rather, to make do with exhibiting the vast treasure of his unappreciated and unutilized abilities, which he regards the community as having ignored.

The **obtuse angle** is so conspicuous a deviation from the standard among right-handed writers that it suggests the existence of a reason sufficiently strong to have caused the choice of an angle of writing that is at such perverse variance with the rule. Graphological experience demonstrates that the obtuse angle of writing primarily reflects biological changes taking place at various stages in the personality's development. These changes are functionally accompanied by inducements and rationalizations of a psychodynamic kind, since the act of undertaking a change usually involves two conditions:

a) a person's seeking a solution that would relieve him from discomfort and suffering caused by his current circumstances;
b) his mental readiness to exert himself to adjust to new requirements resulting from changed circumstances.

Two crucial questions must be raised at this point: What is the nature of the difficulties or troubles that have befallen the right-handed writer of the obtuse angle? And what sort of solution, if any, may be expected from — or rather achieved by — a person's changing over to the obtuse angle of writing? There is no single, unequivocal answer to these questions. Because of the great variety of sources and motivations for the adoption of an obtuse angle of writing, I shall differentiate its manifestations with respect to Potencies G, H, and I.

POTENCY G is connected with the **reformist type** of existential adjustment, by which an individual seeks on the one hand to eliminate the harmful effects of a distressing experience in his private life, and on the other hand to compensate for personal misfortune or unhappiness by transferring his initiative and energy to the social domain, with the aim of improving human existence through reforms undertaken in various areas of community relations.

The Type-G writer's incentive for "reforming" the slant of his writing in an obtuse angle often derives from aesthetic sensibility, artistic talent, educational aptitude, and diplomatic skill that may be put to the service of the community. However, not infrequently, the social channeling of the reformist type derives from a deeply repressed experience and/or firm conviction and self-admission on the part of Type-G of his having to endure an insurmountable affliction of a biological, psychodynamic, or mental nature. In this case, Type-G's transference of his energies to the social realm greatly facilitates his efforts in maintaining a relatively productive mode of existential adjustment.

Nevertheless, the very fact that a right-handed writer should resort to the obtuse angle of writing is fairly clear evidence of his laboring under a deeply entrenched assumption that he is incapable of being himself and behaving like the majority of his fellows (who write with an acute or right angle). His sense of discomfort prompts him to act differently from others, and with an appearance of originality that is in keeping with his particular compensatory wishful anticipations.

Type-G's duality, consisting of the tension between his private existence and his "socializing" activity, finds expression in personal disillusionment and excessive caution — even suspicion — with regard to other persons, an attitude that causes him to maintain a distance between himself and others. Paradoxically, he is also drawn to maintain some sort of effective tie with the community.

Not surprisingly, the Type-G writer's existential adjustment conveys the impression of a Janus-faced personality whose diplomatic manner of dealing with his fellow man leaves one guessing about which of his two faces is the dominant one. In this he calls to mind the Hebrew proverb, "Honor him but suspect him."

POTENCY H refers to the **Joblike-Wolfish type** of existential adjustment. This dual title was chosen to characterize the two sides of the Type-H writer. On the one hand Type-H's distress and lamentations over his deprivations, adversities, and failures call to mind the Biblical archetype of dispossession and bereavement, Job. On the other hand, Type-H is also inclined to rebel against his troubles and supposed losses; resentfully, he will reject out of hand the fatalistic interpretation that his privations and misfortunes originate in his own particular nature.

Once again we encounter here a facile psychodynamic resolution that consists of an evasion of locating the source of one's frustrations and hardships in one's own deeds and conduct, and choosing rather the less trying way: that of projecting the experience of deprivation onto established social institutions, thereby making of them a scapegoat for one's troubles. Thus Type-H will charge elected representatives with the exploitation and depredation of the helpless masses. Like a raging sharp-toothed wolf, he lashes out at the political leadership and demands that they be punished for their "wickedness" and "evildoing."

The Type-H writer is a self-appointed champion of the oppressed, regarding himself as a just and competent prosecutor, out to rid the world of a corrupt establishment and to restore to the masses their natural right to well-being. However, behind his impressive outward show of altruism on behalf of the community, there lurks not only a brooding resentment of personal privation but something even more sinister. What is at work here is a neurotic mode of existential adjustment which is often accompanied by neurasthenic (weak-nerved) or psychoasthenic (weak-minded) spasms of writing movement that would seem to indicate that Type-H's unfortunate condition requires psychosomatic examination.

POTENCY I belong to the **Instinctual-Anarchic** type of existential adjustment and reveals the agitated instability associated with the earlier phase of adolescence (ages 12-16 approximately) in females, which is the result of the accelerated pace of biological development among women at that period in life, and which is attended by a concomitant disproportionate acceleration of mental maturation. This stage of development is characterized by frequent experience of physiological changes that are felt as sudden onslaughts of hot flushes, sweating, fits of shuddering, and the like. These physical symptoms occur together with emotional perturbation, anxieties, fears of fantastic mishaps, and an excited vacillation between restless gaiety and dejected retreat from participation in the activities of one's companions. Also involved, is an urgent craving for a warm refuge and reassuring comradeship, which is at the same time counteracted by unconscious distrust and withdrawal into one's innermost self, as though in fear of these yearnings.

The existential adjustment of Type-I is highly susceptible to environmental influences and is distinguished by an inclination to capriciousness of mood, fickle-mindedness, and want of mature and responsible self-control and perseverence. Such changeable behavior is quite natural in early adolescence. Usually, at a stage of greater intellectual development and emotional integration, the tendency of the individual is toward increasing self-confidence and stability, a change that can be graphologically diagnosed from the adjustment that takes place in the angle of writing, from the obtuse to the right or acute, and from the consistency with which the new angle is maintained. Experience has shown that such transitions in behavior can take place within a span of two years, and may attest to the individual's increasing capacity for personal responsibility and growing existential independence.

On the other hand, if Type-I's angle of writing continues to exhibit varying degrees of inconsistency in the obtuse angle, beyond the phase of early adolescence (a situation often encountered by the graphologist), this can be taken as a sign that Type I's progress to emotional maturity is being impeded. Such retardation in Type-I's adjustment, if still in evidence up to the age of about 25, is a forewarning of the susceptibility of the particular individual to mental disturbances, especially of a hysterical variety, such as aggressive insistence on one's own priority of preference, displays of prudishness to cover injured flirtatiousness, and constantly making a nuisance of oneself to the community.

Summary and Warning

The description I have presented of the nine types of existential adjustment has been too brief to allow me to do more than consider a few areas and layers of the personality. However, an individual writer's adjustment depends on the proportional extent to which the various potencies described in this paper participate in the functioning of his particular behavior, and the degree to which each of the potencies involved constitute part of his personal style of living.

I cannot caution the reader strongly enough that before an attempt can be made to characterize the specific make-up and composition of a particular writer's existential adjustment, three basic and necessary conditions must be fulfilled:

a) A **qualitative** determination of the graphic components that have been found to be actually present in the homogenous syndrome of each of the participating potencies.

b) A **quantitative** definition of the relative strength (in percentages) of each of the potencies that participate in the individual's handwriting.

c) A **characterization** based on a fixed and constant correlation with the **potential** significance of the relevant graphic component, and undertaken in relation to the relative strength (in percentages) of the above-mentioned quantitatively defined potencies.

No experienced diagnostician, including the scientifically oriented graphologist, would deny that intuition is an invaluable aid in getting at the heart of the problem with which he is dealing. On the other hand, the analyst must always beware lest uncontrolled flights of intuition lead him into interpretations that are unwarranted by the facts. On professional as well as ethical grounds, it is incumbent upon the scientific graphologist to develop a systematic method for analyzing handwriting. And he must always remain on the alert, in order to maintain, as far as possible, a consistent objectivity in his diagnosis of a writer's personality.

Application of the Graphological Typology of the Potencies A-I of Existential Adjustment

The interpretation of the data obtained from Potencies A-I may be used for various purposes and applied in a variety of ways, as for example:

a) In a synthetic characterization of the writer's existential adjustment.

b) To inquire into the nature of a writer's difficulties or impediments that hinder him in his progress toward a desired goal.

c) In the diagnosis of a person's talents and abilities (intellectual, technical, humanistic, etc.) for the purpose of vocational guidance.

d) For graphological testing of prospective marital compatibility between couples contemplating marriage.

e) As a diagnostic tool, to be used in conjunction with the tools employed in psychology and psychiatry, in defining and interpreting disturbances in mental functioning.

f) For inquiring into findings of antisocial behavior and criminal tendencies.

g) For educational purposes by applying the findings of graphoanalysis to teaching.

NAME INDEX

SUBJECT INDEX